IT'S ABOUT THE
MONEY!

IT'S ABOUT THE
MONEY!

The Fourth Movement of the Freedom Symphony:
How to Build Wealth, Get Access to Capital, and
Achieve Your Financial Dreams

The Reverend Jesse L. Jackson, Sr.,

and

Jesse L. Jackson, Jr.

with Mary Gotschall

TIMES BUSINESS

RANDOM HOUSE

Grateful acknowledgment is made to the following for permission to reprint previously published material:

Bloomberg Press: Chart, p. 94, from *The Latino Guide to Personal Money Management,*
p. 57. Copyright © 1999 by Laura Castañeda and Laura Castellanos. Used by
permission.

*Consumer Credit Counseling Service®, a division of Credit Counseling Centers, Inc.,
and a member of the National Foundation for Consumer Credit:* Chart, p. 21.
Copyright © 1994. Used by permission.

Alfred A. Knopf, a division of Random House, Inc.: "Mother to Son" from *Collected Poems*
by Langston Hughes. Copyright © 1994 by The Estate of Langston Hughes. Reprinted
by permission of Alfred A. Knopf, a division of Random House, Inc.

Times Books, a division of Random House, Inc.: Chart, p. 22, "The Rule of 72," from
100 Questions You Should Ask About Your Finances by Ilyce R. Glink. Copyright © 1998
by Ilyce R. Glink. Reprinted by permission of Times Books, a division of Random
House, Inc.

ISBN: 0-8129-3296-x

Random House website address: www.randomhouse.com
Printed in the United States of America on acid-free paper

9 8 7 6 5 4 3 2

FIRST EDITION

BOOK DESIGN BY JOSEPH RUTT

To Matilda Burns, Jacqueline Jackson, Sandra Jackson,
and Marilyn Jackson

FOREWORD

When asked to write the foreword for this book I was elated. Elated by both the subject matter and the author.

The topic of this book is of the utmost importance. The great challenges of the future are twofold. The first is attaining economic equality through jobs and the access to capital and resources that will build the foundation for *all* Americans to be part of the prosperity of our country. The second challenge is knowing *what* to do with these resources and capital once they are in your hands. And that's where *It's About the Money!* comes in. As Jesse Jackson, Sr., and Jesse Jackson, Jr., say, a person who lives in a capitalist society without knowing how to manage money is like a fish who doesn't know how to navigate in water. Each of the twelve chapters in this book is filled with essential information that clarifies and simplifies all the financial areas in your life, from saving to homeownership to investing. My favorite chapter, of course, is "Entrepreneurship," because that topic is wound up in the fabric of my life. Fifty-four years ago I started the company that publishes *Ebony* and *Jet* with $500, a very small amount of capital then and now.

The Reverend Jesse Jackson, Sr., and his son Jesse Jackson, Jr., are uniquely qualified to write this book. Reverend Jackson is a preacher who teaches, a salesman who creates new markets, and a spiritual entrepreneur who makes bigger economic pies for everyone. He has created a new vision of economic salvation, and he climbed the mountain with Martin Luther King, Jr. Congressman Jackson represents a district in Chicago that has experienced a loss of companies and jobs to other areas. He knows firsthand the challenges many people face in building the good life for themselves and the importance of getting access to that capital and managing it well.

I first met Jesse Jackson, Sr., when he came to Chicago as a young man and I gave him his first job. Though he was penniless and unemployed, I knew he was destined to be somebody and make a major imprint on the course of history. Since I was right about him from the beginning, I believe I am more qualified than anyone else to say that all Americans are indebted to this young man who has grown into a modern giant. As early as 1967, *Ebony* called him "The Apostle of Economics," and today he is still preaching spiritual and economic salvation and showing us the way to find success in the market of the new millennium. Reverend Jackson and Congressman Jackson give new meaning to what I call "The *Ebony* Idea," that no American business can reach its full potential without dealing creatively with the $500 billion black consumer market. So, to "The *Ebony* Idea," I would like to add "The Jesse Idea": That this $500 billion—which will surpass the $1 trillion mark by 2011—must be well managed and well invested.

So take the words, take the wisdom, take the vision and the road map that Reverend Jackson and Congressman Jackson have so thoughtfully presented here for you. Implement what they say, and you'll break the shackles of your financial burdens in order to breathe the sweetness of economic freedom in the twenty-first century. The time is now. Because, truly, "It's about the money."

—John H. Johnson
Chairman, Publisher, and Chief Executive Officer
Johnson Publishing Company

CONTENTS

Foreword   vii

Introduction: We Must Learn
to Become Owners, Entrepreneurs,
and Shareholders   3

1. Making Your Money Work for You
Through Consistent Budgeting
and Saving   13

2. Debt and Credit   33

3. Mortgages and Homeownership   53

4. Insurance   71

5. How the Market Works   97

6. Investing   125

7. Using the Internet   145

8. Dealing with Major Life Events   169

9. Retirement Planning   187

10. Avoiding Scams: Don't Let Anyone
Use You for a Cat's Paw   207

11. Entrepreneurship: A Time-Honored   223
    Road to Wealth in America

12. The Importance of Educating the Young   247

    Index   271

IT'S ABOUT THE
MONEY!

Introduction: We Must Learn to Become Owners, Entrepreneurs, and Shareholders

When I was a child growing up in Greenville, South Carolina, my grandmother Matilda Burns left a powerful imprint on me. She worked as a maid, cleaning people's homes, and didn't earn much. She didn't have a checking account, and she couldn't write. But she subsidized our family with her presence and her prudence. She took a little and did a lot with it, in the proud tradition that characterizes African American women in this country.

Grandma never believed in living on credit. She didn't owe anybody anything. She baked her own bread and biscuits. But always, always she taught us to save money as a cushion between yourself and disaster. She taught us to sacrifice for what is really important. A few times, as a child, I painfully watched her borrow $11 to pay back $22 between Christmas and Easter. I would see her go to work with runs in her stockings so that I could have matching socks and not be laughed at in school and discouraged. She sacrificed for an investment in my education.

"We're not poor," she used to tell us. "We just don't have enough money."

She made well enough do. "If you don't have enough meat, use what you have and make gravy," Grandma would say. "Stretch it out." If a mother has five children and two pork chops, she will not conclude that she has three excess children. She'll cut the pork chops up into five pieces and make gravy. These lessons endure.

My grandmother had a very strong commitment to the Lord. When we built a new church, my pastor, D. S. Sample, had a drive to raise money for the building fund. She stood and made her commitment to the building fund. Every Saturday, in her backyard, Grandma would fry fish and make ice cream; then my brother and I would deliver chitlins, rice, slaw, and greens to people's houses, until she raised her quota to build the new church. She was not able to write a check to the church: instead she lived her commitment, through her actions, and made well enough do. She stretched it out.

When my daughter, Santita, was born, rather than give her the usual baby gifts of clothes or toys, as our college friends did, my grandmother gave her a 25-cent-a-week insurance policy to help pay for her college education. She understood the value of investing in education and developing human capital.

Because of Grandma's strong influence on my life, when my wife, Jackie, and I were first married, we practiced sound principles of financial prudence. When we got our first apartment, we bought nothing on credit. We bought nice used furniture, waxed the floors, and used throw rugs. We went to the lumber company and got two doors and placed them on bricks close to the floor; then we put pillows on them and used it as a sofa. We had a music box for entertainment. It was cozy. It was ours. We were in no debt. And except when we finally bought our house and leased a car, we were very conscious of living just beneath our means.

When our five children came along, we invested in their education. We made that a priority, because we knew that if they had an education, nobody could take that away from them. They could go on to do great things. Jackie and I lived a high-risk life, involved in demonstrations and civil disobedience jailings, while we were in college, to break the shackles of legal segregation. But we knew that if either of us died, the best insurance for our children was to develop their intellect. I believe strong minds break strong chains.

My friend the late Lemond Godwin and I once discussed what we could leave our children that would be lasting. We could

1. make them smart and teach them to learn in their formative years.

2. develop their character, so they could be trusted.

3. teach them a work ethic.

4. teach them fiscal discipline.

5. teach them a sense of religious values.

As a result of that investment in our children's education, today my son Jesse Jr., who is a coauthor of this book, is a congressman and a lawyer; my daughter, Santita, is a professional singer; Jonathan, who has an MBA, is a business professional; Yusef is a lawyer and entrepreneur; and Jackie II is in graduate school, studying biology. We're proud of all of them.

Investing in human capital was what was important to us—not buying a bunch of material things. In our family it was our habit at Christmastime to give one another the most minimal of material gifts. We taught our children that family members, alive and warm, are the lights on the Christmas tree. Every year for the past thirty years we've spent Christmas morning with our family and members of our organization and with inmates at the Cook County Jail—where, with each passing year, unfortunately we see too many familiar faces. But we go to provide hope, and we seek to show the children that we take there an alternative to that place. The authentic meaning of Christmas is about saving people from debt and oppression, not plunging yourself further into it. It is about emancipation.

On a personal level, that is where the impetus of this book came from: the values that I learned in my own family as it pertained to financial prudence, discipline, saving, and investing. Just as a squirrel stores nuts for the winter, so must we all carefully save and invest for the future.

This book must also be viewed in the historical context of the civil rights movement, to which I have devoted my life. I view the economic emancipation of African Americans as the fourth phase on a historic continuum. If I were to compose a four-movement Freedom Symphony, the first movement would be the emancipation of the slaves: a two-hundred-year battle, rooted deeply in our Constitution—a season of walls that limited movement and roofs and artificial ceilings that limited growth. The second movement would be another one-hundred-year struggle to end legal segregation—more walls and roofs. The third movement would be the enfranchisement of all Americans, eighteen and older, through passage of the Voting Rights Act. The fourth movement—the final stage of the struggle—would be access to capital, to resources, to financial leverage—the democratization of capital. Hence this book. You could succeed at all the previous three movements, but if you didn't succeed at the fourth, you might starve. That's how crucial economic emancipation is. People of color and the working poor have won everything they've fought for: the right to organize, the right to form unions, and the end of racial and gender barriers as a matter of law. But we've not fought the battle for access to and democratization of capital. It's the ultimate battle. It's the unfinished business of our struggle to make this a more perfect union for all Americans, in which no one will be left behind.

Each phase of the civil rights movement had a how-to component. African Americans had to learn how to make the transition from slavery to freedom. We had to learn how to interact with whites on an equal footing in business, politics, education, and other realms of life, once segregation was ended. We had to learn how to participate as citizens in a democracy, voting in elections, when that had been denied us in the past.

The fourth phase—economic emancipation of our people—is no different. We must learn how to manage money and grow money in a capitalist society. We must learn how to be owners and entrepreneurs, shareholders rather than sharecroppers. We must learn how capitalism works and promote financial literacy among ourselves and our children. Failing to understand the role of money in a capitalist system is like being a fish that doesn't know how to navigate water.

For many people who were enslaved or colonized under capitalism, without democratic rights and legal protection, who were victims of exploitation, the very word *capitalism* sets off a tremor and a reaction. But slavery and oppressive systems have existed in capitalism, socialism, communism, religious orders, and monarchies. We must not resist learning how the system in which we live operates. Our values will determine what we do with the system and how we direct it. But first we must learn to navigate these economic waters.

This fourth phase is a continuation of Dr. Martin Luther King's vision. Dr. King's first assignment to me in 1966 was to serve as the national director of the Southern Christian Leadership Conference's Operation Breadbasket, which was the economic wing of the organization. Reverend Leon Sullivan, pastor emeritus of Zion Baptist Church in Philadelphia, Pennsylvania, and founder of Opportunities Industrial Centers International, brought the idea of ministers fighting for jobs and rights, leveraging consumer strength, to Dr. King. I have been blessed to take it to some advanced stages. The church's role in expanding economic options is a powerful one.

We challenged the exclusion of African Americans and Hispanics from business and worked to open up franchises, loans, and investment for African American and Hispanic entrepreneurs. Eventually Operation PUSH and LULAC, a Hispanic organization, began to do joint negotiations. That cooperation between blacks and Hispanics must be expanded. Dr. King understood that equal opportunity required entry into the marketplace and access to jobs, education, and private investment. The Wall Street Project—launched in 1997 by the Rainbow/PUSH Coalition—is a tribute to Dr. King's realization that dreams and visions are not enough to achieve economic emancipation of those left behind in our society: instead structural problems require structural solutions.

These lessons derived from our experience are not for blacks only. Now I'll remind you of how Dr. King spent his last birthday, January 15, 1968. That morning he had breakfast with his family at home. Then later in the morning, in the basement of Ebenezer Church, he convened African Americans from the rural South, some Hispanic workers, farmworkers, Native Americans, whites from Appalachia, Al Lowenstein and

Jewish allies from New York, and labor allies. There we worked as a coalition, trying to chart a course—a march to Washington—a multiracial, multicultural coalition, seeking jobs, income, economic security, and economic inclusion for all Americans. We saw then the need to build a vertical bridge from the "haves," living in the surplus culture, to the "have nots," living in the deficit and debt culture. In the long run it would be mutually beneficial for both groups.

Today we come to Wall Street to move corporate America through enlightened self-interest. It is in America's compelling national interest to tear down the walls that have limited growth and denied economic opportunity for all its citizens. Inclusion is the key to economic growth. Blacks, Latinos, women, and rural people in places like Appalachia need to be viewed not just as consumers in our society, but as people of diverse talents and training, with investment potential and underutilized skills.

Investors who speculate in emerging markets overseas too often forget that a far larger emerging market exists right here at home. African Americans as a group have $500 billion in purchasing power; Latinos have $350 billion. Let's harness the money, market, and talent that we have right here in America. Let's greenline redlined neighborhoods and rebuild scorched-earth communities. Let's create incentives to invest and hedge against risk at home, as we do abroad, to expand our economy. The new chains of slavery for the working poor are credit card abuse, using credit cards as a substitute for money and taking on excessive amounts of debt, on the one hand, then using lottery tickets or gambling boats as the plan for instant recovery.

This book is about building wealth. Our focus is on wealth, not just income, and this is a crucial distinction. It's not how much money you make that's important—it's how much you keep. Income is how much you make; wealth is how much you keep.

It's About the Money! will furnish you with real-life examples of people who came from humble backgrounds but who rose in life by successfully gaining mastery of their own personal finances.

The new chains of slavery for the working poor are credit card debt and lottery tickets. But we are going to tell you how to free yourself of those chains. We'll tell you about Helene Moore,* a black woman and divorced mother of three children, who works as a secretary on the South Side of Chicago. She earns $30,000 a year but had racked up $26,000 in debt from credit cards and auto loans. It seemed overwhelming. Then she sought help from her pastor, Reverend James Meeks at the Salem Baptist Church, which my son Jesse Jr. attends. After listening to his stirring sermons, entitled "Debt Free in 2003," she was able to embark on a plan to pay off all her debt by the year 2000 and remain debt-free.

This is a fine illustration of how churches can play a leadership role in the economic emancipation of our people. They can lead by example, through their marketplace initiatives, some of which we describe in this book. They can promote the formation of investment clubs at their churches and implement financial ministries to teach key personal finance skills to members of the congregation. They can practice sound financial stewardship of church funds and help rebuild their communities in the process.

Most poor people in America are not black and brown; they are single, white, female—and invisible. Kathy Goe was one of them.

We'll tell you about Goe, a thirty-nine-year-old disabled woman in Appalachia who lived in a trailer in Lee County, Kentucky. It was so ramshackle that she had to stuff rags under the door to keep the wind from whistling through during the winter. Then her pastor, Reverend Herman Newton at the Beattyville Christian Academy, told her about Habitat for Humanity. It's a nonprofit Christian group that builds homes for low-income people. You have to be willing to put in "sweat equity" on your home—and Goe did just that. She hammered. She stood up the first wall of her house. She worked on every phase of building it, even though she had never done construction work before. Today she has a beautiful home in the mountains and continues to do volunteer work for Habitat, both here and abroad. "The Lord always works it out," says Goe.

We'll tell you about Deborah McGriff, a middle-aged woman in Milwaukee, Wisconsin, who joined an investment club and whose eyes

---

*Pseudonym.

were opened to the thrill of investing. She and a group of other black women of all different ages and backgrounds launched the Phenomenal Women's Investment Club, using materials furnished by the National Association of Investors Corporation. Each woman contributes just $75 a month to the club's portfolio, and in the three years the club has been in existence, their portfolio has almost doubled. They begin and end each meeting with a prayer.

People can learn about personal finance at any age—and the younger the better. We'll tell you about Richard Anderson Jr., a seven-year-old boy in Brooklyn, New York, who—at his tender age—is already an avid investor, looks up corporate data on the Internet, and has given speeches about investing at the New York Stock Exchange.

We'll also tell you about entrepreneurs who created wealth by starting their own company, like Alex Bambara, an African immigrant from Burkina Faso who came to America about ten years ago with just $150 and is now launching a successful gourmet bakery with annual profits of $150,000, thanks to free advice he received at the U.S. Small Business Administration.

We'll tell you about Henry Ford, a fifty-eight-year-old African American man in Cleveland, Ohio, who was a factory worker at the Euclid division of General Motors, which makes heavy construction equipment (now called Euclid-Hitachi). He was there for thirty years and worked his way up in the company. Because he participated in Euclid's 401(k) plan, he now has a comfortable pension for his retirement.

You can learn this. All you need is the proper spirit, the right frame of mind. As Jesus taught us in the Book of Matthew: "Ask, and your prayer shall be granted; search, and you shall find; knock, and the door shall be opened unto you. For he that asks receives, he that searches finds, and to him that knocks, the door shall be opened."

Accumulating wealth—as distinct from just making a big income—is the key to your financial independence. It gives you control over assets, power to shape the corporate and political landscape, and the ability to ensure a prosperous future for your children and their heirs.

Wealth is not about showy consumer goods, which quickly depreciate in value, like clothes or vacations. Instead wealth "signifies the command over financial resources that a family has accumulated over its lifetime, along with those resources that have been inherited across generations. Such resources, when combined with income, can create the opportunity to secure the 'good life,' in whatever form is needed—education, business, training, justice, health, comfort, and so on," note Melvin Oliver and Thomas Shapiro, authors of the 1995 book *Black Wealth/White Wealth*. Wealth is used not just to pay the rent or buy groceries, but to create opportunities, to free you to pursue your dreams.

Income—without wealth or a steady plan of savings and investment—is just flash without cash. There's nothing behind it. It can be gone in an instant. If you work for a company, you could be downsized or fired and your salary would evaporate overnight.

Stories abound of prominent people who came from humble backgrounds, excelled in sports or the arts, and commanded high salaries but then lost them. They were cheated by unscrupulous advisers or were simply reckless with their money. Although they were rich, they practiced the habits of the poor, and that led to their undoing. Great successes like Elvis Presley have lost as spectacularly as they have won, in the realm of financial management.

Elvis Presley loved giving Cadillacs to friends and even strangers, knowing they could never afford to buy such items on their own. When he ran short of money he'd simply go out and make more. He'd call up his manager, Colonel Tom Parker, and ask him to book another concert tour. During the 1970s Elvis could pull down about $130,000 a night at such gigs.

Despite his millions, Elvis was living paycheck to paycheck. Basic rules of personal finance apply, no matter what the size of your bank account.

A high income—in and of itself—doesn't guarantee wealth. Many accumulate wealth on relatively low incomes, thanks to prudent saving and investing. Whatever your income, you must carefully plan how to grow your money, then monitor your financial affairs to make sure your plan is properly carried out. You can't just put the whole thing on autopilot and walk away. You must be vigilant. You must keep tabs on your money, even if you hire professionals to manage your funds for you.

It's About the Money! will teach you those skills. This is not a "get rich quick" book. Instead, this is a book that will give you steady, time-honored techniques to accumulate wealth. It will prepare you for a lifetime of wealth building and train you to pass on these skills to your children.

Every great journey begins with a small step. Remember, as the great abolitionist Frederick Douglass put it, "You are judged not by the height you have risen, but from the depth you have climbed."

The fourth movement of the Freedom Symphony is the battle to provide greater access to capital and economic power to underserved America. All of underserved America. Black America. White America. Brown America. Red America. Women in America. Now that we have ended legal apartheid, it is time to tear down the economic partition and build bridges to wealth and growth.

Thirty-four years ago African Americans staged a peaceful march in Selma, Alabama, to protest disenfranchisement of African Americans in the state. The march was led by John Lewis (then head of the Student Nonviolent Coordinating Committee and today a congressman from Georgia) and Reverend Hosea Williams of the Southern Christian Leadership Conference. When the marchers arrived at the crest of the bridge, they were greeted by a sea of Alabama state troopers, who came charging at them, beating them with nightsticks and bullwhips. The marchers didn't have any weapons. They didn't have any computers, or any Web site, or any fax machines. All they had was their bodies, a spirit that would not surrender, non-negotiable dignity, character, and a will to suffer and sacrifice for the high ethical and legal principles they held dear.

Today, in the fourth stage, we must add to that awesome arsenal of weapons our capital. We have mountains and oceans behind us, but by comparison, mere hills and rivers in front of us. In the struggle for access to capital, we have money, markets, talent, and location. Now we must apply the focus and the discipline.

We have now arrived at the moment in our history when we can move from working, consuming, and spending to saving, investing, and building equity. We have now arrived at the moment in our history when we can finally realize Dr. Martin Luther King's dream for all Americans.

—Reverend Jesse L. Jackson, Sr.

CHAPTER 1

Making Your Money Work for You Through Consistent Budgeting and Saving

The moral imperative of our day is to leave no one behind.

B arkin' Bill Smith is a blues singer who plays at famous clubs like Buddy Guy's Legends on Wabash Avenue in Chicago. Some of the most talented musicians in the world, such as Stevie Ray Vaughan, Eric Clapton, Willie Dixon, and Otis Rush, have played there. The club's founder, Buddy Guy, revolutionized blues guitar playing and jammed with greats like Muddy Waters and B. B. King.

Barkin' Bill is tall and dapper, gliding about elegantly in a gray tweed jacket, sporting a dark fedora, with just the hint of a smile. He carries an elaborately carved walking stick and looks as if he might break into dance any minute. Far and away he is the best-dressed guy in the place.

He's seventy years old, working hard, traveling to clubs all over the country. He claims that he's never been sick a day in his life, adding that he feels great. "I'm just as limp as a dishrag," he says.

Barkin' Bill clearly loves life. He has a big, full-throated laugh, and his exuberance is infectious.

He's not only a terrific entertainer, he's an entrepreneur as well. He and his band, Cold Sweat, have CDs they'll sell you for $15. Everybody at Buddy Guy's seems to know him. They come up and greet him, and he talks animatedly with all of them. Barkin' Bill sells a few CDs in the process. He knows how to market. That's why he's not old, broken, and broke.

He's making a good living. The night before, he earned $1,100 at a club in Indiana.

There's only one problem. Ask him what he does with the cash he earns and he replies: "I keep it in a lockbox at home."

It's all about the money. There are still too many people out there like Barkin' Bill. Talented. Energetic. Hardworking. Well dressed. They have their act together. They're enjoying life.

But ask them about how they handle their money, and they give you a blank stare.

So many people say, "Money doesn't grow on trees." We challenge that. You can grow money on trees, but you have to plant it in money mud. So many of our churches take up collections on Sunday morning, put the money in a lockbox Sunday night, then deposit the funds in a low-yielding savings account for months or even years, passing up the chance to earn a higher rate of return on their investments. We know of one case where a pastor friend of ours was trying to raise $1.5 million to buy some property and build a new church. The church eventually raised $1 million, but they held $900,000 of that money in a low-yielding certificate of deposit (CD) for seven months. This is not the way to make money grow.

Too many people don't have their share of the money, their share of the wealth, their share of the equity. It's not that they can't win it. They're losing it by forfeit. Keeping their money in a lockbox is one of the ways they're losing it. When thousands of African American churches across the country tie up their money in long-term, low-yielding savings accounts, they're also losing the chance to build wealth, and their communities are losing out, too.

Money can grow on trees, but you have to plant it in money mud. A money tree will not grow out of a lockbox; but it will grow out of the fertile soil of prudent saving and investment. Ted Turner, the multibillionaire entertainment mogul, recently gave away $1 billion to a number of good causes. It was money that he earned from his extensive array of investments. He didn't have to do a day's work to get it: he simply let the money work for him. He's an example of someone who knows how to grow money on a money tree.

Affluent people make the choice to save, invest, and follow a disciplined financial plan to insure a prosperous future for themselves and their children. You can make that choice, too. For African Americans to succeed in the fourth great phase of the civil rights movement, it is a choice that our community *must* make.

Handling your money wisely is not just the right and prudent thing to do economically. It's also supported by Scripture. The Bible has many parables in which people are rewarded for financial prudence.

For example, there is the famous parable about the talents in Matthew (25:14). A man was going on a journey and called his servants and entrusted his property to them. To one, he gave five talents; to another, two; and to the third, just one. A talent was an ancient coin used in the Holy Land. Each servant was given sufficient talents "according to his ability," says the Scripture. Then the man went away.

The first fellow, who had five talents, went out and traded with them and made five more. The second fellow, who had two talents, traded with his and made two more. "But he who had received the one talent went and dug in the ground and hid his master's money," says the Scripture. This is like putting your money in a lockbox or under the mattress.

After a long time, the master came home and settled accounts with them. The first servant who had doubled his five talents to ten came forward and told what he had done. The master praised him and rewarded him. The second fellow came forward and did the same, with his two talents that had become four. Likewise, the master praised him heartily and rewarded him.

But then the third fellow—who had just one talent that he had buried in the ground—came forward. "Master, I knew you to be a hard man, reaping where you did not sow and gathering where you did not winnow," he said. "So I was afraid, and I went and hid your talent in the ground."

The master answered him angrily: "You wicked and slothful servant! You knew that I reap where I have not sowed and gather where I have not winnowed? Then you ought to have invested my money with the bankers, and at my coming I should have received what was my own with interest."

The master took the talent from him and gave it to the first servant, who had ten talents, then declared: "For to every one who has will, more will be given, and he will have abundance; but from him who has not, even what he has will be taken away."

So don't you be like the fellow who buried his money in the ground. Do something with your money. Make it work for you. As the Bible teaches, using your talents tends to multiply them. This works not only in the spiritual realm, but also when it comes to money.

The biblical parable teaches us about the value of investing money at a bank and drawing interest. This is a crucial concept.

We urge you: Set up an account at a bank, credit union, or savings and loan association (S&L). There are some compelling reasons to do this. Among them:

- Money held there is safe from fire, loss, or theft.

- You can earn interest on money deposited in savings accounts.

- Having an account eliminates fees charged for cashing payroll checks and other checks.

- Maintaining a checking or savings account makes it easier to get good deals on credit cards and loans.

- Depending on the type of account, deposits at most financial institutions are protected by federal government insurance, through the Federal Deposit Insurance Corporation or the National Credit Union Administration for up to $100,000.

Banks, S&Ls, and credit unions resemble one another in terms of services provided, although there are some differences. Commercial banks offer a variety of services, including checking and savings accounts, loans, safe-deposit boxes, investment services, financial counseling, and automatic bill payment.

Savings and loan associations historically have accepted savings and only furnished home loans. But that's changing. Many of them now provide most of the services offered by commercial banks.

Most checking and savings accounts at banks and S&Ls are federally insured by the Federal Deposit Insurance Corporation (FDIC) for a maximum of $100,000. To check out the insurance status of a bank or S&L, call the FDIC at 1-800-934-3342.

Credit unions are not-for-profit cooperatives, owned by their members. They're not open to the general public. Instead, to become a member you must have some common association, such as the same employer, union or place of worship. Some credit unions serve a particular geographic area, and you can join if you live or work in that region. The services that credit unions offer are much the same as those offered by banks, and can be less expensive than the fees charged by banks and S&Ls. To find out whether you qualify to join a credit union and to obtain the names of those located near you, call the Credit Union National Association at 1-202-682-4200, or contact your state credit union league. Most credit unions are federally insured by the National Credit Union Administration for a maximum of $100,000.

You may also want to look into community development banks and community development credit unions. They tend to be located in areas that are traditionally underserved by financial institutions, such as low-income or minority neighborhoods. The American League of Financial Institutions is a trade group representing African American–, Asian American–, and Hispanic American–controlled S&Ls and savings banks nationally. To obtain a listing of all their members, you can call them at 1-202-857-3176. Among their members are Carver Federal Savings Bank in New York, the largest African American savings bank in the country; Berean Federal Savings Bank in Philadelphia, Pennsylvania, the oldest continuously operating African American thrift in the United States; Broadway Federal Bank, located in Los Angeles, the oldest African American savings and loan association west of the Mississippi; and Illinois Service Federal Savings and Loan in Chicago. Another group active in developing communities nationwide is America's Community Bankers, a trade group representing 2,000 savings and community financial institutions and related business firms; you can phone them at 1-202-857-3101.

With the rise of the Internet, many banks and other financial institutions now offer online banking services as well. But even with a basic account at a bank or similar institution, you'll be able to move funds around electronically. That is, you'll be able to use "direct deposit" and "preauthorized payments." The first feature enables your employer to deposit your paycheck directly into your account every month; the second allows regular bills—such as your rent or mortgage—to be deducted from your account automatically. Many institutions also have automated teller machines (ATMs), so you'll be able to deposit or withdraw money from your account using a computer terminal.

Before selecting the right bank or financial institution, shop around. Visit a few banks, credit unions, and S&Ls, and compare features for convenience—namely, location, hours open, and ATM access. Then compare all additional costs, including monthly charges and fees for ATM usage, check writing, and/or failing to maintain a minimum balance. Find out how much you need for an opening balance, and whether or not your account will earn interest.

Compare the cost of cashing a $1,000 check through a checking account or a check-cashing service, and you'll quickly see the benefits of maintaining an account at a financial institution. Banks and credit unions often don't charge their customers anything to cash a check. But according to the Consumer Federation of America, the average cost of cashing a paycheck at a check-cashing store in 1997 was 2.3 percent of the amount of the check; 2.2 percent for a Social Security check; and 9.4 percent for a personal check. These may not sound that high, but the figures quickly add up. Cashing your $1,000 check every month for an entire year would run you $276, $264, and $1,128, respectively.

Having a checking or savings account at a bank, S&L, or credit union will save you these exorbitant fees.

To open an account, you will need money to place into it, your Social Security number, and a picture ID, plus one other form of identification. With a checking account you'll get a checkbook, and you will need to learn to balance it so you don't "bounce" checks, or write checks when your account does not have sufficient funds to cover the amount. Bounced checks can be costly. You might have to pay a service charge of $10 to the bank and another $20 to the store or company that you wrote the check to. In addition, always write your checks in ink, so no one can erase them or alter them.

What are some of the other lessons about money that we can learn from the parable of the talents?

First, think about how you can increase your assets. Even if you have only a few extra dollars after all the bills are paid, find out ways in which you can put your money to work. Avoid credit card debt and lottery tickets. Slowly and steadily save and invest any extra money so you can build a nest egg for the future. The man with the five talents now has ten and a more secure future. The one who buried his money faces tough times.

Second, rent out your money. Money is bought and sold in the marketplace, like anything else. People pay a price for money, just as they pay a price for bread or eggs or chicken. And the price of money—known as "interest"—fluctuates depending on the number of buyers and sellers in the marketplace. This process is known as "supply and demand."

Interest rates go up and down on money—higher or lower, driven by market demand. If you keep your money in a lockbox, you can't lend it to others and collect interest from them and make a profit on it. You can't grow money on the money tree. When you make a bank deposit, you rent your money to the bank. The bank pays you "rent" in the form of interest. If you don't take your money down to the marketplace, you can never get anything for it. You can't invest it. It's just sitting there idle.

By depositing your money in an interest-bearing account, you'll benefit from the principle of "compound interest," which means that your money earns interest on the interest that it accrues, as well as on the original principal amount. Interest may be compounded daily, monthly, twice a year, or once a year, depending on the financial institution. Over time this really adds up. Even small amounts can become big ones over a period of years. As you can see from the following chart, $1 invested at a 5 percent annual compounded rate of interest more than doubles, to $2.08 (rounded) after fifteen years—and this takes place without your ever having to add more money to that initial $1 investment.

Thus your money can double and triple in value, given a long enough time horizon. The accompanying chart on page 22 called "The Rule of 72," shows you a quick way to compute this. You divide 72 by the interest rate that your money is currently earning to figure out how many years it will take your funds to double.

As you can see, if your money is earning 6 percent a year, it will double in twelve years; if it's only earning 2 percent per year, it will take thirty-six years to double. The rate of return you earn on your money makes a huge difference in how much you end up with. And you should always think about how you can achieve the biggest profits over time. Another way of saying this is, how can you maximize the return on investment on your money? How can you get the biggest bang for your buck?

The third lesson from the parable is that there is a trade-off between risk and reward when it comes to money. The higher the risk, the greater the reward. So you want to balance the return on your money with a reasonable amount of risk—one that you can live with.

Here are several different ways in which you could use your money, with varying degrees of risk attached to each:

1. You could invest it in a money-market account, currently yielding about 5 percent in interest. A money-market account is a hybrid between a traditional checking account and a savings account. It pays higher interest rates than other bank accounts do. If you put your funds into this type of account, your money will be "liquid,"

Compound Interest Table

The Amount to Which $1 Will Accumulate at the End
of the Specified Number of Years

Years	4%	5%	6%	7%	8%	9%	10%
1	1.0400	1.0500	1.0600	1.0700	1.0800	1.0900	1.1000
2	1.0816	1.1025	1.1236	1.1449	1.1664	1.1881	1.2100
3	1.1248	1.1576	1.1910	1.2250	1.2597	1.2950	1.3310
4	1.1697	1.2155	1.2625	1.3108	1.3605	1.4116	1.4641
5	1.2165	1.2763	1.3382	1.4026	1.4693	1.5386	1.6105
6	1.2652	1.3401	1.4185	1.5007	1.5869	1.6771	1.7716
7	1.3158	1.4071	1.5036	1.6058	1.7138	1.8280	1.9487
8	1.3684	1.4775	1.5938	1.7182	1.8509	1.9926	2.1436
9	1.4232	1.5513	1.6895	1.8385	1.9990	2.1719	2.3579
10	1.4801	1.6289	1.7908	1.9672	2.1589	2.3674	2.5937
11	1.5393	1.7103	1.8983	2.1049	2.3316	2.5804	2.8531
12	1.6009	1.7959	2.0122	2.2522	2.5182	2.8127	3.1384
13	1.6649	1.8856	2.1329	2.4098	2.7196	3.0658	3.4523
14	1.7315	1.9799	2.2609	2.5785	2.9372	3.3417	3.7975
15	1.8008	2.0789	2.3966	2.7590	3.1722	3.6425	4.1772
16	1.8728	2.1829	2.5404	2.9522	3.4259	3.9703	4.5950
17	1.9477	2.2920	2.6928	3.1588	3.7000	4.3276	5.0545
18	2.0257	2.4066	2.8543	3.3799	3.9960	4.7171	5.5599
19	2.1067	2.5270	3.0256	3.6165	4.3157	5.1417	6.1159
20	2.1909	2.6533	3.2071	3.8697	4.6610	5.6044	6.7275
21	2.2786	2.7860	3.3996	4.1406	5.0338	6.1088	7.4002
22	2.3697	2.9253	3.6035	4.4304	5.4365	6.6586	8.1403
23	2.4645	3.0715	3.8197	4.7405	5.8715	7.2579	8.9543
24	2.5631	3.2251	4.0489	5.0724	6.3412	7.9111	9.8497
25	2.6656	3.3864	4.2919	5.4274	6.8485	8.6231	10.834
26	2.7723	3.5557	4.5494	5.8074	7.3964	9.3992	11.918
27	2.8832	3.7335	4.8223	6.2139	7.9881	10.245	13.110
28	2.9985	3.9201	5.1117	6.6488	8.6271	11.167	14.421
29	3.1184	4.1161	5.4184	7.1143	9.3173	12.172	15.863
30	3.2432	4.3219	5.7435	7.6123	10.062	13.267	17.449

To calculate interest: Take end-of-the-year value × % interest to determine current year's interest and add to year-end value. Example: End-of-year value (1.04) × 4% (.04) = current interest (0.416). Add 1.04 + 0.416 = 1.0816.

Rule of 72

The Rule of 72 will give you a quick calculation of how quickly your money will grow.

72 ÷ Interest Rate =	Time Needed to Double Your Money
1.0%	72.0 years
1.5	48.0
2.0	36.0
2.5	28.8
3.0	24.0
3.5	20.6
4.0	18.0
4.5	16.0
5.0	14.4
5.5	13.1
6.0	12.0
6.5	11.1
7.0	10.3
7.5	9.6
8.0	9.0
8.5	8.5
9.0	8.0
9.5	7.6
10.0	7.2
10.5	6.7

Source: *100 Questions You Should Ask About Your Personal Finances* by Ilyce R. Glink. Published byTimes Books, a division of Random House, Inc.

which means you will have access to it in case you need it for a big, unforeseen expense or to pay taxes. This is a good way to invest funds for the short term.

2. You could invest it in a mutual fund composed of shares of different stocks, or else invest in individual stocks outright. Over time, if you ride out all the up-and-down cycles, investments in stocks have outperformed all other investments, yielding an average of 11 percent compounded per year from 1926 to 1997. Thus, as the Rule of 72 chart illustrates, your money would double in about seven years at this rate of return.

3. You could invest it in bonds, or debt instruments—also known as "fixed-income securities." Their historical yield is lower than that of stocks, but over time they have proven to be less volatile than stocks, and municipal bonds—issued by states, counties, and other local governmental entities—can provide you with a tax shelter. From 1926 to 1996, long-term corporate bonds had a compound annual return of 5.6 percent; long-term government bonds, 5.1 percent; and Treasury bills, 3.7 percent.

4. You could invest it in a combination of stocks and bonds. Many people choose this strategy, because owning some bonds enables you to offset downturns in the stock market. It reduces the risk, as well as the reward, of just owning stock.

5. You could invest it in real estate, such as a house. A home may appreciate in value over time, and it will also allow you to get a tax break—the mortgage interest deduction—as well as build equity.

   If you keep your money in a lockbox, it's just sitting there, doing no good. You are not benefiting from the time value of money. That is, a dollar today is worth more than a dollar tomorrow, or a year from now, or five years from now. Why? Because if you had the dollar today, you could invest it and make even more money with it.

The fourth lesson from the parable is that money that is idle depreciates over time. That dollar you are given a year from now—as well as the $1,000 not placed in a savings account or invested—is losing value.

But how could that be? Isn't $1,000 that's safely locked up worth $1,000 a year from now, or two years from now, or ten years from now?

No—because it is not protected against the ravages of inflation. If you just sit there and do nothing with your money, its value will be eroded over time. The face value of the money will still be $1,000, but its purchasing power—what you can actually buy with it—will have shrunk.

Inflation means a period of generally rising prices for goods and factors of production—rising prices for cars, houses, and televisions, but also for the materials and equipment used to build the cars, houses, and televisions. Over the course of the past one hundred years there's been a general upward trend of prices. With this rise in prices comes a decline in purchasing power. If your dollars are worth less today than a year ago, then you won't be able to buy as many things as you could a year ago. Inflation is minimal at present—3 percent to 4 percent a year—but it hit 13 percent in 1980. Even at low rates of inflation, the value of money declines. Your $1,000 today will be worth $970 a year from now if inflation is 3 percent. And it will be worth just $941 a year after that, assuming inflation continues at 3 percent annually. And so on.

Inflation can really whittle away your retirement savings if you aren't careful. The dollars you set aside for retirement at age twenty-five often shrink in purchasing power by the time you hit seventy. If prices rise at an average rate of about 3 percent a year, the real purchasing power of a dollar held for forty-five years will be cut in half once and then a second time during that period, if you do nothing with your money.

Thus you need to seek a return on your money that is greater than inflation, so the value of your money will grow over time rather than being whittled away.

As we have seen, opening a checking and savings account at a reputable financial institution ought to be one of your top priorities. Once that's done you need to create a financial plan. Think of this as a road map of how you'll accomplish your financial goals.

Achieving your financial goals involves choices. Just as a company has a balance sheet with a bottom line, so do you. You make choices each day that will have an impact on your bottom line. You need to make the same types of choices as the rich person does: choices that will add to your wealth over time, not detract from it. Like a squirrel that buries acorns in the earth to get ready for winter, you need to save and invest regularly and consistently, year after year, to create wealth. Calculating your net worth is a useful exercise. You can call the Consumer Credit Counseling Service (CCCS) at 1-800-547-5005 and get a worksheet to help you calculate your assets and liabilities (what you owe to others). The difference between these two is your net worth.

You want to calculate your net worth so that you can ascertain exactly where you stand financially. This is what you would have if you suddenly had to sell all your belongings to pay your debts. Is your net worth a positive number or a negative number? If it's negative, you're living beyond your means. You're not able to save and invest, because all your money is being drained away to pay off creditors, such as banks, department stores, and home-equity lenders. You are not building wealth; you're building debt. In the next chapter we'll tell you how to work out from under that mountain of debt. You'll want to update your net worth statement every year to see how you're doing.

As we said, achieving your financial goals involves choices. You want these choices to have a positive, not a negative, effect when it comes to your bottom line. Some choices you make will have an impact over a period of years, while others will be short-term.

Benita Tardy of Milwaukee made some wise long-term choices about her finances. When she was a teenager she faced a decision all teens have to make: how to spend her Saturday afternoons. Instead of staying at home and watching TV, or going to the mall and spending money, she got a series of jobs and saved what she earned. Let's say she earned $6 an hour on Saturday and worked for five hours. That's $30 per day, $120 a month, and $1,440 per year. After two years her earnings were $2,880, and by the time she graduated from high school she had $4,320.

Tardy opened up an interest-bearing passbook savings account at TCF Bank, which she has kept to this day. With it she bought certificates of deposit, which are interest-bearing instruments that mature in three months to five years and pay a stated rate of interest. Hers paid about 5 percent. These are a good way to save money in the short term.

While attending high school, Tardy held a series of jobs, doing clerical work, security, parking, cashiering, day care, and teaching. During the summertime, when school was out, she worked two jobs. None of them paid very much, but she always managed to save some of the money.

"Pay yourself first—I practiced that," she says. "I just disciplined myself. I knew where my money was going, and I had a goal in mind." Tardy wanted to buy a house, something that she could pass down to her children and an asset that would appreciate in value. That was her dream, and from the age of seventeen onward she worked steadily to achieve it.

Tardy saved little bits of money, here and there. She used coupons whenever she shopped at the grocery store. She bought items on sale. She had credit cards but spent modestly and was always careful to pay off the balance every month. She avoided spending money on the latest fads—whether it was new clothes, a hairdo, or fancy manicures—that other young women in her neighborhood were buying. She had grown up as an only child, and her mother, a single parent, had studied accounting and taught her the value of saving money.

In addition, she paid her bills on time, every month, realizing the value of good credit. If you don't pay your bills on time, it will cost you more money in the long run. You'll be charged late fees or extra finance charges. If it's a utility bill you've failed to pay, your service could be disconnected. Your lights might go off, or your stove won't turn on. To avoid this, you need to pay all your bills as they come due, and you will want to set up a system to make sure you follow through with this. It could be a payment calendar, in which you write the bills off on a calendar every month on the day you pay them.

By saving steadily in this fashion, Tardy was able to sock away $8,000 by the age of twenty-three. Recently she got married, and she and her husband, Adrian Thomas, a twenty-six-year-old sports coordinator, were able to buy a house. Both had excellent credit, so they qualified for a mortgage loan at a very favorable interest rate. In addition, thanks to their thriftiness, they could easily afford the $2,000 down payment on the $42,000 property.

Currently Tardy works as a program assistant for Milwaukee's Center for Teaching Entrepreneurship, set up in 1991. Through the free seminars given there, she's helping to empower other African Americans.

In order to save on a regular basis like Tardy, you must first figure out where your money is going every month. You need to make a family budget, listing all your monthly expenses in one column and your sources of income in another. The accompanying chart offers a sample budget for you to fill out, furnished by the Consumer Credit Counseling Service, a nonprofit group that helps people manage their personal finances.

Family Money Management System

Expenses	Weekly	Monthly	Week 1	Week 2	Week 3	Week 4	Adjustments
Mortgage/Rent Payment							
Electric							
Gas							
Water and/or Sewage							
Telephone							
Property Taxes							
Homeowner/Renter Insurance							
Grocery Purchases							
Work Lunches							
School Lunches							
Beverages							
Toiletries							
Cigarettes/Tobacco							
Automobile Payments							
Automobile Insurance							
Auto Repairs/Maintenance							
Gasoline/Oil							
Public Transportation/Parking							
Medical Insurance							
Life Insurance							
Doctor							
Dentist							
Medication(s)							
Family clothing							
Laundry/Dry Cleaning							
Haircuts							
Pet Expenses							
Newspapers/Magazines							
Children's Allowances							
Tuition and Books							
Child Care—Work							
Child Care—Recreational							
Christmas/Hanukkah							
Birthdays and/or other Gifts							
Church							
Other Donations							
VCR Tape Rentals							
Cable TV							
Movies and Concerts							
Sports (Bowling, Golf, Hunting)							
Clubs and Hobbies							
Lottery—Bingo							
Meals Out							
Trips and Vacations							
Child Support and Alimony							
Savings, Bond/Regular							
Savings Emergency Only							
Charge Accounts (list)							
Miscellaneous—Other							
Total Monthly Expenses (D)							

They have offices around the country, and you can call them at 1-800-547-5005 to set up an appointment with one of their counselors.

You need to track your expenses for a period of time—three to six months would be good—to see your patterns of spending. Where is all your money going every month? What are your weak spots? Do you tend to blow a lot of money on lottery tickets, dining out, or buying fancy clothes? You may be surprised to learn that even little things add up. That extra cup of coffee at $1.50 a day is costing you $400 over the course of a year. Figure out where you are overspending, then think about ways you can cut back.

Think of your household budget as a big slab of bacon. You want to cut out the fat and keep the lean. You're the one who has brought home that bacon. The "lean" part of your budget consists of items that you really can't cut. These are called "fixed expenses," and they are the same amount each month or each quarter: your mortgage or rent, car payment, student loans, health insurance, and so forth. Then there are "variable" expenses, which vary in amount from month to month, like the telephone bill, utilities bill, and food and transportation costs. There may be some room to cut here.

But the "fat" part of the budget consists of "discretionary" expenditures, which are not necessities—these are the items that you choose to purchase. These are "wants" and not "needs." You could do without a lot of them. Thus, in this category you have expenditures for vacations, bowling, movies, eating out at restaurants, buying a giant-screen TV, getting the latest sport utility vehicle, and on and on. As you can see, you could live without these items. You could make the choice to cut some (or all) of these and to save the money and put it to more productive uses.

Too many people buy what they want and beg for what they need. They spend themselves into poverty. They end up poor because they're gullible and greedy.

Instead of spending money on unnecessary items, you could decide to save and invest at least 10 percent of your salary every month. Many people find it easier to save if they allow their bank to automatically remove that amount from their paycheck and deposit it into a savings or investment account. Second, you should establish an emergency fund, amounting to three to six months of your annual living expenses, to tide you over in case you lose your job or some other calamity strikes.

When it comes to trimming the fat out of your budget, you can be quite creative. You don't have to live like a pauper. You can still enjoy life. The key thing is to make thriftiness a way of life.

For example, to save some money every month, you could

- get a second job.

- buy a used car rather than a new one. Have a mechanic inspect it first to insure it's in good shape.

- buy your clothes and household items from secondhand stores. You can find some excellent bargains at such places. No one has to know that your Donna Karan dress had a previous owner.

- make presents for friends and family instead of buying Christmas or birthday gifts. Bake them a cake; knit them a sweater; throw a party for them in a nearby park; grow a garden and give them some fresh vegetables. Offer them a service, such as baby-sitting or mowing their lawn. Whatever your talents may be, use them. In addition to money, you have many other resources that can be put to good use: your time, talent and knowledge are among them.

- create your own business by using your talents. Perhaps you could open a child care center in your home, or do sewing, carpentry, or other handyman work, and charge a fee for it. Your family may be able to pitch in and help you. We will discuss entrepreneurship later on in the book, along with organizations that can help you launch a business.

You need to adopt the habits of the well-off instead of the habits of the poor. Instead of spending a big wad of money on clothes, look how the children of the rich wear uniforms at their private schools. They've removed the status value from clothes, and we could do that, too. Many people who feel a sense of personal inadequacy cover that up by

spending lots of money on fancy clothes. Let's sew our own school uniforms and use the entrepreneurial services of a neighborhood seam-
stress to do so.

You must insure that your income exceeds your expenses every
month, by as large an amount as possible. You must live below your
means so that you can have money to save and invest.

There are programs around the country to help you get on a budget
and stick with it. We mentioned CCCS. Redonna Rodgers, who is executive director of Milwaukee's Center for Teaching Entrepreneurship,
runs another such program. Her organization offers a free program
called Teach Me Some Cents, to get low-income teenagers aged twelve
to seventeen to budget, save, and plan for the future. Her group has
worked with dozens of young people in Milwaukee's schools and encouraged them to open checking and savings accounts and begin saving
consistently.

Their programs drive home the economic consequences of various
actions: for example, having a child. Benita Tardy teaches one work-
shop geared toward teens that advises them what they'd be getting
themselves into, both financially and emotionally, by having a child.
"Having children out of wedlock is going to cost you money," emphasizes Tardy. The workshops show you the numbers, right there on the
blackboard. A child can cost you tens of thousands of dollars by the
time he or she reaches age eighteen.

"Your life is your business, and your business can be your life" is the
motto of the center. "We ask the kids: Are you living a life of profit or
loss—socially, financially, and spiritually?" continues Rodgers. The
young people are encouraged to set financial goals, then begin the
process of saving and investing to attain those goals, get an education,
and plan their lives.

They teach the kids that your savings account is like a bill—a bill to
yourself, to pay yourself first every month—however much you can
reasonably save: the more the better. They teach the kids not to over-
spend, by writing down all their purchases and keeping track of how
much they've spent. That helps you see what you do with your money.

"If you can save forty or fifty cents on a product at the store, that's your money," Rodgers explains. "The bottom line is that at a certain point, no matter what your life was, you make choices. You have a certain amount of personal responsibility. And that determines what your future will be."

Rodgers, aged forty, grew up poor in Chicago and recalled how her own family "kept a stash" of money at home in a little container. The family didn't keep their money in a bank. "My father had this thing about white institutions," she says. He didn't trust them, so they didn't put their money there. Her father was a salesman who frittered away money freely, never saving for the future. There were six kids in the family, and her mother stayed home to raise them.

Today Rodgers runs the center and educates young African Americans about the financial consequences of their actions. She's joined an investment club—the Phenomenal Women's Investment Club of Milwaukee—which we'll tell you more about in the chapter on investing. A graduate of Monmouth College, she hopes to get a graduate degree in economics one day.

Don't spend money just for pleasure; use it to build wealth and, in so doing, acquire power to manage and control your life, she advises. There's a big difference between power and pleasure. Because many black people have felt denied for so long where material goods are concerned, they're particularly inclined to spend money on "flash"—flashy clothes, expensive cars, fancy jewelry.

"Now that we have the opportunities to get these things, we get the 'surface' things—the look: the clothes, the jewelry, the car," says Rodgers. "You fake it till you make it. But very few of us make it. You make less than other people, and you spend more. It's all going to the suits and the shoes."

These items don't build wealth and rapidly depreciate in value. Added to this is the fact that white people in America are born with more assets than blacks. After the conclusion of slavery, the advantages that whites had didn't end. So this combination of factors has tended to cause black wealth to lag behind white wealth.

Rich people tend to have certain habits that poor people would do well to emulate. For example, rich people understand that you shouldn't fritter away your money on such baubles as cars and clothes, which quickly depreciate in value. This was a point driven home by the book *The Millionaire Next Door.* The authors, Thomas Stanley and William Danko, found that American millionaires tend to drive old cars, live in modest houses, and wear cheap suits. Instead of spending all their money on consumption, they make saving and investing a way of life. And they pass on these skills to their children. You can do this, too.

Living above your means is a financial sin—and the wages of sin is economic death. The rock-and-roll legend Elvis Presley, though fabulously wealthy, squandered his money on fancy cars and often found himself living paycheck to paycheck. Although he was rich, his habits were poor. And he paid the penalty.

"You have to do certain things so your family won't just survive, but thrive in our economy," summarizes Rodgers. "You have to work your way out of a situation where you have just enough to make ends meet. You have to build a foundation.

"If you're exposed to it, you can have it and use it," she adds. "You can come out of the dungeon and out of the dustpile. You have to have the discipline to sacrifice something today, so you can have something greater tomorrow."

CHAPTER 2

Debt and Credit

Capitalism without knowledge of or access to capital leaves only the "ism," the margins, the bark of the tree. Ideas without capital, dreams without capital, opportunities, contracts, farmland, mineral resources, and potential without capital is like a fish having everything but water.

Chiffon Jones* works for a Fortune 500 company on the South Side of Chicago and lives nearby. She's a stylish woman, attired in a chic beige suit, wearing exquisite jewelry, and carrying a Gucci bag.

This was her downfall, however: she loved beautiful things and freely went out and bought them. And bought them, and bought them.

"I was a shopaholic," confesses Jones. "Shopping made me feel better. It was definitely recreational."

But, she acknowledges, "it was also bondage." Jones shopped compulsively. Two closets in her house overflowed with her outfits. She also bought clothes and other items for her husband, as well as for her two sons, aged ten and twelve. She was passing on the addiction to the next generation. She was passing on the addiction of more clothes than they needed, of living beyond their means. She began hiding all the clothes and jewelry so that her husband wouldn't find out about it.

"I had so much that I was ashamed—really ashamed of it," she re-

---

*Pseudonym.

calls. "I realized that I had to change my behavior. I couldn't go to the mall anymore. I didn't need to buy the twenty-third black suit that I didn't already have." Jones adds ruefully: "I have lived for American Express."

When she was growing up, in a family of eleven children—six girls and five boys—she wore faded hand-me-downs. "I didn't have enough," Jones continues. "I was deprived as a child." She had shoes with holes in them and made do wearing her sisters' old dresses.

Nor did Jones's parents ever teach the kids anything about money. Her father was a carpenter, while her mother stayed home and raised the children. She remembers them cashing checks at storefront check-cashing places, and there was never any talk of saving for the future. When Jones went off to college, where she majored in business, her father would always send her money, and she always went shopping and spent it. It was in college that she started acquiring credit cards; she ran up regular balances that she didn't pay off in full every month but instead "rolled over," meaning that she paid interest on the remainder of the money owed. This went on every month, and she never looked at how much interest she was being charged. Yet some credit cards charge interest as high as 21 percent per year, so over the years she was paying thousands of dollars in finance charges.

What happened to Jones happens to too many young people in college. They are heavily marketed to by credit card companies, start using several charge cards, and by the time they graduate they're burdened by massive credit card debt—often in addition to their student loans. Debt becomes a way of life. They get married and are in debt. They send their children to college and are in debt. We need to break those chains of debt that are enslaving us. We can never build wealth until we free ourselves from the corrosive habit of living in debt.

Jones felt her compulsion to shop stemmed from a spiritual sickness. She was also concerned about passing the habit of overspending on to her children. So she sought guidance from Reverend James Meeks, pastor of her church, Salem Baptist. Meeks, who is pastor of the church that one of the authors (Jesse Jackson Jr.) attends, is a young, dynamic preacher who regularly draws crowds of five thousand people to his Sunday morning sermons. The crowds are so large that the church quickly fills up, and the rest of the people have to go to the "overflow room" in a church building next door and watch the service on a big screen. Another 1,500 turn out for his Wednesday evening Bible study classes.

Reverend Meeks is the pastor of an area of the South Side of Chicago known as Roseland. It has experienced a massive loss of industries in recent years. Companies left; banks and insurance companies redlined his community. The absence of capital and jobs broke the spirit of many people living there. There are vacant lots, abandoned houses, and a surplus of liquor stores that emerged as anesthesia for their pain. Reverend Meeks began organizing people, like Ezekiel in the Valley of Dried Bones, to renew their self-confidence. He led a drive and got the city to pass an ordinance to close down one-third of the liquor stores in the neighborhood. Then he took the semi-abandoned corner of the biggest former liquor store and turned it into the most modern, privately owned bookstore in the city. His church is now buying the shopping center as part of their effort to revitalize the neighborhood.

Reverend Meeks's congregation is encouraged to wear regular clothing to church. They don't have to own a fancy dress or suit, although the service is formal and the spirit is high. The material costs are low.

Many of our churches breed material needs, as do many of our public schools, with peer pressure to buy expensive clothing. Our schools should be focused on learning, not on modeling.

Reverend Meeks is renowned for bold sermons, such as "Why Are We Stuck at the Bottom?" which analyzes why many African Americans are clustered far down the economic ladder.

Through one of his many innovative programs, which focuses on the role of the church in community development, Meeks succeeded in establishing Salem Baptist Church's flourishing bookshop in what was formerly the largest liquor store in the neighborhood. He's also been instrumental in reducing the number of liquor stores in the neighborhood by one-third. And he has compiled educational materials warning the parishioners of the folly of throwing their money away on lottery tickets.

When Chiffon Jones came to him last year, worried about how her recreational shopping had spun out of control, he realized that she was not alone in her problems with credit cards; many of his other parishioners were awash in debt, too. Indeed, many of the people who live there have "unacceptable" credit. This can arise for a variety of reasons. It may be that they had gone into bankruptcy, defaulted on a loan, or their home was foreclosed and the lender took it from them. Moreover, major industrial shifts—beyond the control of the residents of the community—had left many people living there high and dry. Over the past couple of decades industrial companies, such as meatpacking firms, had moved out of the area, thereby eliminating jobs and leaving lots of people unemployed. Many of the area's residents were left in the lurch financially, and their abysmal credit ratings reflected that. Some were in denial about this state of affairs. Jones recalled that one time when she had to pass out church flyers to the homes of parishioners, she opened many of their mailboxes and saw stacks of letters there—mostly unpaid bills. People had so many bills that they had simply stopped opening them.

Meeks saw an opportunity here: he could break some new ground and use the pulpit as a way to teach parishioners key financial skills. This could become an important mission of the church. Many other black churches around the country have embarked on innovative personal finance ministries as well. Reverend Kirbyjon Caldwell, pastor of the Windsor Village United Methodist Church in Houston, is a fine example. Under his leadership the church now has more than 11,000 members and 120 ministries, including programs on job placement and financial planning. In Chicago Bishop Arthur Brazier's Apostolic Church of God has succeeded at building a multimillion-dollar shopping center in their neighborhood. The shopping center contains a chain grocery store and drugstore and is the cornerstone of economic revitalization in the area.

Reverend Floyd Flake, at the Cathedral Allen AME Church, in Queens, New York, has created businesses, employment, schools, and houses. He has effectively used the resources of the congregation to massively transform his community. And in New York City Reverend Wyatt Walker, pastor of the Canaan Baptist Church in Harlem, is another example of how pastors at black churches can take a leadership role in rebuilding their communities and teaching a new financial culture to their flock. Reverend Walker, the former executive director of the SCLC and one of Dr. King's cellmates in jail, has done the most to build affordable housing in Harlem. These examples can be multiplied.

Moreover, there is support in the Scripture for this. The Bible has scores of passages reinforcing the theme of financial prudence, including repayment of debt. "The wicked borrows and does not pay back, but the righteous is gracious and gives," as Psalm 37:21 teaches us. Faithful management of money will yield a surplus, which is a major goal for Christians, enabling them to tithe to the church and thereby respond to the needs of others.

Meeks came up with a series of four sermons, entitled "Debt Free in 2003," specifically addressing ways in which people could set up a plan and extricate themselves from debt in a timely fashion. (To order audiotapes of the sermons, you can call the church at 1-773-371-2300.) He also enlisted Jay Anderson, a member of the congregation who works in the financial services industry, to develop money management seminars at the church to educate the parishioners.

"Debt has become a strong man that is keeping us from being financially free," Meeks told the congregation. "Mark said in 3:27 that you cannot enter a strong man's house and spoil his goods unless we first bind the strong man. Debt has entered your house; now you got to get him out of your house. . . . You got to bind the strong man."

And here's how Meeks told them to do it: Rather than just paying your bills every month and your mortgage over a thirty-year period—which is the conventional way of doing things—take a different approach. Pay off all your debts early—including credit card bills, mortgages, and car loans. In so doing, he told them, they would save tens of thousands of dollars in interest payments, which they could then invest. Over a period of twenty or thirty years, by steadily rechanneling the amount they used to pay in debt every month into investments in mutual funds, which pool investors' money in a diversified portfolio of securities, they would eventually have a sizable nest egg, assuming a compound interest rate of 10 percent annually. (The stock market has returned 11 percent, compounded annually, from 1926 to 1997.) They could eventually live off their investment income, if they saved and invested enough.

Instead of being in hock to the credit card companies or the mortgage lenders, "You've got to get to the point where somebody's paying *you* on *your* money!" intoned Meeks.

Paying off your credit card debt on time always makes sense. Paying off your mortgage early makes sense for many people; but if mortgage rates are low, and if having the tax-deductible mortgage interest from a home loan reduces your tax burden by a significant enough amount, then from an economic standpoint you may be better off keeping your mortgage. Plus, with a mortgage you can borrow on a tax-deductible basis against the full value of your home to pay for your children's college education. So before you decide to pay off your mortgage early, you'll need to examine your overall financial situation carefully and see what is the best course of action for you.

For Jones, Reverend Meeks's sermons were an answer to her prayers. Following the plan, she wrote down all her debts in a notebook—all the credit card obligations and other bills and all the balances. It was a long and tortuous process, but it had to be done.

There was the department store, where she bought a suit for $300 and was paying 21.6 percent interest on it. There was a finance company, which was charging her 30 percent interest on $12,000 of debt; a jewelry store was charging her 21 percent; 22.9 percent interest on a $900 computer; another finance company, 24.9 percent on a $7,200 loan for new windows on her house; the bank from whom she had borrowed $25,000 for a home-equity loan at 14 percent, to pay income taxes and other expenses; a major credit card company, 17 percent; 12 percent for time-share vacations in different places, such as Cancún, Mexico; two car payments, for a new Ford and a Mercedes. All told, it came to a whopping $80,994 as of June 1998.

Nonetheless, between the two of them, Jones and her husband, who is a business executive, were affluent. Their combined salaries came to about $132,000 a year. They had bought a house and were in the process of selling it and moving to another home. But they had almost no savings. Everything was being drained away by debt.

"I never looked at how much interest I was paying," says Jones. Yet some of the bills had been accruing interest for years.

Under the debt-free program at Salem Baptist Church, Jones wrote down how much interest she was paying on each of her bills, using the church's chart. She then calculated what she would save if she started paying off the debt quickly rather than spreading it over many years.

For example, on the bill of $2,086 for jewelry, if she simply paid the minimum—$54 a month on that one—it would take her 5.36 years to pay off all the debt, and over that period of time she would have paid a total of $1,392.07 in interest: 67 percent of the original price blown away on finance charges. Similar scenarios emerged on all her other bills.

"When I looked at it like that, and saw it on a piece of paper, something started to shake," recounts Jones. "It made so much sense to me. I stopped charging things."

Then she began paying off the bills, one at a time, starting with the small ones and working up to the bigger ones. It gave her a sense of accomplishment. "It's all spiritual to me," explains Jones. "I started cleaning out stuff—getting rid of the clutter and making things orderly. Then I was able to give and tithe regularly to the church. Things started happening. More money started coming in. My husband got a promotion and became a manager." The Joneses sold their home and made a sizable profit on it, which enabled them to buy their new home and pay off even more debt.

"I stopped shopping, and God opened all kinds of doors," she continues. For one week Jones wrote down every dime she spent. "It brought tears to my eyes—how much we were wasting," she says. "We were making good money, but wasting most of it."

The Joneses cut back on their lifestyle. They started going to the dollar show at the movies instead of paying full price. The family canceled their annual vacation to the Wisconsin Dells, which is a scenic area in the state, and thereby saved $2,000, which they used to pay off debt. Jones started getting her nails done once every three weeks instead of every two weeks. It costs her $25 for a manicure, so this ended up saving her $217 over the course of a year. It's not a big sum of money, but it adds up. All these little changes add up. As a result, they were able to pay off the $80,994 in just one year.

She also got rid of all her credit cards, except for the American Express Gold Card, which she pays off every month. She barely charges anything anymore. Following the Debt Free in 2003 plan, she and her family will also pay off their mortgage early, in just five years, by making extra payments each month.

She has started teaching her children about debt. Both her boys now have savings accounts—something she never had as a child—and she encourages them to regularly deposit their allowance there.

Nowadays she carries her notebook containing her mortgage payment schedule with her everywhere. "This is my Bible," says Jones. "And I tell everyone about it."

Like Chiffon Jones, you may have a problem with buying things. You may be constantly desiring the latest stereo, the newest appliances, the most up-to-date television, the finest suits and shoes.

As Reverend Meeks told the congregation, quoting 1 Corinthians 13:11–12: " 'When I was a child, I talked as a child, I felt as a child, I reasoned as a child; now that I am a man, I have done with childish ways.'

"It is childish behavior to want to buy everything you see and to not take control of your financial destiny!" he thundered. "Children do that. Kids have no regard for what things cost. They see a pair of Air Jordan sneakers, and they want them. When we were children, we acted like that."

Maturity, he continued, consists of "the ability to know what's best and to sacrifice for what's best.

"There comes a time, black man, black woman, when somebody is going to have to become spiritually mature. Somebody is going to have to become financially mature. Somebody is going to have to say, 'It's time for us to take control of our financial destiny!' " continued Meeks.

Reverend Meeks's wife, Jamella, led by example. Often the wives of pastors in our churches are seen as the fashion pacesetters. Pastors' wives are prominent, visible women in our churches. It's part of our tradition to fast and pray for spiritual strength. As a form of fast, Jamella chose not to buy any new clothes for a year. Many others began to follow that model.

The Meeks family also sets an example by living in the community in which Salem Baptist Church is located. The presence of prominent people like the Meekses can have a galvanizing effect and provide hope for people in the community.

Helene Moore,* who works as a secretary in the South Side of Chicago, has also used the Debt Free in 2003 program with great success. She's middle-aged and has three grown children. She currently makes $30,000 a year, but she had racked up credit card debt and car loans of $26,000 by the time she entered the church program last July.

She used to look at her bills and wonder, Why can't I finish paying off these things?

At Salem Baptist's program, she learned why. They taught the congregation about how interest payments work. "We were educated," notes Moore.

Following the church program, she started paying her debts off gradually—first $50 a month, then $100. She's got a ways to go, but she's on track to pay it all off in the year 2000. And as part of her commitment to her faith, she tithes 10 percent of her salary to the church. That 10 percent enables this church to grow: scholarships, job creation, bookstores, and so forth.

"I always tried to pay more than the interest," says Moore. "I paid my payment plus more than what the finance charge was." She cut back on her expenses and started bringing her lunch to work. She uses coupons whenever she buys groceries. Instead of going to see first-run movies, she waits and rents the video. And although she loved shopping for shoes and blouses, she made herself realize that she already had enough. She didn't need any more. She quit buying. And she was not tempted to start up again.

Certain stores allowed her to pay her bills in person. So every month "I would take my payment in the day they were due," says Moore. "And

*Pseudonym.

it strengthened me to walk in that store and be able to make my payment and not shop, and not even look."

She advises her kids: "I don't care what time of the year it is, what store you go in. There's always going to be sales. So forget the credit cards, forget the shopping, get out of debt."

Moore grew up in a small town in North Carolina and was one of a family of ten children. Her father worked as a hired man on other people's farms, and her mother was a homemaker. They had a big garden, with rows and rows of vegetables. There was always plenty of fresh produce, and they had big dinners of pork chops, chicken, beans, ham hocks, collards, biscuits, and cornbread. They lived in a little three-room home with an outhouse, and her brothers slept on cots in the hallway.

"We picked cotton, raised peanuts and tobacco," recounts Moore. All the kids worked. They were poor and rarely traveled out of their little town, but "there was so much love in our family," she recalls. "Our backyard was so big that we played baseball in it. We just enjoyed and loved each other."

Years later, when it came to paying off her debts, Moore says, the key thing was this: "I know what I owe. I started examining all my bills to see what I'm paying. I started logging everything, putting it on paper where it's visual."

Do you know what you owe? How much are you paying on your debt? The accompanying chart, furnished by the Consumer Credit Counseling Service (CCCS), shows you how much interest you pay every year for different amounts of credit card debt at different interest rates. The CCCS is a nonprofit organization, run by the National Foundation for Consumer Credit, that works with consumers to help them get on sound financial footing.

The "APR" column in the chart stands for "annual percentage rate" (APR), which means the annual cost of using credit, stated as a percent. It incorporates standard fees and interest into one number. Note how a higher interest rate makes a huge difference in how much interest you pay. If you carry an average daily balance of $3,000, for example, you'll pay $360 each year at 12 percent APR, but you'll pay $660 per year if your APR is 22 percent.

Compare Costs of Credit

The interest you'll pay each year if your average daily balance is:

APR	$1,000.00	$3,000.00	$5,000.00
12.0%	$120.00	$360.00	$600.00
13.0%	$130.00	$390.00	$650.00
14.0%	$140.00	$420.00	$700.00
15.0%	$150.00	$450.00	$750.00
16.0%	$160.00	$480.00	$800.00
17.0%	$170.00	$510.00	$850.00
18.0%	$180.00	$540.00	$900.00
19.0%	$190.00	$570.00	$950.00
20.0%	$200.00	$600.00	$1,000.00
21.0%	$210.00	$630.00	$1,050.00
22.0%	$220.00	$660.00	$1,100.00

Source: The National Foundation for Consumer Credit.

Borrowing money on credit cards costs more than just the APR, however. Some credit cards charge you an annual fee; many also impose late payment fees and fees for racking up debt in excess of your credit limit. You need to find out what "hidden" fees are associated with your credit card and shop around for the best deal. There are over six thousand companies that issue credit cards in America, with annual interest rates varying from about 22 percent down to 12 percent, so you have plenty to choose from. To locate the best deals on credit cards, the CCCS recommends that you contact a company called CardTrak, P.O. Box 1700, Frederick, Maryland 21702; phone number 1-800-344-7714. Ask for their "CardTrak Credit Card Checklist," which costs $5 and features an updated, monthly listing of credit cards that offer low interest and no annual fee.

In addition, for those trying to rebuild damaged credit, a "secured" credit card could be the answer. To obtain one of these, you make a deposit with the financial institution issuing the card. Your deposit—often $300 to $500—is used as collateral. The amount deposited is the credit card limit. Usually, if you use the card responsibly for six months to a year, the status of your card will be upgraded to a standard, "unsecured" credit card. The downside is that these cards frequently have expensive transaction fees and application fees. To obtain the latest listing of the best deals on secured credit cards offered by American banks, you can contact CardTrak's secured card hot line at 1-800-874-8999 and request their report. It costs $10.

Credit is essentially a way of buying something now and paying later. It comes in a number of different forms, such as credit cards, personal loans, lines of credit, mortgages, and store charge accounts.

A good credit rating is crucial for everyone. But a rising percentage of Americans have ignored this fact. Personal bankruptcies hit an all-time high of 1.4 million in 1998, according to the National Foundation for Consumer Credit.

"People tend to spend as much as they make," summarizes Joanne Kerstetter, president of the Consumer Credit Counseling Service of Greater Washington, D.C.

"This is an issue that affects all income groups," she continues. "We see cases of people making half a million dollars a year who get into debt over their heads." The average person whom CCCS works with earns $38,652 a year. But the organization also sees college students, retirees, divorced people, the unemployed, and those facing major medical expenses. The whole gamut of humanity walks through their doors. "Financial problems can hit any age group and any income," points out Kerstetter.

The root of the problem lies in poor money management skills, she adds. Because no one is required to study personal finance in school, many people enter the working world with no knowledge of how to manage their own money.

CCCS is part of a nationwide organization, with over 1,400 branches all over the United States, that works with consumers on a free or low-cost basis to help them sort out their credit problems. They can help you with credit card debt, budgeting, mortgage counseling, and tax issues, and all their services are confidential. They can also help you practice "preventive" steps that will keep you from getting into financial trouble in the first place. You can contact them by calling the National Foundation for Consumer Credit at their national headquarters in Silver Spring, Maryland (1-800-388-2227) or by visiting their Web site at www.nfcc.org.*

---

*Chapter 7 explains the use of the Internet and Web sites.

CCCS counselors have seen two major trends in consumer credit over the past few years. First is a lack of savings. This can be devastating, because if a crisis hits, people have nothing to fall back on. Before they started to turn over a new leaf, Chiffon Jones's family had no savings, despite the fact that she and her husband earned a good salary.

The second trend is that people are not budgeting their expenses. As a result, they live beyond their means. It creeps up on them gradually. On weekends they go to the mall and engage in "recreational shopping," thereby blowing a big wad of money. They rack up huge credit card debt on multiple credit cards and are continuously in hock. Helene Moore found herself in this situation. Other people start spending excessively as college students, then, upon graduation, get saddled with both credit card debt and student loans.

Americans have been taking on more and more debt with more and more abandon. As of February 1999 Americans had amassed $1.3 trillion in outstanding installment debt—that is, long-term debt that features "buy now, pay later" terms. This represented an increase of 7 percent from the previous year, according to the Federal Reserve. And in 1997, the most recent year for which data are available, debt totaling $247.4 billion was handed over to collection agencies, which recovered $32.2 billion that year, according to the American Collectors Association, a trade group based in Minneapolis.

Once your debt is handed over to a collection agency because of your failure to pay, you've got a blot on your credit rating. This is something that you want to avoid. After a bill is overdue for some time, credit card companies and other creditors often sell the debt for pennies on the dollar to these collection agencies, which are allowed to keep anything they can get from the debtor. Modern debt collectors can use high-tech software and computers to quickly do a search on you, so there is no place to hide. Debt collectors will phone you, write you, or go see you in person—but they will track you down.

To avoid this scenario, use debt sparingly. Save it for major wealth-building assets such as a house, a business, or a college education. Also, beware of cosigning a loan with someone else, because the amount of the loan you cosigned for will appear on your credit report as though you had borrowed the money yourself. When you cosign a loan or credit card, you're agreeing to pay back the entire amount if the person you cosign with fails to do so.

The National Consumer Law Center (NCLC), an organization that is nationally renowned for its expertise on the rights of consumer borrowers, has an excellent book, entitled *Surviving Debt*. In it they discuss in great detail the best ways for consumers to deal with debt collectors, home foreclosures, automobile repossessions, bankruptcy, and other topics. They talk about laws that are designed to protect the consumer as a borrower. They advise against using a for-profit debt counselor, as this field has become "a significant consumer ripoff." Debt counselors are people who will charge you money to help you get out of debt. "The charge for such counseling will almost always exceed the value of the counseling," warns the NCLC. Moreover, many of these counselors will steer you toward unscrupulous lenders, who charge exorbitant interest rates and take advantage of people with financial problems. You should also avoid firms that offer to "fix" your credit, because they cannot change any accurate information in your credit report. Going to a respected nonprofit group for debt counseling is the best course of action. Try the CCCS, whom we've mentioned, or Debt Counselors of America, at 1-800-680-3328 (Web site www.dca.org).

If you are in serious financial straits—possibly on the brink of bankruptcy—the NCLC offers some sound advice. They urge you to prioritize your debts and pay them off in order of importance. The overarching principle in setting your priorities involves understanding the concept of "collateral." Collateral is property that a creditor has the right to seize if you do not pay a particular debt. The most common forms of collateral are your home, in the case of a mortgage, or your car, in the case of a car loan.

Determine which of your debts are "secured"—by some sort of collateral—and which are not. The latter is called "unsecured" debt. You should almost always pay off secured debts first, because if you don't pay them, you stand to lose significant assets.

For example: Always pay family necessities first—namely, food and essential medical expenses. Then pay housing-related costs; utility bills; car loans if you truly need your car; child support debts (if you don't pay these, you could go to prison); and income taxes. On the other hand, loans without collateral are low priority. This includes most credit card debt, doctor and hospital bills, and any professional services, such as hiring someone to do your taxes. Because you have not pledged any collateral, there is nothing the creditors can do to you in the short term. Student loans are also medium-priority debts, because most are backed by the United States government, and federal law provides special collection remedies. Another thing to remember: Refinancing your debt is rarely the answer. "It can be very expensive, and it can give creditors more opportunities to seize your important assets," warn the NCLC authors. "A short-term fix can lead to long-term problems." You can get a copy of *Surviving Debt* for $17, plus shipping costs, by contacting the NCLC's Boston headquarters at 1-617-523-8089.

"The most important thing people need to know about credit is that it's just like a report card," explains Bill Cheeks, an African American who is vice president of consumer education at Atlanta-based Equifax, the largest and oldest credit-reporting agency in the United States. "It's your report card on how you pay your bills and how you manage your bill-paying history."

You have to manage your credit. You can't just assume it will take care of itself. To do this, you need to get a copy of your credit report on an annual basis and review it. You can do so by calling or writing any one of the three biggest credit-reporting agencies in the United States. Their names and addresses are as follows:

Equifax Information Service Center
Attention: Consumers Dept.
P.O. Box 105873
Atlanta, Georgia 30348
Phone: 1-800-685-1111

TransUnion Corporation
National Consumer Disclosure Center
P.O. Box 390
Springfield, Pennsylvania 19064-0390
Phone: 1-800-916-8800

Experian (formerly TRW)
P.O. Box 2104
Allen, Texas 75013-2104
Phone: 1-888-397-3742

The bureaus may charge you a fee of about $8 for a copy of your credit report. However, if you've been denied credit because of information in your credit report, all three bureaus will provide a copy free of charge.

Once you've received a copy of your credit report, make sure it's accurate. Under federal law you've got the right to have any incomplete or inaccurate information corrected by a credit bureau at no charge.

Having good credit is essential to achieving many major goals in life, such as

- buying a car

- renting an apartment

- getting a credit card

- being hired for a job

- obtaining auto insurance or life insurance

- qualifying for a mortgage loan on a house

- arranging for utility services in your house, such as gas and electricity

- becoming eligible for a bank loan to start a new business

- qualifying for a student loan to finance your education.

When you attempt to do any of the above, the person reviewing your application will pull one or maybe even two or three of your credit files from the major credit-reporting agencies. They do this in order to get the lowdown on you. They want to find out whether you're a deadbeat who doesn't pay his or her bills on time—and if you are, they aren't going to be inclined to do business with you. They simply can't afford the risk of not being paid back. Or they will charge you much higher interest rates than they would an individual with a good credit rating, to compensate themselves for taking on this higher risk.

Once you reach age eighteen your credit starts being tracked by these companies, if you've applied for credit. For example, if you've obtained a credit card, a credit history has automatically been started on you. To maintain a pristine credit report, you'll need to pay your bills promptly every month, whether it be your mortgage or rent, a student loan, an electric bill, or a credit card bill. Even if you can't pay your entire credit card bill every month, you must still pay the minimum every month to keep your credit intact. Having too much credit or too many outstanding balances are examples of why your request for credit might be declined.

You can request a credit report about yourself maintained by a credit-reporting agency. There are several things you need to pay attention to on such a report. First, make sure your name, address, Social Security number, and place of employment are accurate. If you've gotten married and changed your name recently, inform the credit-reporting agency. Also, when you apply for credit, make sure you use the same name all the time.

As Cheeks explains, "My name is William P. Cheeks. Most people call me Bill. But I never fill out any credit applications with the name 'Bill.' Instead I always use 'William P. Cheeks.' " This reduces the likelihood that credit-reporting agencies will confuse you with someone else. In addition, always write legibly when filling out any credit application, so that the information can be accurately transmitted to the reporting agencies.

The Equifax credit report, for example, has a heading entitled "Credit Account Information." Under it is a subheading entitled "Status." This is a very important section, perhaps the most important of all. This is where your "grades" on your credit report card are listed. Your goal—like that of an A student—is to have perfect marks, and in this case, that means having all 1's. The grading system here, instead of A through F, is 0 through 9. Basically, a grade of 1 means you have "paid as agreed," and you are up-to-date on all your obligations. This is what you should aspire to—a grade of 1 in every category. A 9, by contrast, means that the obligation has been charged off as a bad debt, which is the very worst classification.

Under this section, if there are accounts listed that you have since closed—such as a department store credit card you canceled—be sure to call the credit-reporting agency and let them know.

In addition, if you're about to make a major purchase, pull your credit file to make sure everything is complete and accurate.

Under the section entitled "Public Record Information" in the Equifax report, creditors will look to see whether you have any court records or filed for bankruptcy. There are two types of personal bankruptcy: Chapter 7, a category for people who declare that they can't pay any of their debt; and Chapter 13, for individuals who can pay off a portion of their debt. Creditors look more favorably on the latter group, because they seem to be making a good-faith effort to pay back their debts. It takes ten years for a Chapter 7 declaration of bankruptcy to be removed from your credit report but just seven years to remove the Chapter 13 bankruptcy, as well as to clear the credit rating of those who have failed to pay their bills on time.

Personal bankruptcies are a topic of some concern among creditors, since such bankruptcies have hit an all-time high in America—nearly double what they were in 1990. Bankruptcies are up 80 percent in the last five years alone, as the following chart indicates:

Number of People

Year	Filing for Bankruptcy (Chapter 7 or Chapter 13)
1998	1,398,182
1997	1,350,118
1996	1,125,006
1995	874,642
1994	780,455

Source: Equifax, Inc.

Creditors are concerned about these soaring bankruptcies, because they lose an estimated $40 billion a year in bankruptcy proceedings. Most credit card debt is currently forgiven in bankruptcy, so borrowers can make a fresh start. But there's a move afoot in Washington, D.C.—led by a lobby composed of some of the nation's biggest banks, retailers, and credit card companies—to make it harder for people in debt to do this.

Next on the Equifax credit report comes the section entitled "Collection Agency Account Information." This includes accounts that creditors have turned over to a collection agency. In the collection area, over 50 percent of the items are health-care-related, points out Cheeks. So make sure you follow up on the payment of bills by insurance companies and other agencies. If you receive two bills, follow up in writing, and keep a record of whom you talked with at both the insurance company and the medical facility. You need to find out if the insurance company will pay for a given medical bill. Then send a copy of the letter from the insurance company to the medical facility, so that the payment process is clear to everyone involved.

The "inquiry" portion of the credit report—which is at the bottom, under the heading "Companies That Requested Your Credit File"—is also worth noting. Let's say, for example, that you decided to buy a television set. You went around to five different stores and filled out credit applications at each so that you could pay for the TV over time, if you decided to buy it. All the stores, in turn, got a copy of your credit report. You now have five inquiries on your credit file. Let's say that in a couple of months you apply for a car loan.

"These loans will present some problems," warns Cheeks. "The finance company would look and say, 'Why did this person apply to five different companies one or two months ago?' It could delay or even prevent you from getting that auto loan."

So you want to be sure to minimize the number of inquiries about your credit. Use such inquiries sparingly.

The credit score is an important number to acquaint yourself with. It's not part of your credit file. Instead it's used by the credit grantor during the credit application process. A credit score is a composite that indicates how likely you are to pay on a loan or credit card under the agreed-upon terms. It's one piece of information credit grantors use when evaluating your application for credit. Your credit score may be based solely on information in your credit file with credit-reporting agencies. Other scores may be based on a combination of credit information and other data that you supply on your credit application. Having a regular job, maintaining a checking and savings account, and paying your bills on time can all help raise your credit score.

For advice on how to avoid credit problems, the Consumer Credit Counseling Service offers its clients some cardinal rules. Among them:

- Live below your means. This is the only way that you will be able to save and invest money over time. For example, avoid buying a house that is too expensive, which will make you "house poor."

- Keep your fixed expenses as low as possible. Don't obligate yourself to long-term installment debt, in which you "buy now, pay later." This will enable you to handle any sudden financial changes, such as the unexpected loss of your job.

- Get rid of all your credit cards but one. Pay off your credit card debt in full every month.

- Write down your goals for becoming debt-free. Set a date for achieving your goals. And stay focused.

We would add: Never let yourself waver from the spiritual side of this. Recognizing the spiritual dimension of managing money enabled Helene Moore, Chiffon Jones, and others to stay on the right path. It can do the same for you.

"Do not love the world or what the world can offer," wrote John in his First Letter 2:15–17. "When any one loves the world, there is no love for the Father in him; for all that the world can offer—the gratification of the eye, the pretentious life—belongs, not to the Father, but to the world. And the world, and all that it gratifies, is passing away, but he who does God's will remains for ever."

CHAPTER 3

Mortgages and Homeownership

Inclusion is the key to economic growth. If people have access to capital, they can buy a home and increase their stake in society. . . . Let's green-line redlined America and make the grass grow in scorched areas.

I t's a sultry Saturday morning in Washington, D.C. At a shopping mall in the northeast section of town, tucked in a neighborhood of quaint row houses, a roomful of people is eagerly gathered, watching a video. Rather than spend this summer day at the beach or out running errands, they are preparing themselves for one of the most important events in their lives: buying a home.

Buying a home. This is the quintessential American dream. And in recent years, thanks to the creation of flexible lending programs, it is within reach of more and more people.

The group is gathered at HomeFree-USA, a nonprofit mortgage-counseling agency in Washington, D.C., that works exclusively with moderate- and low-income people, enabling them to successfully buy their first home. Other such mortgage-counseling agencies exist all over the country.

HomeFree-USA works with blacks, Hispanics, Asian Americans, whites, and recent immigrants to the United States. They deal with single as well as married people, gays as well as straights, people with pristine credit and those with a pile of debt. One thousand people a month come through their doors. After five years in business, HomeFree-USA has helped over three hundred people buy homes—and stay in their homes. HomeFree-USA works with new homeowners for two years after they move into their new property, providing advice every step of the way and ensuring that 100 percent of their loans are approved and no one ever "forecloses," which means that the buyer fails to make payments and the lender takes back the house. Theirs is a motivated clientele.

"The people who come here are actively in pursuit of change in their lives through personal finances," says Marcia Griffin, founder of Home-Free-USA. "They have the attitude 'I'm going to do better. I'm going to find the path and the way.' "

She has started a "Homeowners' Mortgage Assurance Program" to prevent foreclosures. If any members have problems paying their mortgages, HomeFree-USA will pay it for them for three months.

Griffin, an exuberant African American woman who hails from New Orleans, has also partnered with 133 black churches in the Washington, D.C., area, because she understands the centrality of religion in the lives of her clientele. The pastors at these churches have become a vehicle through which she can spread the word about financial literacy, especially as it pertains to buying a home.

"Before we're able to impact our people, there has to be a bridge of understanding and confidence building," she explains. "People need to understand: 'This is not nearly as hard as I thought. I really can save.' You need to make a mental change before you can make a financial change." Through their teaching, the pastors of the local churches help bring about this mental as well as spiritual transformation among their parishioners.

In her free seminars, Griffin lays out ten home-buying secrets everybody ought to know. Here they are:

1. The home-buying process has changed. People should no longer just jump out and find a lender. "These days, to get your mortgage approved, you need to start the process much earlier and build good financial skills," explains Griffin, a veteran of the mortgage-lending industry. Such preparation is important for everybody—

but especially in the African American community, where a large percentage of those who apply for a home loan are denied. The reason is "lack of knowledge on the part of our people," notes Griffin. "Knowledge breeds confidence."

2. You need to get your credit, savings, and financial picture in order before beginning to search for a house.

3. Watch out for mortgage loans featuring high interest rates and high "points," which are the fees a lender charges to process a loan. That's a treacherous combination, used frequently by predatory mortgage lenders who are out to rip you off. Points are the fees a lender charges to process a loan and usually are based on the size of the loan. One point typically equals 1 percent of the amount of the loan.

4. Before buying a home, always get it inspected. Don't ask a Realtor to find you a home inspector, though, because all too often their interests are allied, they work together, and they won't necessarily give you an objective assessment. Instead contact the Better Business Bureau or the American Society of Home Inspectors at 1-800-743-2744. Most home inspections cost between $200 and $350. It's worth the price, given the high cost of home repair.

5. Know your credit score before you start looking for a home. The mortgage industry looks at your credit score. You need to understand what will make it increase or decrease. (We discuss credit scores in chapter 2.)

6. Know where your mortgage loan will come from before you start looking for your home. What lenders are you going to go to? What government agencies could you look to for assistance?

7. Before you start looking for your new home, if you can spend ten hours on prepurchase counseling or education, "this will triple the chances of your success in keeping your home," Griffin advises. "Information is power. Lenders look at these ten hours very highly. It'll cause them to look more favorably on your loan."

8. Everybody in the home-buying business who advertises does not
    have your best interests at heart. The mortgage industry is a
    business, and like all businesses, their goal is to make money. You
    have to have some basic knowledge under your belt to protect
    yourself before you approach professionals in this industry.

9. Don't hesitate to ask mortgage professionals to explain their
    lending programs in simple language. Have them break down
    complicated topics into plain English. Above all, don't feel
    compelled to sign things you don't understand. You're going to
    have to pay the money back on any loan you take out, so it is
    absolutely essential that you understand the terms of the loan—
    how much interest you will have to pay over what period of time
    and how many points. A "point" in real estate language is 1
    percent of the amount of the loan.

10. Get out a magnifying glass whenever you see small print on a
    contract. Usually it relates to money.

Owning a home can increase your net worth and for many families
ranks as the biggest financial commitment they will ever make. Historically houses have appreciated over time, so if you select a house in a
promising neighborhood and maintain it well, you'll often be able to
sell it for more than you paid for it, after a few years. Your mortgage interest and property tax, as well as certain moving expenses, should be
tax-deductible. There's also a "capital gains" tax benefit: if you sell a
home after living in it for at least two years, up to $500,000 profit is ex-
empt from federal income tax if you're married ($250,000 if you're sin-
gle). Experts say that if you're planning to live in the same place for
more than seven years, it doesn't make sense to rent, when you could be
building equity in a home.

"Home equity" is the part of your home that you own outright; it is
the difference between the home's appraised value and the balance of
your mortgage loan. You can borrow money against your home by obtaining a home-equity loan, if you needed to raise a large sum of money
to pay for your children's college education, for instance. With a home-

equity loan, you can borrow on a tax-deductible basis against the full value of your home and deduct the interest payments up to $100,000. Contact the National Home Equity Mortgage Association at 1-202-347-1210 (Web site www.nhema.org) to find names of reputable lenders who do these transactions.

"There's a tremendous positive impact that homeownership can have for low-wealth borrowers," comments Craig Nickerson, vice president of Community Development Lending at the Federal Home Loan Mortgage Corporation, known as "Freddie Mac." "There's no better way to create wealth for people of low income." By way of example, he pointed out that the average net wealth of homeowners in America is $90,000, versus only $4,000 for renters.

Freddie Mac is a private company created by the federal government to provide funds to mortgage lenders. Both Freddie Mac and "Fannie Mae," which is the Federal National Mortgage Association, increase the liquidity of the nation's mortgage market by buying mortgages from lenders and repackaging them into securities that are then used as collateral for securities sold on Wall Street. This is the origin of the "mortgage-backed" securities industry. Because of this arrangement, the lender gets payment immediately and can go ahead and make more mortgages, thus fueling homeownership in this country.

In the last five to ten years, Freddie Mac and Fannie Mae have begun offering increasingly flexible loan products to meet the needs of low-income people and minorities. The overall homeownership rate in America is at an all-time high of 66.7 percent. Minorities are gaining in homeownership, but they still lag behind whites by a significant percent: 72 percent of whites own homes, compared with 46.9 percent of blacks and 46.2 percent for Latinos, according to the Department of Housing and Urban Development (HUD).

"The travesty is that there are tens of thousands of families out there who don't believe homeownership is attainable," explains Nickerson. "They may be the third generation of a family of renters. Or they may have been rejected once and never tried again."

But there are new programs to help close that gap in homeownership. Thanks to these initiatives, minorities' homeownership rates are growing twice as fast as those for whites: according to HUD, a total of 39 percent of new homeowners since 1994 are minorities, although minorities account for just 24 percent of the population. These programs have the potential of reviving declining neighborhoods. Homeownership in a neighborhood correlates with more stable families, greater wealth, less crime, and better self-esteem among residents.

If you are a low- to moderate-income person, there are many lenders willing to lend you the money for a mortgage, such as banks, mortgage companies, and savings and loans. Plus, there are African American institutions that have historically provided money to help black families buy homes. You can find a list of minority-owned commercial banks by contacting the National Bankers Association at 1-202-588-5432. The National Partners in Homeownership, a coalition of sixty-six national groups representing the housing industry, lenders, nonprofit groups, and all sectors of government, has also launched initiatives to close the homeownership gap. You can find out about these and other programs by calling Community Connections, at 1-800-998-9999. Most states have affordable housing programs as well. You can contact your state housing agency, whose number is available by calling the National Council of State Housing Agencies at 1-202-624-7710.

A few people are fortunate enough to be able to pay cash for a home, which will save thousands of dollars on mortgage interest costs. Alternatively, you may find an owner who will let you "assume the mortgage," which means that once you make the down payment, you just keep paying the existing mortgage. Such mortgages can be hard to find, but they can be a good deal if you get one written with a very low mortgage rate.

Most commonly, however, you will borrow the money to buy a house from a bank, thrift, or credit union. Before approving your mortgage loan, lenders look for a solid employment history, such as two years or more with your current employer, and a good credit rating, for at least the past year, according to the American Bankers Association.

In addition, lenders these days will make loans to people with less than perfect credit records, although such loans will be more expensive than conventional ones. However, steer away from the subprime lend-

ing market, which charges people with spotty credit histories higher interest rates than they could get elsewhere. The subprime lending market, which we discuss in chapter 10 ("Avoiding Scams"), sometimes
charges rates as high as 250 percent per year, according to *Consumer Reports*. These loans, which are legal in most cases, account for an ever-
growing segment of the consumer lending industry: they represented
15 percent of home-equity loans in 1997, according to the Federal
Trade Commission, and 8 percent of new car financing and 14 percent
of used-car loans, according to a recent dealer survey by J. D. Power and
Associates. These predatory lenders, who often work out of their cars,
might knock on your door or call you on the phone. Abuses are increasing, especially against the poor, the elderly, and minorities. If you
have a poor credit record and are trying to get a mortgage loan, contact
HUD, Fannie Mae, or Freddie Mac for recommendations about reputable lenders.

How costly a house can you afford? A general rule of thumb is that
an affordable home costs 2½ times the gross annual salary of the potential buyer or buyers. In addition, lenders generally require that monthly
housing costs plus any long-term debts should not exceed 36 percent of
your monthly gross income. Your monthly mortgage payment is the
combination of the "principal, interest, property taxes, and insurance,"
or PITI. The principal is the amount of money you borrowed, and in the
early years of the mortgage the bulk of your payment goes toward the
interest rather than the principal, in a process known as "amortization."
Fannie Mae can provide you with charts to show the maximum loan
amount you qualify for. Lenders also recommend that the monthly
housing costs themselves—namely, the mortgage payment, property
taxes, insurance, and, if applicable, condominium or cooperative fee—
should not total more than 28 percent of your monthly gross income,
although this is a conservative figure and not by any means a hard and
fast rule. There is a lot of flexibility here, depending on the type of loan
you take out.

Your "gross" income refers to all the money you earn before you pay
taxes or deduct any expenses. A "condominium," or condo, is a unit
that you own in a multifamily development and is often an apartment

or town house. You own the unit you buy, but you must pay a monthly maintenance fee on it, along with the mortgage. Tenants jointly own common areas, yards surrounding the buildings, parking lots, and recreational facilities. In a "cooperative," also known as a co-op, you don't own the property you live in; instead you buy shares of stock in a corporation that gives you the right to live in a particular unit. Usually these are apartment buildings. The biggest drawback for co-ops is that owners are jointly liable for all debts pertaining to the complex, so if a fellow tenant is sued for an accident involving negligence on common grounds, all the tenants will be held liable in the insurance policy. Similar to a condo, you pay a monthly maintenance fee and a mortgage, and both co-ops and condos generally have rules that govern what changes you can make to your unit, for example.

Before you actually begin looking for a home, go to a lender and get "prequalified" for a loan. This will tell you whether you qualify for a mortgage and how large a home loan you could be eligible for. This is a free service. You need to provide the lender with data such as your income, assets, credit report, debts, expenses, and marital status.

Always shop around and seek out the best deal on a mortgage loan. Check with at least six different lenders when looking for a mortgage. To do this, read the local newspaper listings of mortgage loan rates; call up banks, credit unions, savings and loans, and mortgage companies; and visit relevant Web sites. Some of the major home-buying Web sites you'll want to check out include Fannie Mae, www.fanniemae .com; Freddie Mac, www.freddiemac.com; HUD, www.hud.gov; E-Loan, www.eloan.com; National Association of Realtors, www.realtor.com; Homeseekers, www.homeseekers.com; CyberHomes, www.cyberhomes .com; Bank Rate Monitor, www.bankrate.com; LoanGuide, www.loanguide .com; and U.S. Department of Veteran Affairs, www.va.gov. You can also phone Freddie Mac (1-888-780-2060) to get information about mortgage rates. In addition, Freddie Mac has issued a new study about the credit disparity between minorities and whites, which you can get free on their Web site or by phoning them.

There are mortgages with different maturities and payment terms. In addition to fixed-rate mortgages, which give you the security of paying the same amount over a set period of time, such as thirty years, there are also adjustable-rate mortgages (ARMs) with interest rates that fluctuate, usually no more than once a year, based on current financial market activity. These adjustments are pegged to an economic index, such as one-year Treasury securities, plus a fixed number of percentage points. Initial rates will be lower than on a fixed-rate mortgage, to compensate you for taking on the additional risk of fluctuating rates in the future. If rates rise dramatically, you'll end up paying more than you would on a fixed-rate loan. However, by way of protection to home buyers, the federal government requires a cap on adjustable-rate mortgages that limits the total the rate can increase over the life of the loan to 6 percent.

Interest rates change often, even daily, so you will want to record the date of your rate quote for your mortgage loan. One way to evaluate the interest rate paid is by examining the annual percentage rate (APR). It indicates the "effective rate of interest paid" per year, which includes points and other closing costs and spreads them over the life of the loan. The APR provides you with a common point of comparison when looking at mortgage loans, but you need to examine the whole product before choosing one. You also need to think about the different maturities of mortgage loans. Rather than getting the conventional thirty-year fixed-rate mortgage, you could get a fifteen-year fixed-rate mortgage. And you would save a tremendous amount in interest costs in doing so.

The best deal for you is to seek the shortest length of loan with the lowest possible interest rate. Let's say you take out a $100,000 home mortgage loan at an interest rate of 8 percent. If you were to take out a fifteen-year mortgage versus a thirty-year one, you save a whopping $92,078.75, which you can then invest in stocks, mutual funds, or other investments, thus reaping a handsome return on your money. Plus, with the fifteen-year loan you build equity faster, because more of your payment goes toward the principal. In order for this to work, however, you need to have sufficient income to make the higher monthly payments on the shorter loan.

You need to calculate all your out-of-pocket expenses when buying a home. Keep in mind that there are two basic sets of expenses for home buyers. First is the one-time cost of buying the house, including moving, selling your previous house or apartment if you have one, home inspection fees, and Realtor and attorney fees. In addition to this, you must pay the down payment and closing costs, which vary a great deal in amount, depending on the selling price of the home and the terms of your loan. The amount can be as low as 5 percent to 10 percent of the selling price of the house, but it could be a lot higher. Remember, too, that the down payment takes care of part of the selling price.

Besides the cost you incur at the moment you purchase your home, there are ongoing expenses once you own a house. These include homeowners insurance (usually part of the mortgage payment), expenditures on lawn care, furniture, and interior decoration, and maintenance and repairs, such as hiring a plumber to fix clogged drains, replacing the roof, or installing new appliances. It can all add up to thousands of dollars. You'll need to have a regular savings plan to pay for these items as they pop up.

Many people cite difficulty in accumulating the down payment as their major obstacle in homeownership. However, thanks to programs run by Freddie Mac and Fannie Mae, it's now possible to purchase a home with only a 3 percent down payment and total up-front costs of around $4,000. No application fee or private mortgage insurance is required. The Fannie Mae mortgages are available only to people who earn up to 100 percent of the median family income in their particular region, with exceptions for certain high-cost areas. You can call Fannie Mae to get a list of banks in your area that make such loans. The number is 1-800-7FANNIE, and their Web site, www.Homepath.com, has a great deal of consumer information. In addition, if you request it, Fannie Mae, which is the largest originator of mortgages in the country, will send you their free booklet entitled *A Guide to Homeownership*.

In some cases, if you put down less than 20 percent to purchase a home, you'll have to buy private mortgage insurance (PMI). The insurance premiums are usually added to your monthly mortgage payment. Thus you should ask lenders what the lowest allowable down payment is with and without PMI. Some lenders will also charge you a fee if you pay off your mortgage early. So try to find a loan with no prepayment penalties, if you think you may pay off your mortgage ahead of schedule or refinance your mortgage if interest rates drop.

There are other government programs to help home buyers, as well. They include Veterans Administration (VA) guarantees on loans, which do not require a down payment and usually have low interest rates. Homes must meet VA standards of building and safety requirements, and there is no limit on the dollar amount financed. Only veterans qualify under this program. You can call the VA at 1-800-827-1000 to get more information.

You should get a real estate agent to help you find a home. Their services are free, because agents typically represent the sellers, and their salary is a commission based on the home's sale price. To find a good agent, ask for recommendations from family and friends. Besides showing you homes that are for sale, your agent can give you a comparative market analysis, or CMA, which shows what comparable homes in the area have sold for recently, so you can tell whether you're getting a good price. When you buy a home listed with a real estate broker, remember that the broker works for the seller, not the buyer. Never reveal the highest price you're willing to pay for a home to an agent working for the seller; indeed, it's wise to say nothing about price until you make an offer.

The Internet is a great tool in helping you find the right home. The Web site realtor.com is the Internet site of the National Association of Realtors. By entering the city, state, and ZIP code of the area in which you want to buy a home, plus information about price range, number of bedrooms, and other features you would like, you can see a picture and description of available homes.

When selecting a home, you'll need to consider many factors, such as the location; the quality of the nearby schools, if you have children; the crime rate; and the general economic outlook for the neighborhood. If the neighborhood has thriving businesses, new buildings going up, and well-maintained homes, this bodes well for its economic growth and the price appreciation of houses there. Visit the house in the daytime, in the evening, on weekdays, and on weekends before you buy, to get a real sense of the neighborhood.

You'll need to consider certain structural features about the house. A professional home inspector can help you determine whether the house is sound, in terms of the foundation, roof, plumbing, insulation, and electrical and heating systems. Such an expert can also alert you to termite damage in wooden structures of the house or water damage in the basement. If the house has any problems, you can get an estimate as to how much it would cost to repair them, then bargain with the seller to lower the price on the house accordingly.

How do you know if you're getting a good price on your house? You can look in the local newspaper and often see what comparable homes have sold for in the area. It's also easy to do a price comparison through realtor.com. Normally, homes sell within thirty to ninety days of being listed, but in "hot" real estate markets, where demand outstrips supply, there may be several offers, and properties can move very fast. Sometimes you can get a good deal on a home by finding a "distressed seller," one who is forced to sell because of bankruptcy, foreclosure, divorce, loss of a job, or some other urgent reason. To find such properties, contact the foreclosure department at local mortgage lenders. Call HUD's Federal Housing Administration, since they periodically sell houses carrying federal loans that have been repossessed. And check the probate court for a record of properties being sold through estates; sometimes, when someone dies without leaving a will or heirs, properties are sold by auction for the amount of the back taxes owed. Whenever you buy a property through any of these channels, always be sure to have it inspected first, as it might be in bad shape.

To make an offer on a house, use a real estate broker or lawyer to present a written and signed purchase agreement to the seller, at a set price under specified terms. You must also submit a payment known as "earnest money" to the agent's brokerage firm. This shows that you're serious about the transaction. Amounts vary based on the cost of the property. If the seller accepts your offer and you back out of the deal, you forfeit this money. If the seller rejects your offer, you get back your earnest money.

Let's say you already own a home. When does it make sense to refinance? Experts recommend refinancing your home when the market rate is at least two percentage points below the rate on your loan, so if the interest rate on your mortgage is, say, 9 percent and the rate goes to 7 percent, refinancing is probably a good deal. When you refinance, you will likely pay between 3 percent and 6 percent of the outstanding principal (the amount of the loan) in closing costs, so you want to make sure that the benefits of refinancing outweigh the costs of doing so. It may be cheaper to decrease the number of years of the mortgage or double up on your payments, rather than refinancing.

You can also get a free brochure online entitled "A Consumer's Guide to Mortgage Refinancings," published by the Consumer Information Center, at www.pueblo.gsa.gov. It will help you determine the costs of refinancing and whether it makes sense for you.

Some people decide to pay off their mortgage early and thereby save thousands of dollars in interest costs. You'll need to make a careful evaluation of your own personal financial situation to determine if this makes sense for you from an economic standpoint. But take note that such a practice has a long tradition in the African American community: black churches have a history of paying off their mortgages early and holding a "mortgage burning" ceremony to celebrate that feat. Indeed, it would be hard to find a black church that has ever defaulted on its mortgage loan, and most pay off their mortgages well before the thirty-year note comes due.

Jade Martin* never thought she would be able to afford a home. A single, thirty-six-year-old black woman, she worked as a secretary and earned $20,000 a year. Martin had a few credit card debts, as well as some student loans outstanding from Howard University, where she had obtained an undergraduate business degree in 1986. "I had bad credit," she explains. "I owed money on bills I hadn't paid in a while, plus my student loan was in arrears." Her total debt came to about $2,000. She was renting an apartment in the Shaw area of Washington, D.C., for about $500 a month and thought that she would always be a renter.

---

*Pseudonym.

"I assumed that if you had outstanding debt, you couldn't buy a house," recalls Martin.

Then, one day back in 1997, she happened to be surfing the Internet, looking up information about homes, and stumbled upon the Web site of the Department of Housing and Urban Development—www.hud.gov. There you can click on the name of whatever state you want and find names and phone numbers of organizations like HomeFree-USA, which provide mortgage counseling to low- and moderate-income people. Martin decided that of the three or four agencies listed in the D.C. area, HomeFree-USA seemed to provide the most services. So she made an appointment and went to see them the next day.

Martin met with Freda Williams, a counselor at HomeFree-USA, and became a member of the organization, which cost $75 for the year. As a member she became entitled to attend seminars and counseling sessions. The first thing Freda told her was, "Boost your income a little." So Martin got a second job, working part-time as a data-entry clerk for a federal agency, in the evenings from six P.M. to ten P.M. She did this in addition to her secretarial job, from nine A.M. to five P.M., for a nonprofit organization. For one year she worked these two jobs and paid off all her bills. She got in the regular habit of paying all her bills on time. In addition, she took ten to twelve hours of classes about the home-buying process, offered by HomeFree-USA. The classes dealt with such topics as how to work with a Realtor, down payments, contract negotiations, credit, interest payments, points, closing, and settlement.

"I wanted to get my finances in order, to be mortgage-ready," explains Martin. "I didn't want to be in a situation where I could be exploited in any way."

Williams informed Martin about all the government programs available to help first-time, low- and moderate-income home buyers in Washington, D.C. One of the programs, called Homeownership Purchase Assistance Program, run by the D.C. government, enabled Martin to obtain $19,500 from the city government, to help her purchase her first home. The money is interest-free for the first five years, and then interest is charged at the rate of $15 a month for ninety-nine years. Martin was also able to qualify for a tax abatement on her home, meaning that she didn't need to pay any taxes on her house for five years. In addition, because of her low income, the tax recordation fee of $900 was waived, and the D.C. government paid for an inspection of the house. At that time in Washington, D.C., to qualify for these programs, an applicant had to be earning less than $25,000 a year. There's also a sliding scale for married couples, single parents, and the disabled.

All this culminated in the purchase of a home. Martin was able to buy a historic turn-of-the-century Victorian town house, with four bedrooms, stained-glass windows, and two bathrooms, near Howard University, for $90,000. It was in immaculate condition. Today, because of the increased demand for homes in that area, Martin believes she could sell it for $200,000.

"It's a gorgeous area," she comments. "And it's a mixed community, too. There are blacks, whites, gays—a real mix of people."

She has a thirty-year fixed-rate mortgage, carrying a 7 percent interest rate and 1½ points, which were paid by the D.C. government. She pays just $556 a month in mortgage payments—roughly the same as her old rental payments. But now she's accumulating equity. She has bought an asset that is appreciating in value. She's building wealth.

Other programs around the country are using innovative approaches to help low-income people in rural areas acquire homes, sometimes for the first time in their lives.

Kathy Goe, for example, age thirty-nine, was a single mother living in a "sweatbox" of a trailer in Lee County, in the Appalachian Mountains of eastern Kentucky. The trailer had no air-conditioning and was stiflingly hot in the summertime. When the temperature hit almost one hundred degrees, Goe would take a shower in the tiny trailer, only to find herself drenched with perspiration just minutes later. Then, in the winter, the temperature plunged to the twenties. The sliding door on the trailer wouldn't shut all the way, so Goe stuffed rags along the bottom of the door to keep out the chill, using a small kerosene heater to warm herself. She and her eighteen-year-old daughter Jessica, who lived with her, struggled to survive.

They barely had enough to eat and existed on the largesse of friends and family. Goe had relatives living in the county, who gave her produce from their gardens.

Because of a hysterectomy operation that went awry, Goe became disabled in 1988 and lived on Supplemental Security Income checks from the federal government, which currently amount to $496 a month. As a result of her disability, she can't sit or stand for very long and can't lift anything heavy.

A native of Louisville, which is two hours away, Goe had grown up in a working-class home. Her father had worked as a "dynamite man," handling explosives on construction sites, while her mother had been a nurse's aide. Goe dropped out of high school and married at age fifteen. From that union—which lasted almost nineteen years—she has two daughters, Lisa, age twenty-three, and Jessica, age eighteen.

"The marriage went bad," she recounts. Her husband, a diesel mechanic, developed a drinking problem and became abusive. She divorced him in 1991 and moved to the mountains, where she had relatives.

Lee County, like many counties in Appalachia, is a scenic, rural place, with beautiful mountain vistas, yet it's remote and hard to reach. To get there, you have to leave the main highway and drive along narrow two-lane roads with hairpin curves, winding through the mountains. Off these roads are rutted lanes of red dirt with shacks or trailers at the end of them, where people live. There is some tobacco farming in Lee County, but the biggest employer is a prison—known as the Lee Adjustment Center. The per capita income in the county is just $10,000 a year. The poverty rate is 37.4 percent. Less than 2 percent of the population has finished high school. Fifteen percent of the housing there is considered "distressed," meaning dilapidated, run-down, no indoor plumbing, no heating or air-conditioning. There are tar-paper shacks with big holes in the walls where the wind comes whistling through. Some of the trailers are rusting, and on others the ceilings are caving in.

Poverty is widespread in the region. In Kentucky's ten poorest counties the average poverty rate is 42 percent, with an annual per capita income of $6,472. About one-fourth of the nation's poorest counties is clustered in the Appalachian Mountains of eastern Kentucky and Tennessee.

This was where Goe was living, with no promise of anything better on the horizon. Then one day Herman Newton, who is the preacher at her church, Beattyville Christian Academy, told her about Habitat for Humanity, a nonprofit Christian organization that builds homes with low-income people.

Headquartered in Americus, Georgia, Habitat for Humanity works in the United States and all over the world to eliminate poverty housing. The organization's mission is to build "simple, decent, affordable houses," as they put it. These homes are sold to those in need at no profit, through no-interest loans.

Founded in 1976 by Millard Fuller and his wife, Linda, Habitat for Humanity has currently built more than 80,000 homes, providing shelter to more than 400,000 people worldwide. It has affiliates in every state in America and in sixty-three other countries around the world.

Goe filled out an application. Three months later she was approved.

You have to meet certain criteria to qualify for a Habitat home. The organization serves people whose income is generally 30 to 50 percent of the median income of the area where they live. Kathy Goe easily qualified. The median income in Lee County was $14,800 per year, and Goe was living on far less than that.

Then you have to be willing to put in "sweat equity" on your new home and volunteer 150 to 500 hours for Habitat. Goe was enthusiastic. Starting in 1996, she began putting in 524 hours of work toward her new home.

She cleaned the Habitat dormitory. She worked in the Habitat warehouse. She helped build the first of a series of houses in Lee County, hammering, hanging siding, putting on shingles. She had never done construction work before.

The following year, in 1997, she started work on her own home, along with a number of Habitat volunteers. "I was involved with everything on my home," Goe recounts. "I stood up the first wall. They let me build my bedroom walls. It was awesome."

It took six days to build the house.

Her new home is slate blue, has three bedrooms, a kitchen, living room, and bathroom, and has a beautiful view of the Appalachian

Mountains from one end of the porch. It sits just outside of the town of Beattyville, on one-fourteenth of an acre of land.

Goe participated in Habitat's 1997 Jimmy Carter Work Project, entitled Hammering in the Hills, during which fifty-two families helped build their own houses. The former U.S. president has become Habitat's most famous volunteer. Goe met Jimmy Carter and Millard Fuller, who walked through her new house.

Today Goe pays $215.86 a month on the house—$154 for the interest-free house payment and the remainder for taxes and insurance.

"She put in a tremendous number of hours of sweat equity," says Mindy Shannon Phelps, executive director of the Kentucky Habitat for Humanity in Lexington, Kentucky. "And in the two years since she moved into her home, she's continued that partnership."

Goe continues to volunteer at Habitat, wielding a hammer and helping to build homes with other people. There's plenty of work to be done. One in five families in Kentucky live in substandard homes, according to Phelps. Her organization, which partners with other groups in the state, has already built 636 homes in Kentucky and hopes to complete another 500 by the end of the year 2000.

Goe, who loves to travel, has even gone overseas to work on Habitat projects. She represented Habitat for Humanity in Ireland last year and worked on a "Mother's Day Build" with twelve Irishwomen who came over to build a home in eastern Kentucky. She's gone to Mexico and built houses with Habitat and is going to Honduras. She also does fundraising for the organization.

"Habitat is a godsend," says Goe. "I love Habitat and everything it represents. We're doing God's work. You can't go wrong.

"I thank God for Habitat," she continues. "I went from way-down poverty to where I can hold my head up high."

"We look at everybody we work with as somebody we'd invite in to dinner at our house," observes Phelps. "Kathy said to us: 'I want to be your friend, too.' And she's become one of my dearest friends. It's a blessing."

"The Lord always works it out," concludes Goe.

CHAPTER 4

Insurance

An Ethiopian proverb tells us, "Anticipate the good, so that you may enjoy it."

Anticipate the good. Strive for the good. But prepare yourself for the bad, which can happen to all of us. You may have seven lean years, then seven fat years—so you must be prepared, both spiritually and financially, for the good times as well as the bad.

You need insurance to protect yourself against the calamities that might befall you in life. People are killed in automobile accidents; their houses burn down; they're stricken by a serious disease and unable to work. What then? If you have the proper insurance, your worries will be taken care of. Your family and your property will be secure.

An insurance policy is a contract that guarantees you financial compensation in the case of death, disability, illness, disasters, or accidents. You pay a charge for this, called the "premium." The premium is higher if there's a greater probability of loss. The insurance industry uses actuarial tables to compute the statistical likelihood of such a loss happening to you, given your age, health, and other factors.

———————

For many years white-owned insurance companies would not sell black people insurance. White salesmen would not go to black neighborhoods or hire black or brown insurance salesmen. In response to this discrimination, African American churches and fraternal groups started their own burial societies in the basements of churches. Many of these burial societies later turned into African American insurance companies. They served a need. You could be buried in a grave with a headstone and not in an unmarked pauper's grave. You could be buried with dignity.

These black-owned insurance companies marketed "industrial" insurance policies to black consumers. They were also known as "debit" or "home service" policies and were sold to people with very low income. Premiums might be as low as 5 to 10 cents a week, on a $250 policy that would pay the cost of burial two or three generations ago. The insurance agent came around and collected the money from people's homes each week. But this was not insurance that protected your property against fire or theft, replaced income in case of death or disability, or paid for medical care—functions we commonly associate with insurance today. The right way to think about insurance is as income replacement in case you die or become ill or disabled.

Industrial insurance is "what our parents remember when they think about insurance," explains Calvin Waddell,* a middle-aged African American insurance agent in the Washington, D.C., area. "They would not have available to them the appropriate counsel in the insurance area," he adds. That's why Waddell has purposely chosen to develop a clientele that is 95 percent black. "I'm on a mission to educate and serve," he says. He thinks it's important for his clients to have "one stop" financial planning. Insurance should not be looked at in isolation or bought separately from other financial products, such as investing in stocks, bonds, mutual funds, and annuities. Employee benefit plans and retirement planning are also important aspects of your financial life that need to be considered with insurance.

Some industrial insurance policies still exist. You can still buy them, although the payments are monthly and the insured amounts are written in $1,000 increments. But they're expensive and offer very little insur-

---

*Pseudonym.

ance protection. Instead you need to examine the range of other insurance policies available and find those that are best suited to your needs.

LIFE INSURANCE

Life insurance is the most basic type of insurance that families with dependent children should have. It is used to provide for the survivors in case one or both of the breadwinners dies. Traditionally, men—who were the sole breadwinners in the family—purchased these policies. If the man dies suddenly, this type of insurance replaces a portion of his lost income and provides money to support his spouse and young children.

For example, if you are a forty-year-old man earning $50,000 a year, over the next twenty years that would amount to $1 million. If you were to die suddenly, your spouse and children would be bereft of that income, and their standard of living might plunge. A life insurance policy furnishes them with a safety net in the form of an assured income.

In recent years, with the emergence of two-income couples, single parents, and frequent divorce, life insurance policies have been adapted to fit these new family structures. They can be customized according to your particular situation. For example, if you're a working mother whose income is crucial to the family's livelihood, then your family's life insurance policy should cover both your income and that of your husband. If you're a single working mother who is solely responsible for supporting your children, then you should have a life insurance policy to cover your income until the children are no longer dependent on you.

For single people with no dependents, however, life insurance is not a necessity. Still, you might choose to buy a policy if you would like to provide financially for a family member, such as a niece or nephew, in the case of your death.

How much life insurance should you buy? The National Endowment for Financial Education recommends buying a life insurance policy that has a face value of eight to fourteen times your annual earnings and other liquid assets, if you are aged forty or younger. For older people, multiply your earnings four to ten times.

In calculating how much life insurance you need, you should also think about other factors particular to your own family's situation. You want a sufficient amount to replace your income if you should die. Also think about how much money you will need to pay off major debts or expenditures; come up with a number for that, and add that to the amount of life insurance you buy. Besides providing replacement income if you die, life insurance could fulfill a number of other objectives, such as paying for your children's college education, accumulating money for your retirement or long-term care, or providing ready cash for estate taxes and probate expense at the time of your death. So you need to factor all these considerations into your calculation.

We'll discuss estate planning and probate in more detail in chapter 8. Keep in mind, however, that at the time of your death, if your estate is larger than $650,000 as of 1999, your heirs will be subject to estate taxes, which are sizable, starting at 37 percent and rising to 55 percent for estates worth more than $3 million. Both the federal government and most state governments impose estate taxes. Probate is a court process that identifies the rightful heirs to your estate and the size of the inheritance each will receive. It also takes legal title of your property out of your name and puts it into the name of your heirs. This can be a lengthy and costly process, so you want to avoid it if possible.

You also need to reassess your insurance needs as major life events occur. With the advent of marriage, divorce, or the birth of a child, for example, you must reexamine your life insurance policy and update it to meet your needs.

The "death benefit" is the amount of money paid to the beneficiary if the insured person dies, and it can be paid out in a variety of ways. In a "lump sum" arrangement, you receive the full payment of the proceeds in one fell swoop. Charles Welch, senior vice president of North Carolina Mutual Life Insurance, the nation's largest black-owned insurance firm, points out, "Life insurance is the only product whereby an estate can be created with the stroke of a pen. If I died, my family would get $1 million, if I'd insured my life for that." The lump-sum payout is the best arrangement, because it enables you to invest the money yourself and ideally get a higher rate of return, rather than letting the insurance company invest it for you. With "fixed installment" payments, the insurance company invests your money for you and you receive it over a set period of time. And with an "interest only" arrangement, the insurance company simply pays you interest and continues to hold on to the principal.

The key is to purchase life insurance when you're young and healthy, not when you're old and in failing health, because this will enable you to pay smaller premiums. When choosing a life insurance plan, be sure to verify the "policy term"—that is, how long you are covered by the policy—as well as the "cash surrender value," which is the amount of money you are entitled to receive from the insurance company when you cancel the policy. The amount of the cash value will be stated in the policy. You need to be aware of how much this is before you sign anything, because it could cost you thousands of dollars if you terminate the policy. Also, inquire about ways that you could turn your life insurance policy into cash, if you needed to. This can be done in several ways, such as borrowing money against the policy's cash value or receiving "accelerated death benefits," if you have a terminal illness and a short life expectancy. Accelerated death benefits (ADBs) allow you to use some of the policy's death benefit before you die, and they have become increasingly common since their creation in 1988. Many insurance companies now offer them as a standard feature of their life insurance policies. ADBs may make sense if you suffer from a life-threatening ailment, such as heart disease or cancer, and believe that you are going to die in about one year or less; they can also be used to pay for nursing home care, for people who have a serious disease. Standard insurance industry practice is to limit accelerated death benefits to half of your policy's full amount.

Life insurance comes in two basic varieties: "term" and "cash value" insurance. Term insurance applies for a specific period of time, often one year, five years, or more, with no savings plan or other features, and is the least expensive life insurance you can buy. It pays a death benefit if you die within the time period of the policy. A young couple with limited cash might find term insurance the best deal. According to the National Association of Insurance Commissioners, "Term insurance generally offers the largest insurance protection for your premium dollar." There are different types of term insurance: annual renewable term, which is renewable each year, is the least expensive of them all and is most recommended by consumer groups. The younger you are when you buy it, the lower the rates, although the premium does increase each year as you get older. Before buying such a policy, be sure to ask the insurance company what the premiums will be if you continue to renew the policy. Find out if you will lose the right to renew the policy at a certain age.

"Decreasing term" is used mainly as mortgage insurance to pay off a home mortgage in case of your death. If you die, the insurance is used to pay off your mortgage. The annual premium stays the same, but the amount of your insurance decreases over time. This tends to be expensive, given the amount of coverage you get.

Cash value life insurance policies charge higher premiums at the beginning than do term insurance policies written for the same amount. The part of the premium not used for the cost of insurance is invested by the company and then accrues a cash value, which can be used in a variety of ways. You can borrow against the policy's cash value and take out a loan on it. You can also use the cash value to increase your retirement income or to help pay for your child's college tuition, without canceling the policy. However, to build up this cash value, you have to pay higher premiums in the early years of the policy.

You need to carefully weigh all the alternative investments out there before you put your money in a cash value policy. Cash value life insurance "costs eight times as much as term" for the same amount of coverage, according to the best-selling syndicated financial writer Eric Tyson. He adds that insurance salesmen are prone to foist cash value policies upon you, since they make bigger commissions from selling them rather than term insurance. "Life insurance tends to be a mediocre investment," he contends, noting that the insurance company quotes you an interest rate only for the first year; after that the company pays you whatever it wants and may penalize you for quitting the policy. Instead of letting the insurance company invest your money, you're better off doing it yourself, through a mutual fund or other investment firm that will bring a higher rate of return.

Cash value insurance comes in three main varieties: whole life, universal life, and variable life. Whole life insurance provides lifelong protection at a fixed premium that is based on your age at the time of purchase. The death benefit is fixed at the time you buy it. In addition, it often comes with a tax-deferred savings plan. Because of the savings feature, the premiums are higher than if you bought term insurance. You can borrow against the cash value of the plan by paying an interest rate stated in the policy.

There are also "universal life" insurance policies, flexible plans that offer adjustable death benefits and let you vary your premium payments. Such policies bear higher costs and fees than whole life plans. The premiums you pay—after subtracting expenses—go into an account that earns interest.

Then there are "variable life" insurance policies, whose death benefits and cash values fluctuate based on a separate fund, which may be invested in an equity, money-market, or long-term bond fund. There is a minimum guaranteed death benefit, but you may pay an extra premium for the guaranteed amount. The size of your death benefits and cash value can rise substantially if the underlying investments do well; on the other hand, they can also shrink if the investments do poorly.

Before you buy a cash value life insurance policy, do a careful financial analysis of your situation or hire an objective financial planner to do one for you. In most cases you'll be better off sticking with term insurance and developing an investment portfolio on your own. As we've said, you'll be able to get a higher return on your money investing it yourself or through mutual funds rather than turning it over to the insurance company and letting them invest it.

The National Association of Insurance Commissioners (NAIC),* a group of state insurance regulators, offers this advice for consumers who are buying life insurance: Get an illustration from the agent or insurance company that explains how the policy works. This will show you what benefits the company guarantees; it will also show you how benefits that are not guaranteed will change as interest rates and other factors fluctuate. It's not a precise predictor of what will happen in the

---

*Not to be confused with the National Association of Investors Corporation (NAIC), which has the same acronym and is discussed in chapter 6, "Investing."

future, however, since no one knows that for sure. In addition, find out whether or not premiums or benefits vary from year to year in your policy; how much do benefits build up in the plan; which part of the premiums or benefits is not guaranteed; and what is the effect of interest on money paid and received at different times on the policy. Bear in mind that state regulations require every new life insurance policy to carry with it a thirty-day "free look" period, during which you can reconsider your decision to purchase the policy. If you choose to cancel during the "free look" period, the company must refund the premium paid. The free look starts once you receive the policy.

If you're considering changing your current life insurance policy, you could contact the Consumer Federation of America, a nonprofit group that is the nation's largest consumer organization. They have a Life Insurance Rate of Return Service that will tell you whether your current life insurance policy is worth keeping. The service, run by James Hunt, a life insurance actuary with forty years of experience, estimates true investment returns on any cash value life insurance policy, whether it be whole life, universal life, or variable life. The service uses a computer-modeling technique to show you how the returns on your cash value policy compare with what you would earn from various alternatives, such as buying lower-premium term insurance and investing the premium savings in a hypothetical alternative investment (like a mutual fund). You receive a computer printout showing you the average annual rates of return for policy holding periods of five, ten, fifteen, and twenty years. The cost for this analysis is $45 for the first illustration and $35 for each additional illustration. You can call the Consumer Federation of America at 1-202-387-6121 to find out more; their Web site is www.consumerfed.org.

HOMEOWNERS INSURANCE

If you own a home and have a mortgage, you must get homeowners insurance; typically, your mortgage lender will require this. Homeowners insurance safeguards the structure and contents of your home, and it also protects you if you're held liable for injury to others. You can insure your home and belongings either for its actual cash value or for its replacement cost. Actual cash value is the amount that it would take to repair or replace damage to your home after deducting for depreciation. Depreciation is an accounting procedure that spreads the cost of an asset over a specified period of time. Thus your seventeen-year-old roof will be valued at less than a brand-new roof, because the old roof may be viewed as almost fully depreciated, or close to the end of its useful life. The replacement cost is the amount of money it would take to rebuild your home and replace everything in it, without deducting for depreciation, if you suffered loss from a peril such as fire or vandalism. You can calculate the replacement cost by taking an inventory of everything you own and coming up with estimates as to what it would cost to replace all of it. Insurers can provide you with worksheets to help you figure this out.

Many insurers require homeowners to insure their homes for at least 80 percent of the replacement cost; if you fail to do so, a penalty is applied and the insurance company will pay for only part of your losses. Most standard home insurance policies cover the contents of your home—that is, your personal belongings—on an actual cash value basis. Many insurers offer an option for you to insure your belongings at replacement cost, and the premium will be slightly higher for this coverage. You may want to consider this option, depending on the value of your personal belongings.

Keep an updated record of the value of your home and possessions. If, for example, you buy a new roof, add a new room, or acquire new appliances, these will all increase the value of your home. If you buy a sofa, a computer, expensive jewelry, a mink coat, or a stereo, these will all add to the value of your belongings. Check with your insurance agent at least once a year to make sure that you have adequate coverage.

If you rent an apartment or condominium, the insurance carried by your landlord will pay for damage to the building or other structural damage, such as to walls, floors, and the ceiling. However, you are responsible for any damage to your personal property, so you will need renters insurance. Generally, this protects your belongings against damages from fire or lightning, windstorm or hail, breakage of glass, explo sion, riot or civil commotion, theft, damage from aircraft or vehicles, smoke, vandalism, and malicious mischief. Those who rent apartments or condominiums should also get coverage for injury to others. If someone is hurt in your apartment, that person can sue you. The amount of liability insurance you'll need varies according to your net worth. Renters insurance policies generally run about $150 a year in premiums for coverage of $25,000 on property loss and $300,000 for liability. In addition, if you buy the policy from your auto insurance carrier, there's usually a 10 percent discount on the price.

If you live in an area that is prone to earthquakes, tornadoes, or floods, you need to get a special homeowners policy to cover these disasters. The Federal Emergency Management Agency offers flood insurance as part of a government program, and anyone can buy it, as long as the community participates in the program. About twenty thousand communities in America are currently enrolled. Call the National Flood Insurance Program at 1-800-638-6620 to find out if your community is involved. Flood insurance is generally not available on the open market. In deciding whether or not to buy flood insurance, consider carefully where your home is located and if it's in an area that is at high risk for such a disaster. If your home is located near the ocean and subject to storm and hurricane damage, then your property is in the highest risk zone. Properties located near a river, lake, or stream may also have a high potential for flooding. In these circumstances, flood insurance might make sense for you. In addition, you should consider earthquake and tornado insurance if you live in certain areas of the country. The cost of insurance for all these disasters varies, depending on the level of risk involved, age of your home, location, amount of coverage purchased, and design of the building. If your area is prone to such disasters, the premium will be higher.

CAR INSURANCE

If you own a car, automobile insurance is mandatory in most states. It covers your car and liability for bodily injury or damage to another person's property.

This is important insurance to have. If you are involved in a car accident, your insurance plan will cover the damage; the plan will also reimburse you if your car is stolen or vandalized. Liability insurance has three key components. Here they are, along with appropriate levels of auto insurance coverage recommended by *Consumer Reports:*

1. Bodily injury coverage, for yourself or others, including death of other people. You should get at least $100,000 per person and $300,000 per accident.

2. Property damage coverage, to cars and other property. States typically require only $10,000 to $25,000, but you should buy coverage of $100,000 under an umbrella liability policy.

3. Medical payments coverage, which pays medical bills for you and your passengers, up to a certain amount, regardless of who is at fault. You may not need any if you have good health insurance, but you may want to carry $5,000 to protect your passengers who may not have health coverage.

You should also get coverage for uninsured or underinsured motorists; this pays the medical expenses if you're hit by a motorist who either doesn't have insurance or doesn't have enough insurance. Collision insurance covers damage to your car caused by a collision with another car or another object, such as a tree. This coverage carries a deductible (the money you must pay to cover a loss before your insurance company begins kicking in any funds), and—as with health insurance—the higher the deductible, the lower your premium. In addition, comprehensive coverage pays for damages caused by flood, theft, fire, windstorms, and other noncollision damages. If your car is valuable, you should get both collision and comprehensive coverage; but you should drop the coverage on an older car that is not worth the cost of repairing. Choose the highest deductible you can afford, preferably no less than $500, but cancel the coverage once its cost equals 10 percent of the book value of your car.

Shop around and compare rates for auto insurance. Every year you should review your auto insurance and make sure you aren't overpaying. Compare the cost of your current coverage with what at least three other companies would charge. In 1990, the average annual auto insurance premium paid on a passenger car in the United States was $573.90, according to the NAIC. Keep in mind, however, that prices vary from place to place. In big cities, where traffic is more congested and accidents occur more frequently, the rates are higher than in small towns. People who have had a history of car wrecks will have to pay more for automobile insurance than those with a pristine driving record.

HEALTH INSURANCE

You should also have health insurance. This will protect you from the escalating costs of hospital fees, long-term illness, doctor visits, and prescription drugs. If you work for a large company, your employer probably provides such coverage, as well as some term insurance in case of your death. Most major medical policies will cover you, your spouse, and your children up to age twenty-three, if they're students. Unfortunately, because of rapidly escalating health care costs, many employers have eliminated health care benefits to workers. As a result, more than 41 million Americans lack any health insurance in this country, and many of them are low-wage workers. We strongly believe that everyone in America ought to have access to affordable health care. Nonetheless, no matter what your situation, you can choose from several health insurance options, which we're going to discuss.

If you quit your job, are forced to work reduced hours, or are fired for reasons other than gross misconduct from a company with more than twenty employees, the federal COBRA legislation (Consolidated Omnibus Budget Reconciliation Act of 1986) requires that your former employer supply health insurance to you for between eighteen to thirty-six months or until you receive a job offer. You have to pay the premium for this coverage yourself, but it still ends up being cheaper than if you had to buy health insurance on your own. You can also obtain coverage for your spouse and dependent children under COBRA.

If you work for a small company or are self-employed, you may have to buy an individual health insurance policy, and this could be expensive. You may be able to find an affordable health care plan through a professional, fraternal, or industry group. Contact the National Association of the Self-Employed (1-202-466-2100), a national organization that offers affordable health insurance plans for their members, to find out about their plan. To keep costs down, choose the highest deductible you can afford to pay, if you're healthy and have money in savings.

When choosing a health care plan, check to see whether it covers existing medical conditions; pays at least 80 percent of your medical expenses; has a lifetime benefit of $1 million; and is "guaranteed renewable." That means that you can renew the policy as frequently as you like, and the insurer can't raise your premiums or cancel your policy if you get sick. If you're unable to find any health insurance, because you can't afford it or have an existing medical condition, contact your state insurance department. Many states offer health insurance to people who have been turned down elsewhere. You should contact your state insurance commissioner to see if your state offers such a plan.

There are two major types of health plans: fee-for-service plans and managed-care plans. A fee-for-service plan, also known as an "indemnity" plan, enables you to see any doctor you like. You must pay an annual deductible. After you've paid that amount in medical bills, your insurance will begin picking up some of your medical expenses—usually about 80 percent. The remaining 20 percent, which you must pay, is called the "co-payment."

Managed-care plans are more affordable than fee-for-service. Often they have no deductibles and smaller co-payments. But the trade-off is that you're not allowed to choose your own doctor. Instead you're given a list of doctors to choose from. If you want to use a doctor whose name is not on the list, you'll have to pay more out-of-pocket costs for your medical bills. In addition, many do not provide coverage for dental care and eye care.

There are a variety of managed-care programs in existence. Two of the most common types are health maintenance organizations (HMOs), which offer prepaid, comprehensive health coverage for hospital and doctor services by contracting with a specified network of health care providers. A second major type, preferred provider organizations (PPOs), are arrangements between those who purchase care—such as employers and insurance companies—and health care providers.

To get free information about the accreditation of hundreds of managed-care plans across the nation, call the National Committee for Quality Assurance (NCQA), a private, nonprofit organization, at 1-888-275-7585 or visit their Web site at www.ncqa.org. In their free brochure entitled "Choosing Quality: Finding the Health Plan That's Right for You," they summarize some important guidelines you should use when selecting a managed-care plan:

1. Investigate quality. Find out whether the plan has been accredited by the NCQA.

2. Evaluate your needs and priorities. Figure out whether the benefits offered fit your health care needs. Ask whether your primary care doctor is included in the plan's network. If not, are you comfortable with the choices the plan offers? Where would you be hospitalized under the plan, and what network of medical specialists would be used? What is the cost—the amount of your monthly premium and other out-of-pocket expenses that you have to pay?

3. Look through the plan's member handbook to find out how the plan works, how doctors are paid, and what your treatment options are.

4. Then weigh all this information and make a decision. Remember that no one managed-care plan offers everything. "While it's tempting simply to choose the plan that costs less, or the plan your neighbor recommends, it's important, perhaps most important, to look for quality first," according to the NCQA.

For another free guide called "Choosing and Using a Health Care Plan," call the Health Insurance Association of America at 1-202-824-1790. You can also find out more about health insurance by visiting various insurance Web sites, such as Insurance News Network (www.insure.com), Insweb (www.insweb.com), and Quicken Insure-Market (www.insuremarket.com).

DISABILITY INSURANCE

You should also have disability insurance, whether you're single or have a family, because a sudden, debilitating illness could wipe you out financially. These policies replace lost income if you're ill or injured and unable to work. To protect yourself, see if your company offers long-term insurance, and if so, buy their plan; such plans generally cost about $200 a year. Otherwise buy your own disability insurance. Typically, independent plans cost about $400 to $600 per year. If you can afford to support yourself for a few months on your own savings or on company sick leave, then buy a plan whose benefits will kick in several months after your disability starts; these plans are cheaper than the ones whose benefits start immediately.

Look for disability insurance policies with the following characteristics:

1. Will replace between 70 percent to 80 percent of your current income.

2. Have fixed premiums and benefits.

3. Cannot be canceled if you file a claim.

4. Pay if you're unable to work at your occupation, as well as if you are sufficiently disabled that you can work only part-time.

5. Provide disability benefits for both accidents and illness. As you get older, it is more likely that you will be disabled from an illness rather than an accident.

6. Pay up until age sixty-five, when you can begin collecting Social Security.

When buying disability insurance on your own, inquire at professional or fraternal organizations to find a policy that offers a group rate for members. Call the Health Insurance Association of America (HIAA), an industry trade group, at 1-202-824-1790 or visit their Web site at www.hiaa.org to obtain their free guides about purchasing health and disability insurance.

Keep in mind that you are entitled to some medical and disability payments from the government. You've already paid into these programs through your tax revenues, so no additional fees are involved. Social Security, for example, pays disability benefits to people—although these payments are subject to federal income tax if your income exceeds certain limits. In addition, Social Security payments may be reduced or offset entirely by disability entitlements paid to you under other government programs. The rule is that total combined payments from Social Security, workers' compensation, civil service, and military programs cannot exceed 80 percent of average pre-disability earnings. The amount of your disability benefit depends on your average lifetime wages covered by Social Security. (We discuss Social Security in more detail in chapter 9 on retirement planning.) You're eligible for benefits after you have been disabled for five months and if the disability is expected to last twelve months or result in death. In March 1999, the average monthly payment for a disabled worker was $733, or $8,796 a year, according to the HIAA. This isn't a lot, but it is something. In addition, most states offer workers' compensation to employees who are injured on the job or suffer an illness that results from your employment. Ask your employer about this program, or contact the Department of Labor's Employment Standards Administration at 1-202-693-0309.

Social Security also has a program that pays benefits to low-income disabled people. Known as Supplemental Security Income (SSI), it is a financial safety net for individuals who are blind, disabled, or elderly (over age sixty-five) and have little in the way of assets. While no work credits are required to qualify, there is a strict limit on the amount of assets and income you may have in order to be eligible. You are allowed to have a maximum of $2,000 in personal effects and household goods for an individual and $3,000 for a couple. The house you live in is not counted as an asset when determining whether you're eligible. You may also earn up to $85 a month in income and still qualify. Those who earn up to $700 a month can qualify for Social Security disability payments, which is a separate program. In 1999, the maximum federal payment for SSI was $500 a month for a single person and $751 for a couple.

When you turn sixty-five, you will qualify for Medicare, the government-sponsored program that is the largest health insurance organization in the United States. Benefits are also available to the disabled. There are two parts to the program: part A covers hospital insurance, including inpatient hospital services, home health services, and hospice care; part B deals with medical insurance, such as the cost of physician services, outpatient services, and medical equipment and supplies.

Medicare covers only 35 to 40 percent of most senior citizens' health care expenses. The rest comes from private supplemental insurance that you can purchase, known as Medigap, or else it must be paid directly by you. Medicare does not pay for such items as routine physicals, eye examinations, dental care, and most prescription drugs. Nor does it pay for long-term care, although it does pay for some short-term nursing care.

For further information on Medicare, SSI, and disability benefits, call the Social Security Administration at 1-800-772-1213.

A separate government program is Medicaid, which provides medical care to low-income people. Each state runs its own program and determines eligibility requirements, so you need to contact your local Medicaid office to see if you qualify for benefits. There are also programs for low-income Medicare recipients who are not poor enough to qualify for Medicaid. Your local Medicaid office can tell you about them. To find the Medicaid office nearest you, call the Eldercare Locator at 1-800-677-1116.

LONG-TERM CARE INSURANCE

Long-term care insurance is another policy you may want to consider. According to one national study, of the roughly 2.2 million persons who turned sixty-five in 1990, more than 43 percent are expected to enter a nursing home at least once before they die. As you grow older, your risk of needing nursing home care increases. Moreover, women are more likely to need nursing home care than men. The study found that 13 percent of women will spend five or more years in a nursing home, compared with 4 percent of men.

Nursing home costs are high. In 1997 they averaged more than $46,000 per year, according to the National Association of Insurance Commissioners. Medicare does not cover long-term care, nor, in most cases, does the major medical insurance you may have at work; and Medicaid requires you to "spend down" your assets to the poverty level before you can become eligible. As a result, a large private insurance market has developed to pay for all or part of care in a nursing home. Almost all pay a fixed-dollar amount per day, ranging from $40 to more than $100, according to the National Association of Life Underwriters. However, these policies are expensive. Many insurance companies won't even sell you one if you are over age eighty-five and have certain pre-existing medical conditions. And if your assets are less than the cost of a year in a nursing home, it's not worth buying costly insurance to protect such a modest estate. To find out more, request a free copy of "A Shopper's Guide to Long-Term Care Insurance" by calling the National Association of Insurance Commissioners in Kansas City, Missouri, at 1-816-842-3600 or visiting their Web site at www.naic.org. The brochure has worksheets to help you compare different policies and figure out which one would be best for you. Among other guidelines, the NAIC suggests that you should not buy long-term care insurance if you meet the following criteria.

- You can't afford the premiums.

- You have limited assets.

- Your only source of income is a Social Security benefit or Supplemental Security Income.

- You often have trouble paying for utilities, food, medicine, or other important needs.

The NAIC brochure recommends that you consider buying long-term care insurance if you meet the following criteria:

- You have significant assets and income.

- You want to protect some of your assets and income.

- You want to pay for your own care.

- You want to stay independent of the support of others.

(Source: "A Shopper's Guide to Long-Term Care Insurance," National Association of Insurance Commissioners.)

BUYING INSURANCE

When choosing an insurance representative, shop around for the best deal, in terms of premium, length of coverage, benefits paid, and flexibility. There are many kinds of insurance policies, and we've discussed a number of them, such as life insurance, homeowners insurance, disability insurance, health insurance, and auto insurance.

Your first step, before approaching an insurance salesperson, is to educate yourself about these products. As *Consumer Reports* has written, "For years, insurance companies have profited from their ability to keep their underwriting standards and policy pricing opaque to consumers." Thus, you need to be armed with as much unbiased information as possible before you talk to an insurance agent.

You can get unbiased information from a number of nonprofit groups that work with consumers, such as the National Insurance Consumer Helpline, 1-800-942-4242; the National Committee for Quality Assurance, 1-800-839-6487; the Insurance Information Institute, which operates the free National Insurance Consumer Helpline, at 1-800-942-4242, and has a useful Web site at www.iii.org.; AARP, the nation's leading advocacy group for older people, 1-800-424-3410; the National Association of Insurance Commissioners, 1-816-842-3600; or your state insurance department. These organizations have free brochures about buying various types of insurance. You can also search the Internet and get quotes in a matter of minutes from several insurance companies on different policies. There are online services such as Quicken Insure-Market (www.insuremarket.com) and Insweb (www.insweb.com), as well as telephone services such as the *Consumer Reports* Auto Insurance Price Service (1-800-807-8050). We discuss using the Internet in more detail in chapter 7. In addition, *Consumer Reports,* a magazine that you can read in the public library, periodically runs articles about buying insurance.

After you've done this preliminary groundwork, contact several insurance agents and see what kinds of plans they offer. Independent agents sell plans from several different insurance companies, while "captive" agents typically work for one insurance firm and sell just that firm's policies. Commissions for both types of agents range from 5 percent to 15 percent, varying by state and by type of policy, and the commissions are not negotiable. However, the advantage of independent agents is that they give you a range of plans to choose from. To find a list of independent insurance agents near you, call the Independent Insurance Agents of America (IIAA) at 1-800-221-7917 or visit their Web site at www.iiaa.org. In September 1999, the IIAA released the result of a one-year study produced by their Urban and Minority Agents Task Force. They surveyed insurance companies, consumers, and regulators to find out trends in insurance in the minority community. You can call them for a copy or read the results of the survey on their Web site.

When choosing an insurance agent, find someone who comes highly recommended. Get at least three referrals from people you trust. Make sure the agent listens to you, reviews your financial situation before proposing a plan, and explains all the fees, charges, and commissions. Ask them if you can speak to some of their current clients as references.

"Insurance is more than a one-step process," says Charles Welch of the North Carolina Mutual Life Insurance Company. "You don't want someone who will push it on you. Insurance firms don't run 'sales,' like automobile dealers. You want to find someone you can grow with and trust."

For those who feel more comfortable dealing with black-owned insurance firms, there are fourteen of them in the United States, and there is a trade group that represents them, called the National Insurance Association. It's based in Las Vegas, Nevada, and you can call them at 1-702-269-2445 to get more information. Their 1999 roster of companies is as follows:

Atlanta Life Insurance Company
P.O. Box 897
Herndon Plaza
100 Auburn Avenue N.E.
Atlanta, Georgia 30303
phone: 1-404-659-2100
Web site: www.atlantalife.net

Booker T. Washington Insurance Company
P.O. Box 697
1728 3rd Avenue, North
Birmingham, Alabama 35203
phone: 1-205-328-5454

Gertrude Geddes Willis Life Insurance Company
P.O. Box 532
2128 Jackson Avenue
New Orleans, Louisiana 70113
phone: 1-504-522-2525

Golden Life Insurance Company
P.O. Box 293
30 Jackson Avenue
Brownsville, Tennessee 38012
phone: 1-901-772-9283

Golden State Mutual Life Insurance Company
P.O. Box 512332
1999 West Adams Boulevard
Los Angeles, California 90018
phone: 1-323-731-1131
Web site: www.gsmlife.com

Majestic Life Insurance Company
1833 Oretha Castle Haley Boulevard
New Orleans, Louisiana 70113
phone: 1-504-525-0375

North Carolina Mutual Life Insurance Company
Mutual Plaza
411 West Chapel Hill Street
Durham, North Carolina 27701
phone: 1-919-682-9201

Peoples Assured Family Life Insurance Company
P.O. Box 1529
886 North Farish Street
Jackson, Mississippi 39202
phone: 1-601-969-3040

Protective Industrial Insurance Company
P.O. Box 2744
2300 11th Avenue, North
Birmingham, Alabama 35234
phone: 1-205-323-5256

Reliable Life Insurance Company
P.O. Box 1157
718 Jackson Street
Monroe, Louisiana 71201
phone: 1-318-387-1000
Web site: Millercompanies.com

Rhodes Life Insurance Company
1716 North Claiborne Avenue
New Orleans, Louisiana 70116
phone: 1-504-943-6621

Universal Life Insurance Company
P.O. Box 241
480 Linden Avenue
Memphis, Tennessee 38126
phone: 1-901-525-3641

Williams-Progressive Life & Accident Insurance Company
P.O. Box 898
348 S. Academy Street
Opelousas, Alabama 70570
phone: 1-318-948-8238

Wright Mutual Insurance Company
2995 E. General Motors Boulevard
Detroit, Michigan 48202
phone: 1-313-871-2112

North Carolina Mutual (NCM), for example, is the largest black-owned insurance company in the United States. It sprang out of an entrepreneurial vision. A little over a hundred years ago, seven African American men gathered in a Durham, North Carolina, barber shop one evening. They decided to start an insurance company—one that would help their own people. The firm, originally called North Carolina Mutual and Providence, was officially founded on October 20, 1898, in the offices of Dr. Aaron McDuffie Moore, Durham's first black physician, who was one of the seven founders. A year later it began doing business selling burial insurance, and by 1907, it started issuing whole life policies in $100, $200, and $500 amounts. The company grew enormously over the years and today has about $10 billion of life insurance in force and over $228 million in assets—and thus ranks in the top 10 percent of the nation's life insurers. NCM operates in fourteen states as well as the District of Columbia, serving a clientele that is about 90 percent black, according to Welch.

If you think you have a good idea of what sorts of insurance policies you need, contact insurance companies that sell policies directly to the public, thus eliminating the middleman. This could reduce the amount you would pay on an insurance agent's commission, although it won't eliminate it entirely. The downside of buying your insurance directly, however, is that you won't get a professional to review your financial plan; you'll simply be sold a policy. You may want the advice of an industry professional before you make such an important purchase. Here is a list of direct-market insurers:

Direct-Market Insurers

Aetna: Life and health	1-800-584-6001
Allstate: Auto, home, renters, and life insurance	1-800-777-3900
Amica: Renters, home, life, disability, health, and long-term care insurance	1-800-992-6422
American Express Co.: Auto, homeowners, and life insurance	1-800-535-2001
Ameritas: Life and disability insurance	1-800-552-3553
American Life of New York: Life insurance	1-800-872-5963
Geico: Auto and home insurance	1-800-841-3000
Provident: Disability and life insurance	1-800-843-3426
Unum: Life, disability, and long-term care insurance	1-800-227-8138
USAA: Life, health, auto, home, and renters insurance (limited to members of the military and their families)	1-800-531-8080
Wholesale Insurance Network: Life insurance	1-800-808-5810

Telephone and/or Online Insurance Quotes

DirectQuote: Life insurance	1-800-845-3853
InstaQuote: Life insurance (www.instaquote.com)	1-888-223-2220
InsuranceQuote Services: Life, long-term care, and disability insurance (www.iquote.com)	1-800-972-1104
Insurance Information Inc.: Life insurance	1-800-472-5800
MasterQuote: Life insurance (www.masterquote.com)	1-800-627-LIFE
Preferred Quotes Insurance Services: Life insurance via e-mail at quotes@pqins.com (fax: 1-888-333-3750)	1-800-333-3750
Progressive Insurance Corp.: Auto, life, and disability insurance	1-800-288-6776
Quotesmith: Life insurance (www.quotesmith.com)	1-800-431-1147
QuickQuote: Life insurance (www.quickquote.com)	1-800-390-8271
SelectQuote: Life insurance	1-800-343-1985
TermQuote: Life insurance	1-800-444-8376

Source: *The Latino Guide to Personal Money Management* by Laura Castañeda and Laura Castellanos, Bloomberg Press, Princeton, N.J. 1999.

Before you buy any insurance policy, verify the licensing status of the insurance agent and insurance carrier, as well as the rating of the carrier. Licensed insurance companies must contribute to a pool of funds that provide consumers with some protection if the company goes bankrupt. All insurance agents and insurance companies have to be licensed in the states where they do business. Their license number is printed on their business cards. You can call your state's insurance department and verify that an agent or company is really licensed.

Choose insurance companies ranked among the very best with regard to their financial stability. Such a ranking indicates that these are the most sound companies financially and the best able to pay insurance claims. You can check the status of individual insurance companies by reviewing ratings from various agencies, such as A. M. Best, Standard & Poor's, Duff & Phelps, and Moody's Investors Service. Insurance agents can also send you the ratings on their companies. Furthermore, you can go to the library and look up the ratings yourself, in A. M. Best's ranking of insurance companies, entitled *Best's Insurance Reports*. And you can get free ratings by calling Moody's (1-212-553-0300), Duff & Phelps (1-312-368-3198), or Standard & Poor's (1-212-438-2000).

Each of these companies uses a different ranking system to assess the financial stability of insurance companies, so you will need to familiarize yourself with it. Upon request, each rating agency will send you a brochure describing their ranking system. For example, Moody's uses a scale starting with Aaa to denote insurance companies with exceptional financial security; Aa is considered excellent; A is good; Baa is adequate; and weak companies have ratings from Ba down to C. Standard & Poor's, by contrast, has a letter ranking as well as a new system of ranking insurance companies that consists of icons, called Standard & Poor's Security Circle Icons; they resemble the oval "Good Housekeeping" seal of approval. The top ranking—AAA—indicates an insurance company that is rated "extremely strong"; AA is rated "very strong"; A is "strong"; and BBB is rated "good." Only the strongest companies are allowed to use the icon, in these top four categories; those of lesser grades cannot, so whenever you see this seal of approval on an insurance company brochure, you know it is in the top tier. Standard & Poor's discusses their rating system and offers free insurance company rankings at their Web site, www.standardandpoors.com/ratings, as well as on www.insure.com.

Finally, keep in mind that your church can serve as a powerful channel to help you educate yourself about insurance as well as other important personal finance concepts. Calvin Waddell, for example, helped create a financial ministry at his church, the From the Heart Church Ministry in Temple Hills, Maryland. The 24,000-member church now hosts monthly seminars on various aspects of personal finance, including insurance, estate planning, financing a college degree, and writing a will. Moreover, the church puts into practice principles of sound financial management, which is a major factor enabling it to grow and thrive and do good works in the community. Reverend John A. Cherry is the pastor. Under his leadership, during the last eighteen years, his church has grown from a gathering of twenty-four people in a District of Columbia storefront to a mega-church with millions in the bank, a national television ministry, two sanctuaries, and a 10,400-seat building under construction.

By practicing sound principles of financial management and teaching them to the congregation, From the Heart Church has been able to do more good for more people. Their ministry has been able to achieve greater goals in the service of God. In one recent act of largesse, the church donated $1 million to build a chapel in Ghana.

As St. Paul taught us in 2 Corinthians 9:6–9:

"He who sows sparingly will also reap sparingly; and he who sows bountifully will also reap bountifully. Each one must do as he has made up his mind, not reluctantly or under compulsion, for God loves a cheerful giver. And God is able to provide you with every blessing in abundance, so that you may always have enough of everything and may provide in abundance for every good work."

CHAPTER 5

How the Market Works

We must expand our focus from the historical race gap to the vertical resource gap, the structural gap. These resource gaps affect whites who live in struggling towns throughout the nation's heartland, just as surely as they affect the African Americans and Hispanics who live in south-west Texas.

The race walls were made illegal. These walls impeded growth. They denied us the capacity to see the whole marketplace. But the vertical gap, the class gap, is growing and devastating and legal.

Every field of human endeavor has its own language. There is a language of love; there is a language of baseball; and there is a language of finance. People who work with money understand the language of finance—and so must you.

It is a field that is rapidly changing and evolving all the time. New investment products are being put on the market; some could be lucrative, others may be financially dangerous. There are periodic changes in the tax laws and forecasts about the economy that you, as an investor, need to stay on top of. So learning about finance and investments is a continual process of self-education.

You can start this process by doing the following:

1. Read one of the business or financial magazines or newspapers, such as *The Wall Street Journal, Barron's, Business Week, Black*

Enterprise, Hispanic Business, or *Investor's Business Daily.* In so doing, you will gradually master financial terms and learn about company news and earnings, as well as larger economic concepts.

2. Subscribe to a newsletter like *Louis Rukeyser's Wall Street,* a monthly publication that features in-depth interviews with experts in the field of investing, along with specific investment advice from top professionals in the industry (1-800-892-9702).

3. Watch television shows, such as Louis Rukeyser's *Wall Street Week* on public television, that feature interviews with investment professionals who dispense advice, as well as CNBC, which specializes in business news.

4. Use services like *Value Line's Investment Survey* to research individual stocks. A subscription is on the expensive side—$570 per year—but you can get it free at many public libraries. Value Line's weekly reports include ratings and forecasts on 1,700 large, publicly traded U.S. companies.

5. Use one of the Web sites and/or the personal finance software packages described in chapter 7, "Using the Internet."

You don't have to read all of these publications; obviously that would be an overwhelming task. You just need to start reading and skimming some of them, on a regular basis, so you will become comfortable with financial concepts. When culling through the business media, stick with the tried-and-true, established publications, and avoid those that have a breathless, "get rich quick" slant.

The earlier you start learning about the world of finance and investments, the better. John Rogers, an African American who is president and founder of Chicago-based Ariel Capital Management, which has $3 billion of assets under management, said he got his indoctrination to finance as a little boy. When he was twelve, his father started giving him stocks as birthday and Christmas gifts. Every three months the dividend checks arrived, and they were a source of great excitement for him. His father let him keep the checks. This early exposure piqued his interest and led him to eventually become a renowned money manager, whose views are quoted today in top financial publications.

"The stock market became a hobby of mine," he explains. "I started looking forward to getting the checks and reading quarterly and annual reports from the companies. My dad took me down to meet his broker, one of the first African American brokers in Chicago. I'd sit there and watch the tape go by." Thus began his passion for investing. Sixteen years ago he launched Ariel, one of the first African American–owned money management firms in America.

There are different ways to get started down the path of financial enlightenment. John Rogers was lucky enough to have been exposed to these concepts as a young boy. But whatever your age, you can learn about this. Some of you will want to be "do-it-yourselfers" and work on your own, at your own pace. Others will find learning about this in a group setting, such as an investment club or a series of seminars at your church or local college, most effective. Still others will prefer to find a financial adviser whom they trust to educate them about money.

Be aware, however, that many financial advisers are trying to sell you their products and services; therefore, to obtain the most objective advice, you'll be better off going to "fee only" financial planners, who do not receive commissions for the products they sell. The National Association of Personal Financial Advisors is a trade group of these professionals; you can contact them at 1-888-FEE-ONLY or visit their Web site at www.napfa.org. Alternatively, you may want to get your initial grounding in personal finance from nonprofit organizations, such as the American Association of Individual Investors, dedicated to providing impartial information to the nonprofessional (1-312-280-0170; Web site www.aaii.org); or the Coalition of Black Investors (1-336-922-6240; Web site www.cobinvest.com). We discuss more about guidelines for choosing a financial planner in the next chapter on investing.

Robert Wynn II, an African American who is financial education officer in Wisconsin's Department of Financial Institutions, commented that investing could be particularly exhilarating for minorities, because of the absolute impartiality of the principles of finance.

"The market doesn't know what color you are," he says. "It only knows what color your money is." He is an enthusiastic member of an investment club in Madison, Wisconsin, where he lives, and in his work he strives to encourage financial literacy through programs across the state.

What we want to do in this chapter is put flesh on the bones by showing you how the capitalist system in America operates and how you can be a part of it.

The key characteristic of a capitalist economy like that of the United States is its constant dynamism and flux. The economy expands or contracts, depending on where it is in the business cycle. New companies are born all the time; they go through a maturation process, rather like a person—of birth, youth, middle age, then decline. All the while they're seeking to maximize their profits. Then other companies with cutting-edge innovations come on the scene and upstage them. In this fashion new industries are born, then wax and wane. Microsoft, for example, the most powerful and profitable company in the computer industry, is just over twenty years old and has upstaged established companies like IBM.

The famous economist Joseph Schumpeter said that a capitalist economy is characterized by "creative destruction." New competitors come into the marketplace, compete away the profits of the older firms, and thus the economy is continually innovating. Profits consist of the money that a company has left over, after expenses and taxes have been paid. They are the reward for those who have succeeded in a competitive marketplace.

Entrepreneurs are the people who start these new companies. Some of these companies are privately held, but others are "publicly traded"—that is, their shares are sold in the stock market. When a fledgling company arrives at a certain level of financial performance, it can make the great leap to selling its shares to the public. There are two major reasons the owners of the company decide to do this. First, going public enables the company to raise the necessary capital to expand. Second, it limits the firm's legal liability should there be a downturn in its fortunes. By going public, the entrepreneurs decide to relinquish some of the ownership of their firm and spread that ownership among many shareholders. By becoming a corporation—rather than a partnership or some other type of entity—the owners' financial risk is limited to the amount of personal capital they have invested.

Why do shareholders decide to buy stock in a company? Quite simply, they want to partake in the company's profits. Each stockholder becomes a part owner of the company. The stockholders have decided that they could get a better return on their money by investing in the shares of a company, as opposed to any other alternative out there—whether it be real estate, a bank certificate of deposit, or a savings bond. They have decided that the return on their investment justifies the risk they are taking by buying the stock. The potential profit, or reward, justifies the risk, which in this case is the potential for losing the money invested.

Over the last several decades stocks have proven to be a good place to put your money, yielding a compounded rate of return of 11 percent annually from 1926 to 1997, despite fluctuations in "up" or "down" markets. A period of generally rising stock prices is known as a "bull" market, while a downturn in stock prices is known as a "bear" market.

Stockholders can make money from stocks in two ways. They may receive cash dividends from the company, which are usually paid quarterly. But they make their greatest profits from capital appreciation, when the stock rises in price and can be sold for more than what the investor paid for it. (Of course, if the stock falls in value, investors lose money.) This is not gambling when it is done correctly. If proper research is done on a company before its stock is purchased, and if its shares are invested in for the long haul—say, five years or more—you are enabling yourself to participate in the fruits of this company's success over time. You should base your decision to invest on solid data, such as the caliber of the company's managerial talent, its superior products and services, its prospects for growth, and its market share. Thus, investing in stocks needs to be the result of a rational, well-thought-out decision. You should not just act on a "hot tip." On the other hand, if the company does poorly and its profits go down, then you as a shareholder will lose money on your investment. There is no guarantee that you *will* make money in the stock market. Individual stocks may fail; but over time the stock market as a whole has risen. In fact, there's never been a twenty-year period in American history when stocks didn't outperform every other investment.

As a result, those who invest in a broad portfolio of stocks for the long haul—with a "buy and hold" strategy—have made money and have received a steady return on their money, balancing risk with reward. This is in marked contrast with people who "speculate," or take on an enormous amount of risk for a potentially huge reward. You can make a killing as a speculator, but if you don't know what you're doing and lack large amounts of capital, you can lose everything. One of the most popular ways to speculate today is "day trading," which involves trying to profit from small price changes in a stock, often on a daily or hourly basis. Traders are less interested in the stock's underlying value and tend to view the stock merely as a piece of paper that can be quickly bought and sold for a profit. This, too, is highly risky, and only a few people come out ahead. According to recent estimates cited in *The New York Times,* 90 percent of day traders lose money. We think you should be very, very cautious about day trading.

———————

The stocks, or "equities," of most companies in the United States are "common stock." By buying these shares, you become a part owner of the company and are known as a "stockholder" or "shareholder."

As we've said, there is no guarantee that you will make money on common stock. In purchasing common shares, you take the risk that the stock could rise or fall in value and may or may not pay a dividend. If the company does succeed, however, you will share in its success from a financial standpoint, because rising sales and earnings translate into higher stock prices.

"Preferred stock" is another type of stock that companies issue. Usually preferred shares are issued by large, mature companies, such as utilities and auto manufacturers. It is called "preferred" because if the company goes bankrupt, preferred shareholders will be paid off ahead of common stockholders, from the remaining assets of the company. In addition, on preferred stock the amount of the dividend is guaranteed and paid before dividends are paid on common stock. The primary advantages of owning preferred stock are the relatively high dividends and the more stable price of the stock, compared with those of common shares. Another variant, known as "convertible" preferred shares, allows you to convert your preferred shares into a set amount of common stock, when certain conditions are met. Owning preferred shares reduces investor risk but also limits your reward, since preferred shares do not appreciate as much as common shares; preferred shareholders will benefit very little if the company's performance, and its stock price, should soar. On the other hand, common shareholders will benefit from an upsurge in a company's earnings, because when a company's sales and earnings rise, the price of common stock will usually follow.

When new companies first sell their shares to the public, they do so through an initial public offering (IPO). The United States leads the world in the issuance of IPOs. For the past couple of decades, these young, high-growth companies have been the engine fueling the U.S. economy. They've been steadily creating jobs, even as giant companies were downsizing.

Entrepreneurs flourish in the United States because of the unique climate for doing business here. America has very flexible capital markets, which are more open and participatory than any others in the world. This results in great liquidity and breadth of shareholders—both institutional and retail. Institutional shareholders consist of organizations, such as banks, insurance companies, and pension funds. Retail investors are individual people, ranging from the well-heeled "high net worth" client to the person of modest means.

Overall, 50 percent of all the stock (equities) in the United States is owned by individuals. By contrast, just 10 percent of all the equities in Europe are owned by individuals. Thus, there is a wide range of stock ownership across the United States, across a broad array of income groups. We see Wall Street as "walled in" for the elite. But the bridge from Wall Street to Main Street is already there, through pension funds and other vehicles that invest the money of working people in the stock market.

Some of these individuals own the stocks outright, while other people own them through their corporate pension plans. Investors fall into two broad categories: individual, or "retail" investors; and large organizations, such as banks, insurance companies, and pension funds, known as "institutional" investors. Many investors—both retail and institutional—own stocks and other securities through "mutual funds." A mutual fund is an investment company that buys and holds the stock of many companies. (Mutual funds also buy bonds and other investment vehicles.) You can buy shares in a mutual fund and, therefore, own stock in a variety of companies. Owning shares in a mutual fund helps you to diversify risk and reduce the volatility, or dramatic swings, in your portfolio.

America also has a sound regulatory structure in place, overseen at the federal level by the Securities and Exchange Commission (SEC), which ensures that the capital markets are run fairly and openly.

When a company goes public, it must file a preliminary registration statement with the SEC, describing the outlook for its business. It hires an investment bank, which is a firm that specializes in raising the capital that companies need for long-term growth. Investment banks advise companies at various stages of development about the best strategies for raising money. Depending on market conditions, the investment bank may advise the company to sell shares in a stock offering or sell debt through a bond issue.

If the company decides upon a stock, or "equity," offering, then the investment bank prepares a preliminary "prospectus," or description of the offering, to obtain indications of interest from potential customers. The company then hires underwriters, who buy the new issue and resell it to the public. The underwriters' goal is to raise capital under the most advantageous terms possible for the company, which is also called the "issuer" of new shares. Generally the underwriters form a syndicate to distribute the shares—thereby reducing their risk—with a lead manager running the deal.

The new company must decide on which stock exchange it should list its shares. There are advantages and disadvantages associated with listing on the different exchanges, because they have different approaches to trading shares and offer different services to the companies that list there. The New York Stock Exchange (NYSE) is the largest and most venerable stock exchange in America and has long been considered the province of top-quality, well-established blue-chip companies. But more and more IPOs are listing on the NYSE. At the NYSE the trading of shares is done by double auction, meaning that offers to buy and sell securities take place side by side; stocks are sold for the highest price, or "bid," and bought for the lowest offer, or "asked" price, which takes place as a result of supply and demand. This all happens on the floor of the exchange, located in New York City. Ninety percent of the orders come through via computer from member firms, but then they are routed through the brokers on the floor of the stock exchange, so that incoming orders can meet all the other existing orders for the stock. A specialist—or dealer—is responsible for maintaining an orderly market in a particular stock. If, for example, the "spread"—or gap between the bid and asked price—is too wide, then the specialist begins buying and selling shares in that stock, thus narrowing the spread and stimulating trading.

The other major exchange—currently the largest and fastest-growing stock exchange in the world—is the Nasdaq Stock Market. It was the first electronic stock market when it debuted in 1971, and many other stock exchanges around the world have since adopted similar screen-based trading systems. Nasdaq's structure allows multiple market makers—or independent dealers—to compete for investors' orders in an electronic trading market, created through a sophisticated computer and telecommunications network. There is no central meeting place for the exchange; instead broker/dealers are connected by the computer of the Nasdaq system and by telephone. Trading is done using this screen-based system. The dealers must maintain an inventory of securities on the Nasdaq Stock Market and announce bid and asked prices constantly. The trading department quotes a "net price" to the customer, which includes the dealer's markup, or profit, on the transaction. The customer is free to negotiate for a lower price, and the order is completed as soon as the customer and dealer agree.

"Market orders" are instructions to buy or sell stock at the best available price and are the most common type of trade. "Limit orders" instruct your broker to buy or sell stock at the limit price—which is the price you set when placing the order—or better.

The American Stock Exchange, or Amex, merged with the Nasdaq Stock Market in November 1998. Amex was created more than a hundred years ago and is headquartered in New York City. Since the merger, Amex continues to conduct trading in the same manner as it did in the past, using a two-way auction process conducted on a trading floor. Both Nasdaq and Amex are owned by the National Association of Securities Dealers (NASD), a not-for-profit organization based in Washington, D.C. Their Web site, www.nasdaq-amex.com, gets an average of 23 million "hits," or visits, per day from people seeking financial information on the Internet, and it was voted Best Financial Site for 1998 by the Web Marketing Association.

Most IPOs in America list on the Amex and the Nasdaq, although many now list on the NYSE. There are also smaller, regional stock exchanges and some new online stock exchanges that are emerging as well.

The term "Wall Street," which is an actual street in New York City, refers to the entire marketplace where stocks are traded. Many firms involved in the stock market are located not just on Wall Street, but in many places throughout New York City, as well as at hundreds of locations around the country and, indeed, all over the world. Every day billions of shares are traded in this global marketplace.

Companies tend to be designated as "small cap," "midcap" or "large cap." "Cap" refers to the market capitalization, which is the price of an individual share of the company—say, $5 a share—multiplied by the number of shares outstanding. Thus a company whose shares trade at $50 each, with 500,000 shares outstanding, has a market capitalization of $25 million. That's considered "small cap." The market cap figure is used to convey a company's heft relative to all the other publicly traded companies out there. Definitions vary for this, and they've also evolved as bigger and bigger companies emerge in the market; but generally, "small cap" companies are those with less than $1.5 billion in market capitalization; "midcap," $1.5 billion to $5 billion; and "large cap," above $5 billion. An even smaller designation, "microcap," is given to companies with total market value of $50 million or less. Generally, buying stock in very small, new companies tends to be riskier than buying shares of large, established firms. We should point out, however, that every company was once small. What counts, as we've said, is a company with good management, a good product, and a good future. Some very big companies have a great future ahead of them. Others do not.

When a stock is "listed" on an exchange, it means that its stock has been accepted for trading on that exchange. It can be "delisted" for various reasons, such as a drop in the company's earnings below a certain level. To be listed, the company usually has to have a minimum market capitalization and have several years of audited financial statements, among other requirements.

These listing requirements at the different exchanges have tended to cause the oldest, largest firms to list on the NYSE. Smaller and younger companies are more likely to be traded on the Amex. The newest firms of all tend to be traded in the Nasdaq market. However, there are important exceptions. Notably, some of the giants in the high-tech industry—such as Microsoft, Intel Corporation, and Cisco Systems—as well as those in other industries have chosen to stay on Nasdaq even after they grew very big.

More and more foreign companies—especially some of the biggest ones—are choosing to list their shares on American stock exchanges. These shares are known as American depositary receipts (ADRs). Many investors like such stocks because they want exposure both to American as well as to foreign markets, for the purposes of diversifying their portfolio. Nowadays you can buy them as easily as you would the shares of an American company.

A registered representative, or stockbroker, who works at a brokerage firm, sells shares of stocks, bonds, and other investments to the public. The title refers to the fact that this person is registered with the SEC and represents the firm's brokers and dealers who actually execute the customer's trades on a stock exchange. The stockbroker gets a commission every time stocks are bought or sold; you need to find out just how much that commission is, since the amount varies in the brokerage industry. In addition, with the advent of the Internet, it is also possible to bypass the stockbroker altogether and buy or sell securities directly, at a deep discount, using online brokers such as Charles Schwab, E*Trade, and DLJdirect.

Brokerage houses typically have several trading departments: one for stocks listed on the exchanges; one for over-the-counter stocks, which are not listed on a stock exchange but can be traded on Nasdaq; and one for various types of bonds. They also have a research department where security analysts size up the investment potential of various securities, an underwriting department for new issues, a corporate finance department for investment banking, a public finance department, if they deal in government securities, and a record-keeping department.

After a company goes public, its shares are traded on a stock exchange, which furnishes the investor with a sufficient number of bids to buy and offers to sell, along with an opportunity to sell shares at any time. This provides investors with liquidity: that is, the ability to transform their shares into cash at any time. Through this process of buying and selling shares, capital is generated for companies, which in turn enables new industries and new jobs to be created.

In its annual report, a company discusses its net profits, or earnings, which are its after-tax profits. This is important information for investors to know. Let's say that the Palomino Corporation, a hypothetical company that manufactures equipment for livestock shows and rodeos, has one million shares outstanding and reported earnings of $750,000 last year. That means each shareholder would be entitled to 75 cents a share ($750,000 divided by 1,000,000). This number is called the "earnings per share" and is closely watched by equity analysts, who are paid to follow the fortunes of publicly traded companies and then issue recommendations as to whether the stock is a good buy. These analysts typically give recommendations like "buy," "hold," or "sell." They make their recommendations based on an evaluation of the company's earnings from prior years, and from this they project future earnings. When evaluating whether a company's shares are a good investment, equity analysts take into consideration such factors as the long-term outlook for the company's industry; its managerial talent; any unique patents, inventions, or other assets it holds; and its financial strength. Some investors use analyst reports when determining which stocks to purchase.

In addition, the annual report always has two important sections that actual and potential shareholders need to review. First is the balance sheet, which shows what the company owns—namely, its "assets"—along with how much money it owes, which is called its "liabilities." The difference between these two is known as "stockholders' equity," which is defined as the net worth, or the stockholders' ownership in a company. Shareholders studying the fortunes of the Palomino Corporation will want to look at how much profit was produced by each sales dollar, as well as how much profit was produced by each dollar of stockholders' equity. Is the company making money from booming sales, or is it simply selling off assets it already has on hand, such as buildings or equipment?

Let's say Palomino Corporation announced a two-for-one stock split. Instead of one million shares outstanding, they now have two million. Each shareholder now has twice as many shares of the company. If the stock price happened to be $15 before, it would now be $7.50. The earnings per share figure is halved. So even though a shareholder has twice as many shares, the total value would be the same. It's the same size pie, just cut into smaller pieces. Unless the dividend is increased, the stockholder receives nothing new when a company's stock is split.

There are several reasons a company decides to split a stock. If a stock price is soaring, many people are reluctant to pay such a high price for the shares, so splitting the stock makes the price more attractive. Although the underlying value of the shares hasn't changed after the stock split, people still feel they're getting more of a bargain when they buy the shares at the cheaper price. In addition, stock splits usually occur when there is a new high in the company's share price, which implies good news about the company's outlook and earnings; so stock splits tend to be viewed as a positive development by investors—a sign that a company is robust. Lower-priced shares also tend to increase the amount of trading in a stock, thus making shares easier to buy and sell.

When you buy a stock, similar to the purchase of anything else, you want to make sure you get a good deal on it and not pay too much. To assess whether a stock price is a fair one, investors look at the earnings outlook, the dividend prospects, and the company's financial health. Then they compare this data with those of other companies in similar industries, as well as with other investment opportunities. Over time, a company's stock price will generally rise or fall, in line with these fundamental factors.

The "price/earnings ratio" (P/E ratio) and the "dividend yield" are two yardsticks commonly used on Wall Street to size up stock prices. The P/E ratio is the relationship between the current stock price and the earnings per share. You calculate it by dividing the stock price by the earnings per share figure: in the case of the Palomino Corporation, if its current stock price is $15 and it has an earnings per share of 75 cents, then its P/E is 20 ($15 divided by 75 cents per share). Generally, a low P/E ratio is considered desirable, and a higher P/E can mean greater investment risk—but don't consider this a hard and fast rule. Sometimes a stock with a higher P/E will be a better deal than one with a lower P/E—if, for example, the profits of the first company are growing a lot faster than those of the second one.

The dividend yield, often called simply "yield," refers to the annual percent return that the dividend provides to the investor. You calculate it by dividing the annual cash dividend per share by the price of the stock. Thus, if the Palomino Corporation pays its stockholders an annual cash dividend of 25 cents, and the stock price is $15, then the return, or dividend yield, is 2 percent (25 cents per share divided by $15).

A stock paying a higher dividend yield is not necessarily more attractive than one paying a lower yield. You have to consider how safe the dividend is and what the chances are that it could be increased in the future. In any case, the P/E ratio and the dividend yield are numbers that are always changing—sometimes fluctuating widely, depending on news affecting a company or its industry.

The members of the board of directors of the company are elected by the stockholders to oversee how the company is run. Shareholders have a say in the operation of the firm, because each share outstanding is entitled to an equal vote in the annual election of the directors.

Every year the directors of the company must decide what to do with the earnings. They may plow them back into the company by hiring more people, enhancing their marketing efforts, or stepping up spending on research and development, in hopes of bringing some new products to the marketplace. Or they can decide to distribute part or all of the earnings to shareholders in the form of a cash payment called "dividends." Each share receives an equal dividend. The directors might, on the other hand, decide not to distribute any dividends at all.

Publicly traded companies regularly provide financial reports to shareholders, lenders, and other potential investors, as well as to the SEC. In addition, most publicly traded companies now have Web sites on the Internet, so that you can get this data online by visiting a company's home page.

Let's say you owned some shares in Maytag Corporation, the well-known appliance manufacturer, founded in 1893 and based in Newton, Iowa, which boasts annual sales of $4 billion. You placed the trade by phone with a full-service broker or else bought shares using an online discount broker via the Internet.

You want to monitor how the stock is doing over the next weeks, months, even years. To do that, you can get a stock quotation online by visiting various Web sites, including that of the New York Stock Exchange (www.nyse.com). You can look up the price of Maytag's stock by entering its symbol—MYG—in the slot called "enter company symbol." Alternatively, your online broker could customize an electronic stock portfolio for you, and you could get a daily update as to the stock's performance. You could also look up the stock price in the newspaper.

Each company has a "ticker symbol" on the stock exchange. When you look up Maytag's name in the financial pages of the newspaper, you will see its ticker—in this case, MYG, with shares trading on the New York Stock Exchange. Companies are listed in alphabetical order. For example, the financial pages of *The Wall Street Journal* on August 19, 1999, gave the following information about the previous day's market activity in this stock:

The column "52 Weeks-Hi/Lo" tells you the highest daily closing price for Maytag shares on August 18—namely, 74^{13}⁄₁₆, or $74.81—as well as the lowest—39^{5}⁄₈, or $39.62—over the past fifty-two weeks. This helps you see whether this stock has been volatile and had a lot of wide price swings. The more volatile it is, the more money you can make or lose in a relatively short period of time. As we explained earlier, the spread is the gap between the highest price offered by the buyer and the lowest price offered by the seller. Beginning in 2000, to simplify things, the NYSE will quote stock prices in decimals rather than sixteenths.

The next column, entitled "Stock," tells us which company stock we're reading about, usually through an abbreviation of its name, and the type of stock. It is common stock, unless it has "pf" attached to it, which indicates preferred stock. In this case, the corporation is Maytag. The next column, "SYM," tells us the symbol, or ticker, which is MYG.

The "Div" column refers to the anticipated yearly cash dividend paid for each share of stock—in this case, 72 cents a share, or .72. If you owned fifty shares of Maytag, you'd get $36 in dividends over the course of a year, probably in quarterly payments.

The "Yld" column refers to the return on your money, per share of stock. The "percent yield," as it is called, is one way to assess the stock's current value. It tells you how much dividend you get as a percentage of the current price. And it allows you to compare your earnings on a stock with earnings on other investments. You calculate it by dividing the current dividend by the current market price, or closing price: hence, for Maytag, .72 divided by $65.50 equals 1.1 percent.

The next column, "PE," tells you the price/earnings ratio. This is calculated by dividing the current price per share by the earnings per share. Experts say there is no perfect P/E, but some investors shy away from companies if they think the ratio is too high. The P/E also enables you to determine the company's latest twelve-month earnings per share, by dividing its current market price by the P/E: thus, $65.50 divided by 19 equals $3.45.

"Vol" refers to the volume, or number of shares traded on the previous day. You multiply by 100 to get the number of shares traded. A stock with high volume, indicated by underlining, indicates keen investor interest; perhaps investors are reacting to news about the firm. In the case of Maytag, 429,500 shares traded on the previous day, August 18, 1999. "Hi/Lo" in the next column refers to the trading price range on that day—in this case, a high of 66$\frac{1}{16}$, or $66.06, and a low of 65$\frac{3}{16}$, or $65.19. Next is the closing price that day: 65$\frac{1}{2}$, or $65.50; and finally, the "Net Chg," which stands for "net change." This refers to the dollar amount by which the closing price per share advanced or declined from that of the previous trading day: in this case, a decrease of $\frac{1}{16}$, or 6 cents.

In addition to selling stock, or equity, another way that companies raise money for investment is through the issuance of bonds. A corporate bond is a debt instrument, like an IOU, in which the issuer—which in this case is the corporation—agrees to pay interest and principal over a specific period of time in return for accepting a loan from investors. There are bonds in different industries, such as public utilities, industrials, transportation, banking, and finance, as well as international bonds, used to finance projects such as the expansion of the business or the acquisition of other companies.

Then there are bonds issued by the U.S. government, known as Treasury bonds, which are sold to pay for an array of government activities. There are also municipal bonds, issued by states, cities, counties, and local government agencies that finance public projects such as the construction of bridges, schools, and highways. There are bond mutual funds, which enable you to buy portions of many bonds, as opposed to investing in just one bond. Similar to stock trades, transactions in the bond markets are reported in bond tables and charts in the business press.

From an investment standpoint, bonds offer different advantages from stocks. Generally speaking, bonds are more conservative investments than stocks and are well suited for people who tend to be risk-averse. Because the rate at which interest is paid and the amount of each payment is fixed when the bond is offered for sale, these are called "fixed-income securities." If you buy a bond when it's issued and hold it until it matures, you will receive regular interest payments at a set rate until the bond matures. At maturity you will get the principal back to reinvest. Over time, bonds offer a lower return than stocks but feature the predictability of steady income. For those who have a short investment time horizon and can't afford to ride out periodic downturns in the stock market (a bear market), bonds could be a good investment. People who are near retirement or already retired might benefit from owning bonds, since they provide steady income. Because of these different attributes of stock and bond ownership, many investors choose to have a "balanced portfolio," which contains some combination of both. We'll discuss that concept in more detail in the chapter on investing.

Some bonds offer special tax advantages. You don't have to pay state or local income tax on the interest from U.S. Treasury bonds, while the interest on municipal bonds is exempt from federal income tax and, in many instances, state or local income tax as well.

Bonds are given credit ratings by the major U.S. rating agencies, such as Moody's Investor Service and Standard & Poor's (S&P). In the case of corporate bonds, the credit rating of the company is determined by how healthy the firm is. The health of the firm is based on its balance sheet, income statement, and other financial data, as well as on its track record of paying back debt in the past. All these factors are analyzed and used to determine the rating. Companies that have the greatest likelihood of paying the money back have the highest bond ratings. Municipal bonds are also rated; in this instance the rating is based on the creditworthiness of the government issuer to pay back the money.

The world of bonds is divided into "investment grade" and "non-investment grade." Moody's rates investment grade bonds from Aaa, which is the highest ranking, down to Baa, which denotes medium quality; S&P uses the grade of AAA for the best quality, down to BBB. Non-investment grade includes companies that have a speculative element, as well as those that might default in the future, and the most highly speculative of all constitute the "junk bond market." These are bonds issued by companies that are either bankrupt or have a questionable ability to meet their cash flow. They're quite risky, and investors taking this risk are rewarded with higher yields. Moody's denotes non-investment grade bonds by rating them on a scale from Ba down to C; S&P classifies them from a BB rating down to D, for default. These ratings affect the interest rate that the borrower must pay to entice investors to buy their bonds. A higher-rated bond issuer is able to pay a lower interest rate, because the risk of default is low, whereas a lower-rated bond issuer must pay a higher interest rate to compensate investors for the increased risk of losing their money.

Bonds are classified according to several factors. A bond's "maturity" is the date on which the principal, or the original amount invested, comes due and must be paid in full to the lender, or bondholder. The investor gets the "par value," or face value, of the bond, at maturity, usually in units of $1,000. There are three types of maturities: short-term debt, which usually matures in a year or less; intermediate debt, which matures in from two to ten years; and long-term debt, maturing in thirty years or more. From an investor's point of view, generally, the longer the term of the loan, the higher the interest rate, to compensate investors for the increased risk of tying up their money for so long.

1.   Bonds are also classified by their interest rate, or "coupon." The interest rate of a bond is set at the time it's issued and remains intact until the bond matures. Some bonds pay a fixed interest rate; others have a "floating" rate that changes over the life of the issue; still others are "zero coupon," which means they pay no interest rate during the term of the bond. Instead they pay the principal amount and the accrued interest in a lump sum at

maturity. Zero-coupon bonds are sold at a deep discount to par value, to compensate investors for the fact that they receive no regular interest payments over the term of the loan. Many people use zero-coupon bonds as a way to pay for major anticipated expenses, such as college tuition.

2. The difference between the discount and par value is the return to bondholders. Par value refers to the stated value of a bond— usually $1,000 or $100. Bonds may be sold at a "premium" or a "discount" to their par value—that is, at some price above or below their face value—depending on market forces.

    The price you pay for a bond depends on a number of factors, such as interest rates, supply and demand, credit quality, maturity, and tax status. Newly issued bonds sell at a price close to par value. But older bonds traded in the marketplace fluctuate in price, in response to changing interest rates. If the price of a bond rises above its par value, the bond is said to be selling at a "premium"; but when the price falls below the par value, it is selling at a "discount." Some people buy bonds and then trade them, hoping to make money on these price fluctuations.

3. The "yield" of a bond is the annual return you earn on the bond. It's based on the price you paid for the bond, as well as on the interest payment you receive. Current yield is calculated by dividing the bond's interest payment by its purchase price. Thus if you bought a bond at $1,000 par value and the interest rate is 8 percent, or $80 per year, then the current yield is $80 divided by $1,000, or 8 percent.

4. The "yield to maturity" on a bond refers to the yield of a bond, or annual return on investment, expressed as a percentage of the cost or current price, taking into account the premium or discount of the bond and the time to its maturity.

5. From the day a bond is issued until it matures, its price in the marketplace will vary based on market conditions or credit quality. A general rule of thumb is that when interest rates fall,

prices of existing bonds rise, to lower the yield of older bonds sufficiently to match the lower interest rate on new issues. Conversely, when interest rates rise, bond prices fall, to bring the yield of older bonds in line with the new issues bearing higher interest. Thus if you sell a bond before it matures, its value will likely be higher or lower than its original face (par) value.

Some bonds have a "call" feature, giving the issuer the right to call the bonds back at a predetermined price, on specific dates, and refinance them at a more favorable interest rate. Bonds are typically called when current interest rates have dropped significantly since the time they were originally issued. It's akin to a homeowner refinancing his mortgage loan when interest rates drop; in so doing, he may save lots of money on interest costs over the life of the loan. The bond issuer also hopes to save lots of money on interest costs by refinancing at a more favorable rate. So before you buy a bond, always find out whether it has a call provision. If it does, be sure to ask for its "yield to call" as well as its "yield to maturity," since bonds with a call provision usually offer a higher return to compensate for the risk that bonds might be called early.

The U.S. government also issues securities, known as Treasury bills, notes, and bonds.

1. Treasury bills have maturities of one year or less; they do not pay interest and are sold at a discount to face value.

2. Treasury notes are coupon-bearing instruments with maturities ranging from two to ten years.

3. Treasury bonds are coupon-bearing securities with maturities greater than ten years.

Treasury securities are considered very safe, the least risky of all securities, since they're backed by the power of the American government to print money or borrow indefinitely.

The government bond market has immense significance to all the other financial markets. Because the U.S. government is widely considered to be the strongest and most stable in the world, with the biggest economy and strongest currency, the interest rate at which the U.S. government borrows money is considered to be risk-free. Other financial markets, with more risk attached to them, must provide a higher interest rate over and above government yields, in order to entice investors. For example, corporate bonds offer a higher reward, or more yield, to investors to compensate them for the increased risk. This is because corporations might default, since corporations come and go, whereas the U.S. government is viewed as rock-solid.

Yields on government bonds are often driven by expectations about inflation, since the U.S. government is the only entity in the market that can create money. By tightening or loosening money through its monetary policy, the U.S. government can have an important impact on inflation rates and thereby keep the economy on an even keel. To slow down an overheated economy where too much money is circulating, the Federal Reserve System, which is the nation's central bank, sells government securities, absorbing the cash that would otherwise be available for lending. To stimulate a sluggish economy, it does just the opposite: it creates money by buying securities.

Thus all the other markets—including stocks, commodities, mortgage-backed securities, municipal bonds, currencies, interest-rate swaps, and others—carefully watch what the government bond market is doing. As government yields rise and fall, yields in other markets often react in tandem.

Corporate bonds are distinct from municipal bonds, which are issued by state or local government authorities to finance various public projects, such as bridges, schools, and toll roads. Municipal bonds fall into two major groups: general obligation bonds, which are backed by the taxing power, or the "full faith and credit," of the government issuing authority, or "revenue bonds," which are backed by a stream of revenues from the project that the bonds are being used to finance, such as a toll road. Unlike corporate bonds, however, municipal bonds pay interest that is tax-exempt, which makes them an attractive tax shelter for some people.

As an investor, you need to keep apprised of the general economic situation in the country. In the business press you can read about important news such as changes in interest rates, tax cuts or hikes, trends in consumer confidence and spending, business plans for future growth, global trade issues, and the accumulation or liquidation of business inventories, as a barometer of whether the economy is poised to expand or contract.

You should also pay attention to what the Federal Reserve System does. It oversees the nation's monetary policy and plays a big part in keeping the country's economy running smoothly. The Fed, as it is called, acts as banker, regulator, and controller of the nation's money supply. It strives to keep the U.S. economy running smoothly and avoid the extreme "boom" and "bust" cycles that can characterize pure, unfettered capitalism. Partly because of the Fed's intervention, for example, the United States has avoided having another severe depression such as that which afflicted the nation during the 1930s.

The Fed has an Open Market Committee that makes daily decisions about monetary policy. It regularly influences the amount of money in circulation when it decides to buy or sell government securities in the open market. If the Open Market Committee thinks the economy is overheating and inflation is increasing, it slows down the creation of new money by instructing the New York Federal Reserve Bank to sell government securities; on the other hand, if it thinks the economy is sluggish, it will recommend stepping up the money supply as a stimulus to encourage companies and consumers to increase spending. The Fed injects money into the economy by buying government securities, thus making borrowing easier and spurring economic growth. In this fashion the Fed can pour several billion dollars into the economy. The Federal Reserve plays a major role in keeping inflation under control and creating the kind of environment that will enable the economy to grow.

The Fed also monitors the business practices of the banks in its system and audits their records. If a bank needs to borrow money, it can do so through a Federal Reserve Bank. There are twelve separate Federal Reserve Banks, with twenty-five regional branches, located throughout the country. The interest rate that the Fed uses to lend money to banks is called the "discount rate." The discount rate is another tool that the Fed uses to steer the economy. It can increase or decrease the discount rate and, in so doing, create a ripple effect throughout the economy. Increasing the discount rate acts as a brake on the economy: it causes banks to borrow less and thereby have less money available to make loans to their clients. Decreasing the rate has the opposite effect: banks tend to borrow more freely, more money is loaned to clients at an attractive rate, and the economy is stimulated.

There are also several important indexes of overall stock market direction you should be aware of, by knowing whether they are rising or falling and by how much. You can compare how well your own stock portfolio is doing relative to the benchmark of overall stock market performance provided by such an index. An index is a list of stocks, bonds, or other securities whose prices are combined in a type of average to come up with a number that represents their collective value. The Dow Jones Industrial Average (DJIA) is by far the most popular indicator of general stock market direction; it is recognized and quoted worldwide. The DJIA represents the average stock price of thirty major blue-chip companies. Following is the list of the companies on the index as of September 1999 (you can also read this list on the Internet, at the DJIA Web site, http://averages.dowjones.com):

THE THIRTY COMPANIES CURRENTLY LISTED ON THE DJIA

Allied Signal Inc.
Aluminum Co. of America
American Express Co.
AT&T Corp.
Boeing Co.
Caterpillar Inc.
Chevron Corp.

Citigroup Inc.
Coca-Cola Co.
DuPont Co.
Eastman Kodak Co.
Exxon Corp.
General Electric Co.
General Motors Corp.
Goodyear Tire & Rubber Co.
Hewlett-Packard Co.
International Business Machines Corp. (IBM)
International Paper Co.
J. P. Morgan & Co.
Johnson & Johnson
McDonald's Corp.
Merck & Co.
Minnesota Mining & Manufacturing Co.
Philip Morris Cos.
Procter & Gamble Co.
Sears, Roebuck & Co.
Union Carbide Corp.
United Technologies Corp.
Wal-Mart Stores Inc.
Walt Disney Co.

This index has changed since the earliest version was created in 1884. Companies are added and dropped. The most common reason they are dropped is that they are acquired by another company or merge with another firm and thereby are transformed into a completely different entity. The DJIA includes substantial corporations that represent the broadest trends in the U.S. economy. These are companies that have a history of successful growth and wide interest among investors. There are no companies in the transportation or utility businesses in this index, however, since there are separate Dow Jones Averages for those types of stocks.

The DJIA is expressed in "points" rather than dollars; thus the business press will report that the DJIA is "11,283.30, down 16.46 points," which means that these thirty stocks averaged 11,283.30 at four P.M. on the close of trading at the NYSE the previous day, down 16.46 points from the close of the session the day before. The average is computed by adding the prices of the thirty stocks, then dividing this number by a factor that adjusts for distortions caused by stock splits or the impact of replacing one company with another on the list; at present this divisor is .19. The index gives you an indication of the overall direction of stock prices. Over time, a general upward trend in the DJIA indicates a bull market, whereas a downward trend signifies a bear market.

The Standard & Poor's 500 Index, first calculated in 1923, is a another closely watched barometer of the stock market. It was designed to provide a broader measure of the market than the DJIA and has the stock of five hundred large companies in it, including four hundred industrial companies, twenty transportation companies, forty utilities, and forty financial companies. The S&P 500 Index is weighted in proportion to the market value of each security in it, and it is widely considered the benchmark for investors in large stocks. In addition, a whole array of mutual funds that track the performance of the S&P 500 Index has been created, which we will discuss in more detail in the chapter on investing. The S&P 500 Index is maintained by the editorial staff of Standard & Poor's, a subsidiary of McGraw-Hill.

Remember, as you learn more and more about finance and investments, be sure to take the long view. Don't be overly concerned by daily blips in the market that may be overly magnified in the newspapers or on television. Focus on long-term performance.

Everyone needs to know how the market works. It's not just for those who happen to be wealthy today. Take Kyle Donovan, a twenty-seven-year-old African American man. He learned about the stock market through his own efforts. He grew up in the housing projects of Bedford Stuyvesant in Brooklyn, New York, raised by his aunt, who lived on public assistance, and his grandmother. His mother and father were "never around," as he puts it.

Growing up in the projects was a harsh life. He looked out the window of his apartment and saw people shooting each other. Donovan personally knew five people slain in their youth. Crack cocaine was wreaking havoc on the neighborhood, destroying people all around him.

"It was about survival, for the most part—day-to-day survival," recounts Donovan, a slender young man with round glasses. "I have no friends from my childhood. They're either dead, in jail, or we have nothing in common."

But, he continues, "I avoided the chaos around me. I didn't want to sell drugs or hang out on the corner." So after graduating from high school and going to community college for one semester, he began working in an ad agency, doing graphic arts, photography, prints, and color murals. He made $6 an hour and discovered he had a flair for this type of work.

Fired by an entrepreneurial vision, he created a darkroom out of his one-bedroom apartment and bought some photographic equipment. Then he started picking up photos at one-hour photo shops and developing them for a profit. He did large blowup prints and other customized projects, over a period of two years.

The business paid for itself. At age nineteen he had his own apartment in Queens and a new car. And he opened a bank account, thus becoming the first person in his family ever to do so.

He developed a grander vision for his business: at age twenty he decided to move to Manhattan and open a custom printing shop, called Custom C Printing. "I had the equipment and the skills," he explains, and he realized that the big money was to be made there.

Seven years later Donovan has a business with annual revenues in the six figures, and counts among his clients giant firms like Dow Jones, EMI Records, and *The New York Times*. Along the way he teamed up with a partner, Manolo Guevara, from Ecuador, who brought some established clients to the firm, and together they bought a three-thousand-square-foot office on East 25th Street four years ago.

Through reading books and studying financial Web sites on the Internet, Donovan taught himself about the stock market and now has a sizable portfolio of mostly high-tech stocks, since he thinks that's one of the hottest areas of the economy. In addition, he's bought some mutual funds for his young daughter. Each day he checks his online portfolio, updated daily, through his discount brokerage firm, Waterhouse Securities.

His latest venture, *NV*—for "new vision"—magazine, is a hip business magazine geared toward young black and Hispanic "Gen-X" urban professionals. It debuted in January 1999 and already has a circulation of seventy thousand nationwide. He hopes to grow it to a two hundred thousand readership over the next three years. It's sold on newsstands across the country. And it is the first black-owned independent magazine to be launched nationally and internationally in over ten years.

"I started it because there was a lack of business information for minorities," explains Donovan. "For African Americans, there was just *Black Enterprise*. It's crazy to think one magazine can serve everyone."

A recent issue had articles entitled "Women on Wall Street," "Understanding the Stock Market," and "A Business Plan That Gets Results." Donovan is even offering shares of *NV* to readers who want to help grow the publication.

"Many of the magazines you see look like us, but they are not owned by us," Donovan wrote to the readers in a recent issue. "We are strong, we are powerful, we are intelligent, and we are the future.

"*NV* was truly a dream. It is because of you that this dream has become a reality. . . . There is particular joy in knowing when something is truly for us and by us. . . . Creating 'our' vision, the 'New Vision.' "

CHAPTER 6

Investing

We need to become investors. We're currently underinvested in the stock market and there are historical reasons why this is so, but it must change. African American consumers currently wield $500 billion in buying power. Hispanics have $350 billion. They purchase a disproportionate share of items like soft drinks, fast food, and athletic shoes. Thus they should become shareholders of the companies they patronize— such as Nike, Coca-Cola, and McDonald's—and exert pressure as shareholders to change the current state of affairs. They could use their leverage as shareholders to see to it that blacks, browns, and women are promoted to the boards of directors of various companies and advance in the business world. As a shareholder and not a sharecropper, you've got access to the floor. Shareholders raise issues like "Who are our vendors and ad agencies? Who's managing our money? Who's on our board of directors?"

D uane Davis Davis, age forty, is a skilled financial professional, having risen to the post of vice president/investment counselor at First Union Brokerage Services, Inc., in Winston-Salem, North Carolina. Moreover, he has been a certified financial planner for the past fifteen years and had seen how good financial planning could transform people's lives, both on an individual level and over the course of succeeding generations. When he began thinking about the power of pooling money in the black community, he decided to start the Coalition of Black Investors (COBI), a nonprofit group that aims to increase black participation in the capital markets, enhance financial literacy, and promote the formation of investment clubs. Among its many initiatives, COBI sponsors the Road to Prosperity Tour, which is a series of day-long conferences around the country about investing; the Black Investors Census, which aims to find out which companies' shares are most widely held in the black community and to encourage shareholder activism; and the COBI National Investment Month, a month-long event that brings together African American investors with professionals from the securities industry, many of whom are also African American. The organization can put you in touch with top African American money management firms, such as Ariel Capital Management, founded by John Rogers; Brown Capital Management, run by Ed Brown; or the Chapman Company, headed by Nathaniel Chapman. For more information, call COBI at their headquarters in Winston-Salem, North Carolina, at 1-336-922-6240.

Davis, along with his wife, Carol, who has a law degree, devised the idea for COBI, and the two are cofounders of the organization. Carol serves as president. The organization's Web site, www.cobinvest.com, has a wealth of valuable articles and information geared to the black investor. Recently, for example, Carol penned an article for the Web site entitled "Driving to the Poorhouse." In it, she discusses results of a recent survey of black investors conducted by Ariel Capital Management, a Chicago-based African American–owned investment firm, and Charles Schwab & Company. The study found that affluent African Americans spend more on car payments than they invest in their children's education. Twenty-nine percent of African Americans said their number one expense after basic necessities is their car payment, followed by their children's education. By contrast, 31 percent of whites said their number one expense after necessities is investing.

"So while black consumers have reached parity with whites in possession and planned purchases of cars, African Americans continue to lag behind in saving and investing," writes Carol Davis. What's worse, cars quickly depreciate in value as soon as you drive them off the lot. This is another instance of all flash, no cash!

Blacks and Hispanics have just one-tenth the wealth of white people. While the most obvious reason for this is long years of legal denial and lack of access to capital, a major reason today is the failure to save and invest. Historically the government helped to create the wealth gap by its largesse to whites only. One example was the granting of radio and TV licenses throughout the twentieth century. Few, if any, African Americans received these licenses. African Americans and Latinos were—and in many ways still are—kept out of the deal stream.

When it comes to individual behavior, however, there are a variety of reasons why many African Americans, Latinos, and others fail to save and invest on a regular basis. Some people, whose parents or grandparents lived through the stock market crash of 1929 and the Great Depression that followed, were raised with the notion that the stock market was nothing more than gambling. It could crash once again, and you might lose everything. But this is no longer true. After the Depression, the government instituted safeguards within the banking industry and securities markets to insure that such a crash would never happen again. The stock market will rise and fall, and there's always risk, but the chances of seeing another Great Depression are pretty slim.

Still others may believe in the biblical idea that "money is the root of all evil" and shy away from investing on religious grounds. But this is an incorrect reading of Scripture. The passage actually reads, "The love of money is the root of all evil" (1 Timothy 6:8). Furthermore, there are numerous citations in Scripture that encourage sound financial management. For example: "Money answereth all things" (Ecclesiastes 10:19). Worshiping mammon is what is evil. Making money into a god is what is evil. But money in and of itself is neither good nor evil: it depends on what you use it for. In fact, money can be used for a variety of good works, including tithing at your church and helping the poor.

Still other people may be intimidated by the language of finance and feel they can never understand it. But saving and investing require only the mastery of some simple principles. We discuss some of those concepts in this book. Plus, you can add to your knowledge of investing year after year, as you go along, by reading more books, studying the business press, watching shows about investing on television, and visiting personal-finance Web sites on the Internet.

Ed Brown, a legendary stock picker, came to investing from an unlikely background. He grew up poor, the son of an African American laborer who picked oranges in Apopka, Florida. But when he was growing up, his grandmother instilled in him the desire to do better. "She took me to the city, to Orlando, and made a special effort to give me something to shoot for. She showed me people sitting behind their desks with shirts and ties," recalls Brown. "She told me: 'If you study hard and work hard, instead of being in soiled clothes in the fields all day, you, too, will be able to sit behind a desk, wear a suit and starched shirt, and be somebody.' "

Brown followed her advice. He became the first person in his family to finish high school. Then he went on to get a BS in electrical engineering from Howard University, a master's degree in electrical engineering from New York University, and an MBA from Indiana University School of Business. "I always tried to excel in academics, since I couldn't play sports worth anything," he comments. For five years he worked as an electrical engineer. But then he switched to investing and rose right to the top. For ten years he was vice president and portfolio manager at T. Rowe Price Associates, the mutual fund firm; then in 1983 he founded his own company, Brown Capital Management. The company currently has $4.8 billion under management. Brown Capital has won the distinction of ranking in the top 25 percent of all money managers nationally. So renowned is Brown for his stock-picking acumen that he was elected to *Wall Street Week*'s Hall of Fame in 1996, an honor accorded by the popular investment commentator Louis Rukeyser. Brown's advice to novice investors is, "Have a planned, consistent investment program over many years."

The good news is that everyone can learn about saving and investing and benefit from the knowledge—even if you've never been involved before. The key thing is to start now.

At the Rainbow/PUSH Coalition, we're actively spreading the word about learning how to invest for the future. For example, we're encouraging schools, churches, and radio disc jockeys to use the Stock Market

Game as a way to teach young people about the market. The game was devised by the Securities Industry Foundation for Economic Education, a nonprofit group, and hundreds of thousands of students participate in the program during each school year. It gives young people the chance to manage a hypothetical investment portfolio and learn money management skills firsthand.

In another initiative led by the Rainbow/PUSH Wall Street Project, we've worked out an arrangement with the New York Stock Exchange whereby four times a year 35 African American and Latino ministers (a total of 140) will go through a one-week intensive training course at the stock exchange, so they can learn how the markets work and pass on that knowledge to their congregations. Pastors can be instrumental in helping lead us from a debt culture to a surplus culture—from a conspicuous consumption culture to an investment culture.

THE BASICS OF INVESTING

In chapter 5 we introduced you to stocks, bonds, and mutual funds, which are some of the most common investment vehicles you're likely to encounter. Before you begin purchasing any of these instruments, you need to decide upon your investment objectives. Are you trying to save for retirement? Buy a home? Pay for your children's college education? You need to clarify your goals and the time frame in which you want to achieve them, then adopt an investment strategy that will enable you to meet those goals.

Consider your time horizon. Younger people can afford to be more aggressive with their investments. If your goals are long-term—say, ten years or more in the future—you can afford to concentrate heavily on stocks, which offer more risk but a higher return. Having a long investment time horizon enables you to rebound from the inevitable bear markets, as well as market "corrections," in which the stock market drops 10 percent or more. As we discussed in chapter 5, a long-term, "buy and hold" strategy, when you select shares of quality companies, works best when it comes to investing. A long investment horizon also enables you to benefit from the "time value of money," which we discussed in chapter 1. This principle refers to the fact that a dollar today is worth more than a dollar tomorrow, or next week, or a year from now, because you can invest the dollar today and benefit from compound interest. Essentially, you earn interest on interest, via a snowball effect, which builds up substantial returns over time, even on relatively small initial investments.

Long-term, stocks have also yielded higher returns than other investments. They have averaged annual returns of about 11 percent, versus 6 percent to 7 percent for bonds and even less than that for money-market accounts and other cash equivalents. Because of these higher returns, stocks held over a long period are more likely than bonds to protect your money against the ravages of inflation.

Over time, some individual stocks have done spectacularly well and made the people who invested in them early on very wealthy. Home Depot, which sells supplies for homeowners nationwide, is an example. If you had bought 1,000 shares of Home Depot stock when it went public in 1981 at $12 a share—a total investment of $12,000—that would be worth $15.2 million in today's dollars, according to Kim Shreckengost, vice president of investor relations at the firm's Atlanta headquarters. Even if you had made a more modest investment of just 100 shares at a total cost of $1,200, your investment would be worth $1.52 million today.

The value of $1 invested at year-end 1976 in 1996 would be worth

- $15.13 if invested in large company stocks ($5.55 if adjusted for inflation)

- $6.19 if invested in long-term government bonds ($2.27 if adjusted for inflation)

Source: Ibbotson Associates.

Older people are best advised to be more conservative with their investments. If you seek current income from your investments—because you're retired, for example—or are close to retirement and want to liquidate your holdings in less than ten years, then you should choose a more balanced portfolio of stocks, bonds, and money-market accounts to reduce risk. And if you have an investment time horizon of five years or less, you should maintain a portfolio that focuses on income investments, such as dividend-paying stocks, bonds, and money-market funds.

A cardinal principle of investing is the notion of "asset allocation," which holds that the most important factor governing the return on your portfolio is the *proportion* of various investments that you hold, whether or not those investments include stocks, mutual funds, bonds, or international investments. Research by Ibbotson Associates shows that the lion's share of a portfolio's return—91.5 percent—is determined by this principle alone. By contrast, "market timing," or the attempt to foretell price changes in stocks and bonds and trade shares accordingly, almost never works and is not a good strategy. Research by Ibbotson shows that market timing helped portfolio performance just 1.8 percent of the time.

Your investment plan should mesh with your tolerance for risk. You need to feel secure about your money. Besides deciding what investment strategy you feel most comfortable with, you must also decide what your stance is toward risk. Do you enjoy taking risks—knowing that in finance, the higher the risk, the higher the reward? Someone with a high risk tolerance will probably be happy with an aggressive portfolio of high-growth stocks or equity funds. Are you moderately inclined toward risk? If so, you would probably like a balanced portfolio of stocks and bonds. If you abhor risk taking and are conservative by nature, then you will want your money invested in steady, reliable vehicles, which offer less upside potential but also less downside. A portfolio with mostly bonds, some cash equivalents, and a little stock might be appropriate.

The discount broker Charles Schwab and Co. provides six sample plans for allocating your assets, ranging from short-term to aggressive. By going to the Web site (www.schwab.com), you can look at their detailed analysis of each plan.

- The short-term plan (60 percent cash, 40 percent short-term bonds) is for those investors who want current income and a high degree of stability in their investments.

- The conservative plan consists of 25 percent in cash, 20 percent in stocks, and 55 percent in bonds.

- The moderately conservative plan is made up of 15 percent cash, 40 percent stocks, and 45 percent bonds.

- The moderate plan has more in stocks (60 percent) and less in bonds (30 percent) and cash (10 percent).

- The moderately aggressive plan has 80 percent of assets in stocks, 15 percent in bonds, and only 5 percent in cash.

- The aggressive plan places 95 percent of assets in stocks and 5 percent in cash and is for investors who want high growth and don't need current income. As you can see, moving from the short-term plan up to the aggressive involves increasing the degree of risk as the amount of a portfolio devoted to stocks increases from zero to 95 percent.

There is a trade-off between risk and reward when it comes to investing. This trade-off is a function of the mix of stocks and bonds held in an investment portfolio. A higher concentration of stocks subjects your portfolio to greater "volatility" or price swings. Stocks are inherently more volatile than bonds, because a stock price will fluctuate more in reaction to bad news about a company than will a bond's price.

Diversifying your portfolio—that is, buying a mix of investments rather than all stocks or all bonds—offers a couple of major advantages: it enables you to increase your return, and it also lowers your risk. A diversified and a nondiversified portfolio can have equal rates of risk, but the former—say, a portfolio invested in a mix of large-company stocks, small-company stocks, and intermediate-term government bonds—can earn a higher rate of return versus a portfolio invested entirely in long-term government bonds.

Diversification—which can be obtained by holding about ten or twelve different stocks in your portfolio—can give you exposure to broad market growth. For example, rather than simply buying three pharmaceutical company stocks and concentrating your assets in just one industry, pick the market leader in that industry, then buy stock in the best auto company, the best airline company, and so on.

Such blue-chip, big-cap companies are safer investments than small companies, which might go under. Big-cap stocks have an advantage in today's market, since much of the trading is done by large institutions with multimillion-dollar portfolios. Institutions can't invest much money in small companies, since they would end up owning them. As a result, both large institutional buyers and foreign buyers favor large-cap stocks, which they can buy and sell easily without distorting the market. This demand ends up bolstering the price of large-cap companies. Small-cap holdings are inherently more risky. It's hard for the average investor to figure out which small firms will end up as winners ten or twenty years from now.

"Dollar cost averaging" is another principle of investing that you should follow. This involves adding to your investments on a regular basis over time. If, for example, you invest a set amount every month, on average you'll end up buying more shares when prices are low and fewer shares when prices are high. The result: Your average cost will be lower. By investing monthly, reinvesting the dividends, and maintaining a long-term perspective, you stand to make the greatest gains over time.

We introduced you to the concept of mutual funds in chapter 5. There has been an explosion of mutual funds over the last few years. In 1980 there were just 425 funds, with $56.9 billion in assets, according to Morningstar, which collects data and tracks mutual fund performance. But by late 1998 there were more than 6,000 mutual funds, with a total of $4.2 trillion in assets.

There's a great array of stock and bond mutual funds, and each type offers a different strategy. For example, income funds seek steady income through dividends; growth funds go after stocks of established companies with earnings that are expected to rise in the long run; aggressive growth funds seek new, innovative, or small-company stocks to get the highest return in a short amount of time; balanced funds offer a combination of stocks and bonds to produce capital gains and steady income; and international equity funds invest only in shares of foreign companies. But the truth is that only 12 percent of all equity mutual funds beat the return on the S&P 500 in 1998. Moreover, only 4 percent of all equity funds outperformed the S&P 500 over the three-year period ending December 31, 1998.

So if you choose to invest in mutual funds, do so carefully. Look at the track record of the portfolio manager. Read and understand the prospectus, as you should before buying any investment. If you're just getting started, you'll probably be better off sticking with a fund that's been around for three years and invests in big companies. Moreover, when evaluating a mutual fund, look beyond last year's performance. A star performer last year may be a laggard this year. Look at the fund's three-year, five-year, and ten-year record.

In the realm of mutual funds, some charge a "load" or sales fee, and others, known as "no-load" funds, do not. It may be worth buying a load fund, once you review its performance and deduct all fees and annual expenses from its annual return. You can, however, be significantly affected by high expenses on mutual funds. The average managed mutual fund carries a 1.75 percent yearly expense ratio. The SEC found that for every percentage point of expenses charged by a stock fund, the ending account balance on an investment held for twenty years will be reduced by 18%. For example, if you invest $10,000 in a mutual fund with a return of 10 percent before expenses, with an the annual operating expense of 1.5 percent, you'd have $49,725 after twenty years. But if the fund had expenses of 0.5 percent annually, you'd end up with $60,858—an 18 percent difference. You can see these examples on the SEC's Web site, at www.sec.gov. Fees can vary widely on mutual funds and consist of "front-end sales charges" or a fee to withdraw, called a "reverse load," "back-end load," or "contingent deferred sales charge." To see if a fund is charging an excessively high or low expense, look at the average expense for a fund in its category. You can obtain this data from Morningstar by ordering their reports for $5 each: call 1-800-735-0700.

Some mutual funds can be purchased for as little as $100, as long as you agree to make monthly contributions of at least $25. For information on these and other mutual funds, you can contact the industry trade group, the Investment Company Institute, at 1-202-326-5800.

The fastest-growing section of the mutual fund industry is an area known as "index funds." Today there are more than 370 of them. Such funds simply track the performance of market indexes, such as the S&P 500. John Bogle, who founded the Vanguard Group twenty-five years ago and in 1975 invented the index mutual fund, has said that such a fund is superior to a managed fund because over a period of fifty years, he knows of no actively managed fund that has beaten the S&P 500 Index by a significant amount. Plus, managed funds cost you more in taxes and charge fees that are often ten times higher than those of index funds.

When it comes to choosing a brokerage firm to handle your securities transactions, you can go with either a "full-service" firm or a "discount brokerage." Full-service brokers can be valuable in terms of giving you expert advice on complicated investments and monitoring your long-term holdings. And it is possible to bargain with them on their commissions and ask for discounts off their commission schedule, which they may give you. But keep in mind that such brokers earn most of their income from commissions, so the more trades you make, the more money they make.

There are many different approaches to investing, so if you use a full-service brokerage firm, you need to find one whose investment philosophy meshes with your own. For example, a "growth" investment strategy focuses on only the very best companies. Only a few industry leaders make the grade and are added to the portfolio. Their shares are held over time, as the companies increase their profits and market share. The focus, then, is on buying quality and holding it. The price of these companies may not make them particular bargains—but investors in them feel that their superior products, technologies, managements, and strategies will ultimately win out over their cut-rate, "bargain" competitors.

"Value" investing, on the other hand, takes a different approach. It seeks bargain-basement prices on companies with extemely low valuations. Sometimes these companies are in dire straits, such as bankruptcy or reorganization. Still another philosophy is that of "growth at the right price," whereby investors seek good deals among second- or third-tier companies.

These are just a few of the many approaches to investing, to give you an idea that there is no one "right" strategy. Many people have succeeded at investing using very different approaches.

On the other hand, discount brokers, many of whom allow you to buy and sell shares directly on the Internet at a very low price, will save you money. Discount brokerage firms won't actively manage your account or give you "buy" or "sell" recommendations on investments. But they can offer you a lower price because they offer a "no frills" approach to investing. Some offer more products and services than others, so you will want to check out several before choosing one. There are several types of discount brokers, including bank discounters, regionals, and deep discounters, plus the big three firms that dominate this industry and have about 67 percent of all customers who use such services: Charles Schwab, Quick & Reilly, and Fidelity. Whichever type of broker you choose, you will want to monitor your investments regularly and make adjustments to your portfolio as required.

Another way to lower commission costs is by direct investing. Through a dividend reinvestment plan, or DRIP, many companies let shareholders use their dividends on the company's stock to buy additional shares. Some DRIPs even provide shares at 1 percent to 5 percent off the prevailing market price. Other DRIPs let shareholders buy stock directly from the company whenever they want. You can also enroll in a company's direct stock purchase plan, or DSP, and begin purchasing shares from the company immediately. In some instances you can get started with as little as $50 and invest as little as $25 a month. To find out more about direct investing, including lists of participating companies, get a copy of *The Motley Fool's Investing Without a Silver Spoon,* by Jeff Fischer. The book costs $15 and can be found in bookstores or purchased on their Web site, at www.fool.com. You can also contact the nonprofit National Association of Investors Corporation, at 1-877-275-6242, for more information on the subject.

Keep in mind that it's a very good idea to reserve a portion of your wealth in cash—perhaps three to six months of living expenses—to act as a financial cushion in case of emergencies. There are three major "cash equivalents" where your money is safe, can earn interest, and can be withdrawn without a penalty: bank accounts, including time deposits, known as certificates of deposit (CDs); Treasury bills; and money-market funds. However, CDs carry penalties for early withdrawal, and Treasury bills may not return all your principal if you cash them prematurely. So of the three, money-market accounts offer the best deal in terms of fairly high interest and quick access to your money. Many money-market funds offer check-writing privileges and can be linked to your brokerage account. There are both taxable and tax-exempt money-market funds, and to figure out which is best for you, you must take into consideration your tax bracket as well as state, local, and federal tax rates.

HOW TO FIND A FINANCIAL PLANNER

Those who have never before had any experience with investing may want some expert advice before plunging in. One way to get that advice is by hiring a financial planner. Such professionals aren't just for rich people; they can also help those who are on the road to building wealth.

At certain junctures in life, such as getting married, starting a family, or buying a house, you will want solid financial advice. If you dislike a do-it-yourself approach to personal finance, or if you simply don't have the time to keep tabs on your investments, then hiring a financial planner may be just the solution.

Here's how to find one: First, you should get a list of names of financial planners and review them. This can be done by calling the leading industry trade groups: the Institute of Certified Financial Planners (ICFP) at 1-800-282-PLAN, or on the Web at www.icfp.org; the International Association of Financial Planning at 1-800-945-4237, or www.iafp.org; and the National Association of Personal Financial Advisers (NAPFA) at 1-888-FEE-ONLY, or www.napfa.org. These groups will provide you with names of financial planners in your area. Look for professionals who have the CFP (certified financial planner) designation after their name, which means they have earned the highest accreditation in the industry.

To become licensed CFPs, financial planners have to pass a rigorous exam—which only about half of all candidates pass; sign a code of ethics; take continuing education classes; and have a minimum of three years of experience in the field.

Besides obtaining names from professional organizations, you may also want to ask around. Get a referral from people you know at work or at church, or ask family members.

Next, you should screen all the potential candidates. Compare their educational and professional background. Where have they worked and for how long? Look for someone who has a proven track record. Ask for names of their current clients, whom you might talk with, as references. Look for advisers who offer a range of services, rather than just a narrow specialty.

There are six basic areas of financial planning—investment planning, tax advice, insurance, retirement planning, cash management and budgeting, and estate planning. Ideally, you would like to find someone who could help you manage all of them.

Check to see if the financial planner has a clean record in the industry. You can do so by contacting the ICFP's Board of Standards (1-303-830-7500) to see if the individual's license is in good standing. You can call your state securities commissioner and see if the financial planner has been found guilty of any misconduct. Call the Securities and Exchange Commission at 1-800-732-0330 to get the name of your commissioner, or the North American Securities Administrators Association at 1-888-846-2722.

You'll need to meet with several of the financial planners you are considering hiring. See if you can communicate well with them and if their way of doing business meshes with your own. You want this individual to structure a personalized plan for you. You will also want to meet with the planner once or twice a year to discuss your progress in attaining your financial goals. Make sure you have good chemistry together, since ideally you will be working with this person for a long time.

Then get down to the nitty-gritty. Ask the financial planners what they charge for their services. Some charge by the hour, while others work on commission. Some charge a flat fee, while others take a percentage of the assets they manage. You need to clarify the billing structure. Also find out every possible way that the financial planner could make money from you. NAPFA recommends fee-only planners; because these planners do not make commissions by selling you certain products, their advice is more objective than that of other planners. But you may be willing to pay a commission if you think that financial planner is particularly talented at managing money. So you must decide what type of fee structure you are comfortable with.

Fees vary depending on where you live, the experience of the person you hire, the size of the firm, and the reputation of the company. They can run from $50 an hour up to $500 an hour. Depending on a client's needs, a financial plan may cost anywhere from $250 to $5,000.

INVESTMENT CLUBS

One of the best ways to learn about investing is through joining an investment club. This is an especially good technique for those who enjoy the do-it-yourself approach.

For example, Deborah McGriff, a middle-aged black woman who lives in Milwaukee, Wisconsin, said she never understood investing until her daughter, Jacqueline, went off to college at Bryn Mawr and studied economics. Her daughter introduced her mother to basic concepts of finance. Jacqueline has since gone on to become vice president of private banking at Chase Manhattan in New York.

This exposure whetted the appetite of Deborah McGriff, who is executive vice president of charter development at the Edison Project in Milwaukee. She decided to start an investment club, viewing it as a great way to learn as well as a means to get together with friends. Thus, the Phenomenal Women's Investment Club was born three years ago— a group of twenty-one African American women of different ages and varying professional backgrounds.

"You have to be motivated to teach yourself through the group," she explains. "If I do it for you, you haven't learned anything. In the investment club, you have to be able to stand by your decisions."

The women set up their club using materials furnished by the National Association of Investors Corporation (NAIC). NAIC, a nonprofit organization based near Detroit, has books, manuals, videos, a stock selection guide, a monthly magazine, and opportunities to buy stocks and reinvest the dividends through DRIPs, which we discussed earlier. There are also brochures about how to start an investment club. Each NAIC club is slightly different, so within their methodology there is room to "customize" each club to suit the needs of the particular members. You can call NAIC at 1-877-275-6242.

"They have everything you need," summarizes McGriff.

When it came to picking members of the club, McGriff chose hard workers, "people who were not afraid of change." They, in turn, brought in friends of theirs. Their commitment was to be intergenerational, so they brought in women from their early twenties, ranging up to retirees in their seventies. They are all black women, many of whom came from careers as educators.

"We wanted to be self-sufficient," continues McGriff. "Since we needed legal advice, we had a lawyer in the club. There is also an accountant and a banker. And our broker, Brenda Purnell at Everen Securities, is an African American woman, although she's not a member of the club.

"We like to give business to the African American community," comments McGriff.

Members of the club work hard. Theirs is not a ceremonial function, where simply showing up at meetings constitutes work. Nor is writing a check every month to purchase stock a sufficient commitment. Instead everyone is required to do research, monitoring a stock that the club owns. Everyone has a job and responsibilities that derive from that. Each person is expected to do at least an hour of research a week.

If members don't pull their weight, they are asked to leave. "We wanted this to be a place where everybody learned and everybody had to contribute," says McGriff.

Members can, however, request a leave of absence if they have a medical problem, a death in the family, or some other emergency.

The Phenomenal Women's Investment Club has divided itself into two industry groups: technology and consumer goods. "We wanted to do our research in small groups," observes McGriff. "People wanted to buy stocks in industries that they understood."

The club owns large-, medium-, and small-cap stocks, but they do not have more than 20 percent of their money in any single security.

"Market leadership is important," says McGriff. "We only buy leading companies in leading industries, and we expect to hold our shares for five to ten years."

The time commitment for members entails one monthly meeting—which lasts about two hours—plus a monthly subcommittee meeting. The club's subcommittees monitor financial publications, then report back to the larger group.

The club's bylaws say that they can buy any securities, as long as they have a simple majority. But McGriff says her club usually gets 100 percent support on all their stock purchases from the members. Everyone's questions are answered.

The club buys individual stocks, eschewing bonds and mutual funds—although this is a decision left up to the different clubs in the NAIC. Each member of the club invests a small amount of money—just $75 each month—in the club portfolio. "Think of this as your play money," explains McGriff. Many of the women also hold separate investment portfolios at brokerage firms.

In evaluating whether or not to buy a stock, the Phenomenal Women's Investment Club looks at criteria offered by the NAIC stock selection guide: a company's growth, sales, P/E or price/earnings ratio, debt level, and management, among other things. The club also goes online and finds information about a company that is a potential candidate for their portfolio. They monitor several financial Web sites. And some members even travel to do research about companies or attend a company's annual meeting.

"NAIC gives you a pretty simple format for analyzing a stock," says McGriff. The format has been used successfully by more than five million people around the country. And NAIC surveys show that their average member receives a 12 percent annual return on his or her investments.

McGriff's club has a spiritual focus. The women start each meeting with a prayer and end with a prayer. The emphasis is on making the meetings exciting and keeping the level of interest high.

All in all, their strategy seems to work: in the three years the club has been in existence, their portfolio has roughly doubled. The goal of the NAIC methodology is to make your money double every five years.

McGriff, who grew up in a low-income family, said her mother didn't invest at all and found saving money to be a major hurdle. McGriff's father, who was in the Navy, died when she was six years old, leaving her mother to raise her two daughters on their father's pension.

Her mother was "frugal and saved money, which must have really sunk in when I was younger," recalls McGriff. "She was always teaching you the importance of not spending every dime you owned. She taught us not to live from paycheck to paycheck, and that helped me save money later in life."

So enthralled with the investment club is McGriff that she is encouraging her husband to join the club, as well as spouses of other club members, and in so doing is looking to create a "couples" club.

McGriff also likes to pass along what she's learned to others. For example, she says her "greatest accomplishment" was persuading her seventy-five-year-old mother to move money from her savings account into a higher-yielding money-market account. "It took me three years to convince her, but I did it," says McGriff. McGriff's mother was wary of the stock market, having grown up during the Depression.

McGriff also saves articles about investment clubs around the country, culled from NAIC's monthly magazine, and tries to find clubs that are doing something interesting that her club might emulate.

The Phenomenal Women's Investment Club has some big goals beyond simply learning about finance and growing their own portfolio. They want to work on establishing a charter school for finance and economics in Milwaukee. In addition, they want to explore how they could help with the economic development of their entire community, through investment in local business.

"A lot of investment clubs, like one in Los Angeles, invest not only in publicly traded companies, but also help rebuild communities," Mc-Griff points out.

Finance, she is convinced, is a language that can be learned just like any other language. McGriff began listening to business news on the radio and watching CNBC, the financial network, on television. "You turn it on and hear some stuff over and over again," she comments. "And after a while, it doesn't seem foreign to you anymore. You just have to be willing to put in the time.

"The stock market has been around so long, and so many people are taking advantage of it," she continues. "Not to is a mistake.

"If I can learn this, then other people certainly can, too," concludes McGriff. "The people in our club were not financial people. They were regular people, like me."

CHAPTER 7

Using the Internet

There is a computer literacy gap. There is a financial gap. A market gap. A vertical employment gap. An access to capital gap. These are structural gaps that demand structural solutions.

If you plant two identical seeds in the ground, feed them, water them, and build a wall between them, one will grow tall and strong and the other won't grow at all. It's not because one seed was better than the other. Or smarter than the other. Or wanted to grow more than the other. It's photosynthesis. One seed was nourished by the sunlight and the other was kept in darkness by the wall.

The Internet is the fastest-growing, most explosive way to communicate in history. It's as important a development as the invention of printing or the telephone or the radio, and it is poised to revolutionize the way business is done, not just in America, but worldwide.

It's also a great boon to you as an individual investor, because it democratizes financial information in a way never before possible. It gives you access to a lot of the same information as a high-paid Wall Street broker working in a skyscraper in Manhattan. Thanks to the Internet, geography is irrelevant. Right from your home, it's easy to get most of the same information about a stock or a bond that the Wall Street guy has. All you need is a computer—and their prices are dropping rapidly, to less than $500—and a phone line. Now that is power!

If you're not ready to buy a computer, most public libraries have them for your use. And in many communities, library staff can show you how to get started using a personal computer.

As recently as three years ago, you had to call a broker at a securities firm and ask him to send you reports about a company, such as Wall Street analysts' recommendations about whether to buy, sell, or hold the shares of different firms. The broker could charge you a hefty fee for doing that. Now, however, you can get lots of that same material online, free, by visiting the dozens of Web sites that have sprung up to provide people with financial information.

Here are just a few things that you can do using the Internet and personal finance software:

1. **Create a budget and manage your household finances.** Personal finance software can help you track all of your deductible expenses—which is useful at income tax time—monitor your cash flow, and reduce your overall debts. Popular software programs are available from Intuit Quicken (1-800-446-8848) or Microsoft Money (1-800-426-9400). Quicken's Deluxe 2000 software costs $49.95, while Microsoft Money's 2000 Standard U.S. Only sells for $34.95. Both companies make a range of products, some of which are designed for home offices. When you call their 800 numbers, tell them specifically what you want to use the software for, and they'll steer you toward the right product.

2. **Pay your bills and do your banking.** More than a third of the country's big retail banks let you bank online, and millions of people have begun using electronic banking. You can check the balances of your savings and checking accounts, transfer money among accounts, and pay bills—all electronically, from your home or office. Ask your bank if they offer online services. Or contact Checkfree, a nationwide online bill-paying service, at www.checkfree.com, about setting up such an arrangement (1-678-375-1608). CheckFree has an online bill-paying service that costs $12.95 a month and will pay up to thirty-five bills per

month with funds withdrawn from your checking account. There are even some purely online banks that you may want to explore, such as Net.B@nk (www.netbank.com; 1-770-343-6006), the largest FDIC-insured bank operating solely on the Internet.

3. **Do your taxes.** Try Intuit's TurboTax (www.turbotax.com). It alerts you to a wide range of possible tax credits and deductions. You can also file your tax returns online, using the software. Intuit will electronically forward your return to the IRS, if you so choose. If your tax return is simple—such as a 1040EZ, for taxpayers who don't itemize deductions—and you want a cheap, quick way to send it to the IRS, use the less expensive TurboTax Online. You log on to the site and answer a series of questions about your income. Your answers are then placed in an electronic version of your return, so you never have to deal with any paperwork. You can also print out a paper version of your tax return for your files. TurboTax costs $39.95 for the federal tax edition and $29.95 for the state edition; both are updated annually to reflect changes in the tax laws.

4. **Buy and sell stocks, bonds, and mutual funds very inexpensively.** You can set up an account with one of the many online brokers. An online brokerage firm enables you to buy and sell securities electronically, on a Web site you can access via a personal computer at your home or office. This service is provided at a fraction of the cost of a full-service broker who interacts with you by phone or in person. Online brokers offer varying levels of research and customer service, so you will want to choose one carefully. Visit the Web site of Gomez Advisors— www.gomez.com—to get a ranking of the best online broker with the lowest fees. Gomez recently selected five online brokers as the best on the Web, based on several different criteria such as ease of use, on-site resources, and overall cost. In order of ranking, they were E*Trade, Charles Schwab, Fidelity Investments, NDB, and DLJdirect.

5. **Get reams of valuable investment advice.** There are more than
    eight thousand investment Web sites out there, so how do you
    choose a good one? Here are some well-regarded ones:

    The Wall Street Journal Interactive Edition (www.wsj.com) is one
    of the few information sites that is not free. It's sold as a combined
    subscription with Barron's Online and costs $29 a year for those
    who subscribe to the print edition of *The Wall Street Journal,* and
    $59 for those who do not. Subscribers get continuous news
    coverage, searchable archives, and access to detailed company data.
    You can customize your own pages to receive breaking news about
    subjects or investments of special interest to you. The SmartMoney
    Interactive feature has interactive tools and worksheets to help you
    calculate things like how much money you'll need in retirement.
    Barron's Online has recent issues of the popular investment
    magazine *Barron's,* as well as penetrating market commentary.

    The Motley Fool, at www.fool.com, is a popular and witty site
    that aims to demystify investing. The site starts investors off with
    basic investment exercises and teaches the fundamentals of stock
    valuation. A companion site, quote.fool.com, has a mix of news,
    quotes, and updates on the market's most active stocks.

    Yahoo! Finance, at quote.yahoo.com, provides you with many
    free services that other sites charge for: Reuters news on individual
    companies; analysts' earnings estimates; and free insider trading
    filings from the Securities and Exchange Commission. It's a very
    simple, easy-to-use site as well.

    A useful book, *The Individual Investor's Guide to Computerized
    Investing,* published by the American Association of Individual
    Investors (AAII), evaluates the merits of more than seventy
    programs and Web sites. You can find this book at your public
    library or order it from the AAII by calling 1-800-428-2244 or
    visiting their Web site at www.aaii.com. The book is $24.95 for
    nonmembers and $19 for members.

6. **Review the balance in your retirement account, such as your
    company's 401(k).** About half of large companies calculate

401(k) values daily, while others value assets monthly, quarterly, or even yearly. So you may want to check the value of your account electronically on a regular basis. Ask your company's benefits officer how to access your account online.

7. **Find the best-priced mortgage lender and interest rates for a home loan.** Eloan.com offers rates from about seventy different mortgage lenders. You can also try www.interest.com and www.mortgage-net.com for basic financial projections, worksheets, and calculators to help you figure out payments on various home loans, either adjustable-rate or fixed-rate. And at www.hsh.com, run by HSH Associates, America's largest publisher of mortgage-rate information, you can read weekly updates of interest rates offered by 2,500 lenders. To make sure you're getting the best deal, compare online mortgages with terms offered by lenders in your area.

8. **Compare the performance of different mutual funds.** Morningstar is the leading provider of mutual fund statistics and analysis in print form to the investment community. On the Internet you can visit Morningstar's Web site— www.morningstar.net—which offers ratings of different mutual funds, performance data, portfolio holdings, and more.

9. **Purchase insurance.** Visit www.quickquote.com to sift through a database of more than a thousand policies offered by some eighteen insurers. InsureMarket, www.insuremarket.com, is run by the personal finance software giant Intuit and restricts itself to a small number of policies from the major insurance firms. But the site also has a calculator to help you figure out how much insurance you need. The key is to use the Internet as a research tool and find a few policies with the best rates. Then call an independent insurance agent to see if he or she can beat the online rates you've been quoted. Remember that no insurer—online or otherwise—can guarantee you a rate until you've had a physical examination from a doctor.

10. **Visit the SEC's Web site, www.sec.gov, to get valuable information from the investor education section.** In addition, you can get free information about almost all the publicly traded companies in the United States.

11. **Find a job.** There are thousands of Internet job boards—such as Monster.com, HotJobs.com, and CareerMosaic.com, which bring employers and candidates together. You can answer an ad at one of these sites or post your résumé there. You can also advertise your skills on your own Web page. The Internet can literally help you find a job while you're sleeping. Consider this: In January 1998, 17 percent of Fortune Global 500 companies were actively recruiting on the Net, according to iLogos.com, a research firm in Ottawa. Just a year later that figure soared to 45 percent. And 65 percent of those job seekers hail from nontechnical professions. One of them, as *Fortune* magazine recently reported, was Bobby Beck, a thirty-seven-year old truck driver who wanted a job that would "get him home to North Texas more than a couple of days a month." He logged on to Layover.com, where truckers can apply for multiple jobs by filling out just one application, and landed a well-paying job at U.S. Express.

12. **Get an accredited university or graduate degree, such as an MBA or degree in computer science, online via "distance learning."** This can qualify you to get a higher-paying job. More and more, traditional "brick-and-mortar" universities are giving way to online ones. Contact the industry trade group, the U.S. Distance Learning Association in Watertown, Massachusetts, at www.usdla.org, to find out more. Their phone number is 1-800-275-5162.

Nonetheless, we don't want you to go overboard with all this. As *Money* magazine sagely warns: "Don't get seduced by technology at the expense of a good, sober investment strategy." Technology is a powerful tool that you can harness—but ultimately you are still in the driver's seat.

It's important for you to be on the right side of the "digital divide." New users continue to flood the Internet, with one-third of the nation now online. But Internet usage is greatest among those with annual incomes of $75,000 or more. If the people who have the most money are online and increasing their wealth, that should tell us something.

Getting online is not a luxury; it's a necessity for you to stay competitive. Technological skills and access to information will be essential in the twenty-first century. The U.S. Department of Labor has estimated that 60 percent of all new jobs are expected to require computer skills by the year 2000. The Internet—and electronic commerce, which involves selling goods and services online—is one of the hottest areas of the U.S. economy. To participate in the new, technology-driven society, you need access to computers, training, and support.

Not only will the Internet help you with your personal finances, it also can lead to a lucrative career, if, for example, you decide to become a computer programmer or get some other job in the high-tech industry. There's a shortage of people with these skills in the American economy. So if you're good, you can command a big salary. Some eighteen-year-olds who are great with computers are being hired right out of high school at $50,000 a year.

If you're not online, and are concerned that you may not be able to afford a computer and the expenses that go with it, help is available. More and more programs are sprouting up to help as many people as possible get online. Community access centers—including schools, libraries, and nonprofit organizations—are playing an important role in this effort.

Here's just one example: About a year ago, 13 Scribes, an African American–owned software engineering firm, launched an innovative program in Atlanta called Computers in the 'Hood. It aims to make technology available to young black people living in the inner city. The firm offers free classes on how to use the Internet. Reaction to the classes was resounding. When 13 Scribes began the classes in September 1997, they were so popular that there was standing room only.

"After seeing this response, we decided we had to do more," explains Bisi Coker, the Nigerian-born marketing director of 13 Scribes. He and his colleagues hope to replicate Computers in the 'Hood in cities around the country.

As part of the program, 13 Scribes has made their office into a "cybercenter." Neighborhood residents can come in, log on to computers, and use the Internet, all free. The firm also markets its own personal computer, known as "the Underground Railroad Package." You can find out more about 13 Scribes at their Web site: www.13scribes.com.

"Our motto is 'From the Underground Railroad to the Information Superhighway,' " says Coker. The computer is powerful enough to get people launched, and printers are also available at reasonable prices. The company has financing plans to help people pay for the computers over a period of time.

These days, because of technological advances accompanied by decreasing prices, you can probably buy a new, more powerful computer more cheaply than buying a used one. Currently you can get a new computer system and a printer with sufficient capacity to go online and do any home office task for about $500, or even less in some cases. Shop around. Check out the business section of the newspaper for good deals on computers. Visit stores like COMPUSA, Circuit City, or Best Buy. You can also buy computers online, at sites like www.gateway.com or www.dell.com.

Here are some other ways that you can get online inexpensively:

- Buy a new computer, and share the cost with several of your friends or family members. That way they can all benefit, for a fraction of what it would cost to buy a new machine for each of them.

- "Barter" with a company that sells new or used computers. Offer to answer phones at their office, do telemarketing, or perform any other skill you might have in exchange for a new or used computer. This way you won't have to pay sales tax on your computer once you acquire it.

- Use the computer at your office, your church, your public library, a local school, or a community college.

- Find out names of community-based organizations that offer computer training and Internet access in your neighborhood by calling some of the following organizations:

1. The National Urban League, a nonprofit group dedicated to helping low-income people attain economic equality, launched its first technology program in 1968. Since then it has expanded its efforts to include 32 different programs. They work with volunteers from industry, such as Bell Atlantic and Ameritech. Their current goal is to build 114 state-of-the-art community technology centers all over the country. Each "digital campus," as it will be called, will train 600 entry-level workers a year in the booming high-tech field. To find out more, you can call the National Urban League's headquarters in New York at 1-212-558-5300.

2. Bill Gates, cofounder and chairman of Microsoft and the richest man in the world, has set up the Bill and Melinda Gates Foundation, headquartered in Redmond, Washington (1-206-709-3100). It had about $17 billion in assets as of September 1999. The Gates Learning Foundation has a program that has pledged about $200 million to bring computers, training, and Internet access to public libraries in low-income neighborhoods across the country. It is known as the Gates Library Initiative and thus far has worked with more than 1,600 libraries. The second program is an Education Initiative, to explore innovative ways to best use technology in kindergarten through twelfth-grade education. In addition, Bill Gates recently announced a pledge of at least $1 billion to pay for full scholarships over the next twenty years for minority students in the fields of education, math, science, and engineering. This is one of the largest philanthropic donations to a specific cause in history. Gates plans to help a minimum of one thousand high school students a year through the program, called the Gates Millennium Scholarships. He has spoken many times about the need to bridge the "digital divide" in society and will especially target his scholarships toward black, Hispanic, and

American Indian students. The foundation's Web site can be accessed at www.gatesfoundation.org.

3. National technology and media associations are leading the charge to bring technology to everyone. Community Technology Centers' Network (CTCNet) is a nonprofit group that seeks to empower all people equitably through technology. You can reach them at their Waltham, Massachusetts, headquarters, 1-781-684-0830, or at their Web site, www.ctcnet.org. CTCNet is an umbrella group for the hundreds of community technology centers (CTCs) that have been started across the country in community centers, housing projects, libraries, after-school programs, and other places. Besides providing Internet access, some of the centers teach desktop publishing, multimedia, and Web site design. For example, Blazers Youth Center (1-323-292-2261), a community initiative in south central Los Angeles, teaches its clientele of predominantly black and Latino youths Web site design and other Internet skills, for a modest fee.

    CTCNet is, in turn, actively involved with the Alliance for Community Media in Washington, D.C. (1-202-393-2650; www.alliancecm.org). They seek to "ensure that low-income, inner-city, minority, and rural constituencies have not only a seat at the table, but a voice that counts," according to the executive directors of the organizations, writing in a summer-fall 1999 issue of their newsletter, *The Community Technology Review.*

Becoming computer-literate can, as we have said, open the door to some high-paying jobs. Every day corporations are becoming more automated, not just in America but worldwide. So the demand for computer professionals continues to increase at a terrific pace.

In Atlanta, for example, twenty-year-old Carlzell Marshall was casting about for something to do after high school. He was thinking about joining the military but for the time being was working at Hardy's, flipping burgers for $5.75 an hour. Then he came upon the Computers in the 'Hood project. Over a period of two years, they trained him to work on building and programming computers, so that today he commands $20 an hour, working as a computer professional on the year 2000, or Y2K, issue for a private company. The Y2K issue is a very important, high-profile undertaking in the United States and abroad to insure that all computers are set up with the correct date for the new millennium.

Marshall's income has gone from $11,440 a year to $41,600 per year: almost a 400 percent increase in just two years! And his chances of promotion in this booming industry are very bright. Currently only about 5 percent of all computer programmers and just 6 percent of computer scientists in the United States are African Americans.

At 13 Scribes Coker said his firm hopes to groom many more young African Americans for careers in the computer business. They've written letters and sent invitations to a variety of black churches in Atlanta about their program, which has been featured on CNBC and CNN.

"We want the churches to help us spread this gospel of the information superhighway," concludes Coker. "Churches could become community centers where people can go and get on the Internet.

"We have to do what we know best," he adds, "and continue to bring people that look like us up."

ELECTRONIC COMMERCE

Go online, and the world of electronic commerce opens up to you. Electronic commerce, or e-commerce, involves buying and selling goods and services via the Internet. This sector of the economy is undergoing explosive growth. In 1998 total e-commerce exceeded $102 billion for U.S.-based companies. By 2002 that's expected to soar to $1.1 trillion worldwide.

In 1998 the Internet economy generated more than $300 billion in U.S. revenue, up from just $5 billion in 1995: an astonishing growth rate in just four years. The digital economy accounted for 1.2 million jobs in 1998 alone.

"In less than a decade we achieved a base of what other industries—like railroads—took decades to build," comments John Chambers, president and CEO of Cisco Systems, Inc., a global leader in computer networking with $11 billion in annual revenues. "And these are much higher-paying positions than the average job in other industries."

The reason these jobs are higher paying is that they are more productive than traditional, non-Internet jobs. According to a new study conducted by the University of Texas and released in 1999 by Cisco, Internet workers are 65 percent more productive than non-Internet workers. The average revenue per Internet employee is $250,000, versus $160,000 per non-Internet business employee. So that translates into higher salaries for those who work in these high-tech jobs.

"Currently the Internet accounts for 1 percent of employment in the United States," observes Ethan Harris, senior economist at Lehman Brothers, a New York investment bank. "But that's a lot for a four- or five-year-old industry, and it's growing very rapidly."

The University of Texas study was done by interviewing more than three thousand U.S.-based companies that generated all or part of their revenues from Internet products or services. You can read the results of the entire study at www.InternetIndicators.com.

"The Internet will combine people and information in virtual global companies," asserts Chambers. He predicts it will transform business around the globe: "Companies that get it will break away. Those that don't will be left behind."

You need to participate in the digital revolution. You could start an online company or go work for one.

Yolanda Robinson Darricarerre has jumped into e-commerce. She is a thirty-four-year-old entrepreneur who runs a Web-based business from her one-bedroom apartment: D.C. Walking Tours, www.dcwalkingtours.com. Her Web site was created to meet the needs of more than twenty million tourists from the United States and abroad who visit Washington each year. She has devised a unique way for people to visit the nation's capital. They can click on her site and book guided walking tours to some of the most interesting places in the city and its environs: Georgetown. Capitol Hill. The Virginia hunt country. Participants can sample fine cuisine, peruse art galleries and museums, and see stately homes and gardens, all led by a knowledgeable tour guide. Her Web site is just a year and a half old, and she already gets about forty thousand hits a month! She makes money from tour operators and from advertisers who see her site as a way to get their message out to tourists.

A black woman who was one of five children raised by a single mother, Darricarerre studied geography and several foreign languages in college. She's traveled all over the world and lived in Spain and France at different times. All this sparked her interest in global business. And thanks to the Internet, she can run an international business from her own home. "I've created a business that still allows me to educate myself," she says. "Everything I do is international. I think like the big boys."

Isiah Thomas, the former NBA star and now an executive with the Toronto Raptors, has jumped into e-commerce.

He and his eight brothers and sisters grew up poor on the west side of Chicago. His father was a truck driver and left home when Thomas was seven years old. Their mother, who worked for the city of Chicago in Social Services, raised them on her own. Sometimes, when they couldn't afford the rent, they were kicked out of their apartment, their clothes and furniture dumped unceremoniously on the sidewalk. When that happened, they lived in their car or found friends and grandparents to take them in.

"I got a Ph.D. from the streets," says Thomas. But his mother pushed the children to go further. Thomas excelled at basketball and won a scholarship to college. So talented was he at the sport that he entered professional basketball in 1981 and became a star of the Detroit Pistons. He was named one of the "Fifty Greatest Players" in NBA (National Basketball Association) history.

What he saw playing professional sports was this: "A fool and his money are soon parted. So many professional athletes came into basketball or baseball and got taken advantage of. At the end of the day, they didn't have anything to fall back on."

Thomas made sure he did have something to fall back on. He earned a BA from Indiana University. He learned other skills above and beyond shooting hoops. From 1988 to 1994 he was president of the NBA Players Association and was instrumental in increasing players' salaries. and managing collective bargaining negotiations.

"By being on a team, you understand the human dynamics of motivating people," he explains. He began developing diverse business interests. In 1993 he and a partner bought American Speedy Printing, a bankrupt Detroit printing company, and built it into the fourth-largest quick-printing chain in the country. Thomas retired from playing professional basketball in 1994 and became part owner, executive vice president, and general manager of the Toronto Raptors professional basketball franchise—the first African American athlete ever to do so. In addition, he became one of NBC's top sports analysts. Recently, Thomas was appointed a member of the Board of Governors of the Chicago Stock Exchange. And he is the founder and principal shareholder of Isiah Investments, LLC, a diversified holding company with multimillion-dollar investments in a variety of businesses.

Thomas, who is now thirty-eight, has recently launched an online business: Isiah.com. Its goal is to link up all the malls across the country and allow people to shop by gift certificate. On the Web site you can select an item, order a gift certificate for it—which will then be sent overnight to you—and redeem it at any mall in the country. The Web site will also get involved in providing innovative financial services online, such as insurance, banking, investments, and loans.

"Our focus is to serve the underserved community," explains Thomas. "I see the Internet and technology as a way to serve the underserved communities without expending a lot of bricks and mortar."

Plus, he added, when you deal online, no one knows what race you are. "All the stereotypes are erased," he comments. "It's the purest form of business you can have."

Besides participating actively in electronic commerce, as these folks have done, you need to be prepared for the fact that your job could be eliminated by the online revolution. For example, the Internet is transforming the travel agency business and traditional airline ticket sales. More and more people are buying airline tickets online (e-tickets), thus saving the time and money of going out and physically buying tickets. This is poised to happen in lots of other industries. You need to think: Could my job be eliminated by the Internet? And if so, how can I train myself for a high-paying job in the digital economy?

THE INTERNET AND INVESTING

The Internet has revolutionized the securities industry, so that today seven million Americans trade online, accounting for 25 percent of all trades made by individual investors, according to the SEC, the government watchdog that regulates the securities industry.

By contrast, not one person traded securities over the Internet in 1994. Imagine that—going from zero investors online just five years ago to seven million today. It's a breathtaking spate of growth. Many have called the present era "the digital revolution" and have said it will profoundly change our lives, just as the Industrial Revolution did in the nineteenth century, and the agricultural revolution before that.

In the coming years even more Americans will trade online, and the number of online brokerage accounts will roughly equal the combined metropolitan populations of Seattle, San Francisco, Denver, Boston, Dallas, Miami, Atlanta, and Chicago. Online brokerage firms are opening new accounts at the astounding rate of 15,000 per day, as of May 1999.

Online brokerage firms exist in cyberspace, although they also have actual, physical offices. Because these firms have very low overhead—and therefore less transaction costs to do a trade—they're able to offer you a very deeply discounted price to buy or sell securities. After all, they don't have to pay for armies of brokers to carry out your trades. Instead, the process is all automated, thanks to the Internet.

Traditional brokerage houses such as Merrill Lynch are revamping the way they do business, as a result of competition from these cheaper, discount brokerage firms.

It turns out this is another great boon for you as an investor. The Internet has revolutionized the whole fee structure of the brokerage business, which greatly benefits small investors. In the past, some brokers tried to get you to buy and sell stocks frequently, so that they could make a commission on each trade. Because of the way they were compensated, this was bound to take place. Many were paid a commission only, based on the number of trades they did, and no salary or very little salary.

But now, with the Internet, a whole new system is evolving. The individual investor is now able to make his or her own trades, with the click of a button on the computer. In this new era, brokers will have to do more than just execute trades—they'll have to provide you with useful investment advice. Their role will be more that of financial adviser, rather than salesman. Their investment advice may end up being more objective, as a result.

The Internet has "done nothing short of changing the way the world works, and the way our nation invests," according to Arthur Levitt, chairman of the SEC. "And I think overall it's changed us for the better."

We've entered the era of "do-it-yourself" personal finance, thanks to the Internet. The individual is able to take more and more responsibility for what goes on with his or her personal finances.

It's akin to what happened with gas stations in the United States, in the 1950s versus those of today. In 1957, if you pulled up to a gas station in America, three guys would run out to service your car. One would pump gas. Another would wash your windshield. A third would look under your hood and check your oil. You may have liked that level of service, but you paid a price for it, reflected in the cost of the gasoline.

Today, think of a modern gas station. You pull up to the self-serve aisle and you pump your own gas. You stick your credit card in the slot and pay right then and there. A little white receipt chugs out of the slot. Boom! You're on your way in a matter of minutes, and never even dealt with a single person. The gas prices are lower at these self-service stations, as compared to full-service ones. So you, the consumer, benefit from the discount, thanks to automation.

A big segment of the securities business is headed the same way. Instead of paying a steep fee for a broker at a traditional, full-service firm, you will be able to cut out the middleman and do the trading directly yourself, thereby saving large amounts of money in the process.

But the Internet brings with it perils, as well as opportunities. Arthur Levitt at the SEC cautioned against investors becoming "manic about the mania" and warned that fundamentals still apply in the securities business. Nor does online investing alter the basic regulatory structure that has governed the securities industry for the past sixty-five years.

In response to the challenges posed by the Internet, investors need to become more educated about investments and take responsibility for the level of risk they're assuming in their investment decisions. The SEC, for instance, is very concerned about the dangers of day trading.

Day trading consists of people who dart in and out of the securities markets rapidly, hoping to make a killing in just one day. Day traders make bets on small upward and downward movements of stocks and then sell their holdings by the end of the day. They can sit in their homes or offices and do day trading thanks to computers. There are folks who become so compulsive about this that they spend all their time at it, mesmerized by the upticks on the computer screen. Lots of them are day trading in volatile Internet stocks, such as eBay, the online auction house, or Amazon.com, the online bookseller, because these stocks are considered very "hot" and have been getting a lot of press lately. It has the allure of a video game or the adrenaline kick that some people get out of slot machines at casinos. There are those who become addicted to it.

Now maybe you've met people like this. Some may tell you that they made a fortune day trading. They will tell you that you are a fool not to be involved in this.

You're wondering: Could they be right? Should I quit my job and stay home all day and try to make a hundred thousand dollars on Yahoo stock? Have I been wasting my life going to this nine-to-five job all day?

Some people argue that day trading is mere speculation, which is nothing new to the securities industry. There have always been a small segment of players in the market who were professional speculators.

But in Levitt's view day trading goes beyond speculation: it is gambling, pure and simple. The difference is that speculation requires some market knowledge, whereas day trading does not.

"I'm concerned that more and more people may be undertaking day trading strategies without a complete understanding of the risk and difficulty involved," comments Levitt. "No one should have any illusions of what he is getting involved in."

The SEC chairman mentioned he had heard of one state in which sixty-seven out of sixty-eight day traders at a firm had lost money. He was concerned about the influx of novice investors who may be "seduced" by the ease and speed of Internet trading and thereby overlook the risks involved. A mythology has evolved about the power of the trader, through books, movies, and television, which leads some people to aspire to that ideal of machismo. Yet the reality is far different.

"As far as I'm concerned, for most individuals the stock market is best used for investing rather than trading. And I think it's important to make that distinction," points out Levitt. "On-line trading may be easy. On-line investing—and I emphasize investing—requires the same old-fashioned elbow grease, like researching a company or taking the time to appreciate the level of risk."

The SEC chairman noted some common misperceptions about on-line trading. First is the notion that the Internet makes it seem as if you have a direct connection to the securities markets. You don't. "When you push that Enter key, your order is sent to your broker, who then sends it to the market to be executed," observes Levitt. However, it's not guaranteed. Lines may clog, systems may break, and orders may back up. A line forms, even with automated systems. Thus some investors may not receive the currently quoted price by the time they get to the front of the line.

How do investors protect themselves from such an occurrence? They could use a "limit order," or an instruction to buy or sell the security at a specific price. In other words, the order can be executed only if the market price has not moved past a certain level. By contrast, a market order buys or sells the stock at whatever price the security is at the time the order reaches the market.

Still another misconception about online trading is that an order is canceled when you hit the Cancel button. But the fact is, it's canceled only when the market receives that cancellation. Investors can, for example, get clobbered when trying to buy shares of a fast-moving initial public offering (IPO) on account of this.

Levitt described how one major brokerage firm wasn't able to process 20 percent of the cancellation orders on a fast-moving IPO. One investor placed an online order for two thousand shares of the stock, thought she canceled it, and then placed another order for one thousand shares. After realizing she had two orders outstanding, she tried canceling both. Instead she owed her broker over $250,000 for three thousand shares, after wanting to invest roughly $18,000.

"Most cases may not be that exceptional, but I urge investors to contact their firms to see they can ensure that a cancellation order actually worked," says Levitt.

On-line trading does not absolve online brokerage firms of their responsibilities to their clients, either. Such firms need to make sure that customer service 800 numbers are being answered and that the firm's compliance department is not overwhelmed with complaints about failures or delays, order execution, and account accessibility.

"Firms have the same duty to their customers to find the best prices, whether they charge $10 per trade or $100 per trade," asserts the SEC chairman.

Another point he emphasized is that firms need to communicate much more clearly to investors. Overall, the SEC has found that most firms address the different types of orders available, but fewer firms address market volatility and how the use of margin can affect online investors. Moreover, "almost none talk about the risks or what to do in the event of system capacity and outage problems."

Finally the SEC chairman said he worried about the way some online brokerage firms advertise. They imply that it's easy to get rich quickly by trading on the Internet. "Quite frankly, some advertisements more closely resemble commercials for the lottery than anything else," he notes. In response, Levitt asked the regulatory unit of the National Association of Securities Dealers (NASD) to hold a roundtable on advertising to improve fairness in that area. The NASD—which issues general guidelines for advertising by securities firms—held two meetings on the subject and plans to post a report about the event on their Web site (www.nasdr.com) in the fall of 1999.

The SEC has also unveiled its new investor education Web page, www.sec.gov. It contains detailed information about online investing, how to detect fraud both on and off the Internet, and other important information about saving and investing.

Still another peril of the Internet is investment fraud. But we'll take up that topic in chapter 10, "Avoiding Scams."

THE RISE OF DISTANCE LEARNING

The Internet will also allow you to get an education online and thereby increase your marketability in the information economy.

Universities of the future will increasingly have to deal with a diverse student body and more and more use of "online," or distance learning, according to Robert Berdahl, chancellor of the University of California at Berkeley.

The campus at Berkeley is a prime example of diversity, he noted in a recent speech. "In total, 44 percent of our students come from families with at least one of these characteristics: from a family of immigrants, have neither parent with a college degree, or come from families with less than $30,000 a year income," Berdahl told the audience.

Moreover, 13 percent of the 1999 incoming freshman class will be black and Hispanic, while 44 percent of the student body is Asian American. Berkeley also has more women students than male students, and white students represent just 35 percent of the entire student body.

Berdahl spoke of how the technological revolution is poised to transform colleges into "virtual universities." It's enabled a growing number of universities to offer accredited programs through "distance learning," whereby coursework is conducted in cyberspace.

For example, Duke offers an MBA through a combination of online courses, encounters with faculty, and two-week residencies at Duke's campus, for less than the cost of a full-time degree program. The University of Phoenix—run by the Apollo Group, a publicly traded company—is the fastest-growing educational institution in America, with sites all over the country. And recently, Harcourt Brace, the publishing company, announced that it was starting its own accredited university that would employ electronic materials.

"The virtual university represents a tremendous opportunity to provide educational opportunities to people who have previously been denied access, either because of cost or location or age," summarizes Berdahl.

According to a new report by Price Waterhouse Coopers, the big accounting firm, there will be a huge shift toward electronic courses, as the trend toward lifelong learning increases demand for education. That report suggests that software will serve about 50 percent of the total student enrollment in community colleges and 35 percent of the enrollment in four-year institutions.

Traditional "brick-and-mortar" universities won't disappear entirely, to be replaced by "online" universities. But they will be changed in how and to whom they deliver an education. Thanks to the Internet, you'll be able to get accredited diplomas wherever you live, whenever you want to do the coursework, for a reasonable price, without having to move or quit your job.

THE HIGH-TECH STOCK MARKET OF THE FUTURE

Another reason you need to be online is because that is where the stock market is headed.

The stock market of the future will be twenty-four hours a day, high-tech, global, and accessible to investors by cellular phones, pagers, and palm-size computers, according to Frank Zarb, chairman and CEO of the National Association of Securities Dealers.

The NASD is an industry group that owns the Nasdaq Stock Market and is the self-regulatory organization that polices Nasdaq traders. The high-tech stock market of the future is a far cry from the early stock exchanges in America. The first stock exchange in the U.S. was established in Philadelphia in 1790. The exchange arose for commercial reasons—to enable private investors to buy and sell a larger and wider variety of shares of companies—but it was also an effort encouraged by the government to lay the foundation for a national economy. It enabled the government to sell shares of the national debt to the public. Alexander Hamilton, the first Secretary of the Treasury, created a national debt—$80 million in government bonds to absorb the cost of the Revolutionary War—and the means to pay for it: a national currency and a national bank to issue that currency. Both government bonds and shares of the bank's stocks were sold to the public beginning in the eighteenth century. In addition, by 1792, merchants on Wall Street, in New York—which had emerged as a center for commercial activity—had begun trading securities over the counter, like any other of their wares. They began scheduling auctions for stocks and bonds, and soon a central auction was orgnaized at 22 Wall Street.

Until recently, the stock market in the United States was much the same as when it began on Wall Street in the late eighteenth century. Then came the Internet and advanced computer and communications technologies, and all that changed.

Zarb said the stock market of the future—which we'll begin seeing by the year 2005—will have these features:

- Trading securities will be digital, global, and accessible twenty-four hours a day.

- People will be able to get stock price quotations instantly and execute a trade any time, day or night, anywhere on the globe, since stock markets will be linked and almost all electronic.

- Trading floors and paper will be rendered obsolete, to a great degree, by competition and technology.

  In fact, both Nasdaq and the New York Stock Exchange are facing competitive threats from new, electronic trading networks that can execute trades less expensively. They are called electronic communication networks (ECNs), and in 1999 the SEC approved a rule that allows them to apply to become stock exchanges themselves.

- Investors will be able to use not only their home or office computers, but also cellular phones, pagers, and palm-size computers to get access to the markets on the Internet. They'll be able to get price quotes and execute trades.

- Investors will even be able to get programmable, computerized reports on the performance of their own personal investment portfolio. And they'll be able to listen to these reports on their car radios while driving to and from work. At their homes or offices they'll be able to get this same information broadcast to them on digital TV.

"All of this will be available in an orderly, fair, well-regulated, and lower-cost environment," Zarb says. Trading will cost less for consumers; markets will have more liquidity; and it will be easier than ever before for companies to raise capital. There will also be improved, high-tech surveillance of trading to protect the integrity of the markets.

The NASD chief predicted that the twenty-first century will usher in multidealer, computer-screen-based, technology-driven stock markets that will be accessible to all. He also foresaw the day when investors around the globe—from the Americas to Asia and Europe—will invest across borders with ease.

The Internet, said Zarb, has truly democratized financial information. "Mr. and Mrs. America are now in the stock market," he declares. When he started out in the industry some years ago, "the market was composed mostly of rich people selling stock to each other." Nowadays that's no longer the case. Forty-five percent, or almost half of U.S. households, now own stock, compared with only 5 percent at the end of World War II. These retail investors account for 75 percent of all Nasdaq trades. In 1980 stocks accounted for just 10 percent of U.S. household wealth; but by 1998 that figure had risen to 25 percent.

This revolution in securities ownership has been fueled by technology and the instantaneous access to information that it accords. About ninety-six million people in the United States now have access to the Internet. Worldwide, half a billion people will be online by the beginning of next year. One survey showed that 54 percent of American homes have computers, which in turn have helped fuel the whole investing craze.

Globally the number of investors is poised to soar. "There are a billion people in China, and as that country modernizes, there will be many millions of potential new investors," declares Zarb. Furthermore, Japan's investing profile is changing, with a greater emphasis on equities.

Another driving force for change is the fact that the economy is becoming more global and more interconnected. Companies, in turn, want to raise capital globally in stock markets that fit their business plans. Many want their stocks to be traded where their products are sold, and "investors the world over want to trade in the U.S. markets, and foreign companies increasingly want to list their traded stocks here," Zarb points out.

"Never before have so many people around the world had access to so much information, with the ability to act on it instantly through advanced technology," Zarb concluded in a recent speech.

And it is this access to information that is shaping the stock market of tomorrow.

CHAPTER 8

Dealing with Major Life Events

Oseola McCarty of Hattiesburg, Mississippi, recently passed away. She worked as a washerwoman for over 75 years and saved every penny, nickel and dime of her earnings to amass a substantial fortune of $250,000. She donated $150,000 of that money to the University of Southern Mississippi, wanting the pennies that she earned washing the clothes of the rich to be used to nurture young minds, to help educate a generation of future leaders, and to have lasting significance long after the money was spent.

T
o every thing there is a season, and a time for every purpose under heaven: a time to be born, and a time to die," Ecclesiastes 3:1–2 teaches us.

We all go through great passages in life. We are all born, and we all die. Looking back over this century, African Americans have faced several great passages, including ending segregation and winning the right to vote. We used to live in a shadow society, in an era of state-sponsored terrorism. No longer. The road has been rocky, the hills have been steep. We made it. We won those battles. The last river to cross is the resource gap, the access to capital gap, the digital divide. We will win these battles, too. When you think about the mountains we have climbed, when you think about the oceans we have crossed, in front of us are just hills and creeks. Let nothing break our spirits. If we have the faith, God has the power.

Let's focus now on the passages that you as an individual must traverse in life. You will no doubt face a number of great milestones, such as going to college, getting married and raising children, buying your first home, building your career, caring for elderly parents, and finally, death: your own and those of close friends and family members.

You need to be prepared for these milestones: spiritually, emotionally—but also financially. All these stages of life must be dealt with in your financial plan. As your life twists and turns, your financial plan must be revised accordingly.

ESTATE PLANNING

Many people do not want to face the reality of their own death, so they avoid writing a will. But it is crucial that you do so. A will is a legal document that tells your heirs how to distribute your money and possessions once you die. If you fail to leave such a document and thus die "intestate," as they say in legal terminology, then the courts and the state distribute your assets.

Rather than let the state distribute your assets, it's far better to write your own will. Everyone needs a will, regardless of the size of his or her estate. And it has become fairly easy and inexpensive to prepare one. The easiest way to do it is to hire a lawyer or a financial consultant who specializes in estate planning to prepare one for you. An expert adviser can evaluate your estate, advise you about the best way to transfer your assets, and show you how to minimize your tax liability. This will ensure a smooth transition for your family members. Moreover, if your estate is larger than $650,000 as of 1999 your heirs will be subject to estate taxes, which are sizable, starting at 37 percent and rising to 55 percent for estates worth more than $3 million. Both the federal government and most state governments impose estate taxes. (Note: The $650,000 amount will increase according to a set schedule until it reaches $1 million by 2006.)

The way your assets are transferred during your lifetime and at the time of your death has a direct impact on how much tax is due on your estate. With larger estates you should definitely hire an adviser to help you take advantage of strategies to reduce your tax burden. For example, one technique consists of setting up trusts, which enables you to leave property to your heirs and allows them to live off the income from that property as long as they live. A "trust" is a legal entity that holds title to your property. Another technique is to give away your property before your death. Each individual can give away up to $10,000 a year to his or her children or other people, without having to pay gift tax on it. Gifts that pay tuition or medical bills or gifts to tax-exempt organizations are also exempt from gift tax.

However, if your estate is small and fairly simple, it is possible to write your own will using computer software or a do-it-yourself guide. You can also buy a generic will at an office supply store. But make sure that any document you prepare yourself meets all the legal requirements for a will in your state.

When you write a will, you need to have records showing how all your property is held and titled, whether it be real estate, investments, insurance policies, cars, boats, or any other items of value. Outline what you own and how you own it. Then decide what will pass through your will and what you will pass down outside your will. You may, for example, want to present your favorite niece with your antique sofa in person rather than writing it into the will. You may also want to make charitable donations in your will and gifts of personal property. You can change or amend your will right up to the time of your death by means of a "codicil," or addition.

When you write a will, the law allows you to select the person who will settle your estate; this person is known as the "executor," if it is a man, or the "executrix," if it is a woman. The executor should be someone you trust to handle your affairs responsibly. It could be a family member, a friend, your attorney, or an institution such as a bank, which takes on what is known as a "fiduciary relationship." A fiduciary can be an individual or a corporate institution that is responsible for acting for the benefit of another party. The executor is in charge of paying medical bills, final debts, funeral expenses, the costs of administering your estate, and your last tax bill to the Internal Revenue Service (IRS). The executor also collects any income owed to you. For these services this person receives 2 percent to 5 percent of all the assets that pass through your will.

After you die, if you leave behind minor children or adult children who are incompetent—that is, mentally or physically unable to care for themselves—then you will need to appoint a trustee (if you create a trust for your children) and a guardian. You could, for example, set up a trust fund for your dependent children after your death, which could contain money that would be invested by the trustee; the return on those investments could then be used to pay your children's living expenses.

A will is a public document and eventually becomes a matter of public record. Before this happens, however, it has to go through "probate," which is a court process that serves two major functions. First, it identifies the rightful heirs to the estate and the size of the inheritance that each will receive. Second, it takes the legal title of your property out of your name and puts it into the name of your heirs. The great majority of wills go through this procedure uncontested. However, it's desirable to avoid probate, because it can be a time-consuming and expensive process, according to the National Association of Financial and Estate Planning (NAFEP: www.nafep.com). "Reliable estimates are that on a national average, probate costs run from 6 percent to 10 percent of the value of the estate," points out the NAFEP. "This means that an estate worth only $200,000 could cost $12,000 to $20,000 on probate. . . . In some cases, probate ends up in litigation that drags on for years. Frequently it leads to huge family battles, and it often causes or allows the decedent's wishes to be ignored." To avoid probate, the NAFEP suggests using a family estate planning trust—either a "living trust" or a "life estate trust." Through these vehicles you avoid probate by titling your property in the name of your trust before your death. This enables you to have complete control of the property during your life, but the trust is considered the legal owner of the property for the purposes of transferring the title. Once you die, a trustee whom you have appointed will handle the transfers or the payments to the heirs you specified in the trust. The trustee can handle everything quickly and simply, without lawyers, court supervision, excessive costs, or delays. The typical cost for setting up such an arrangement is about $1,995, according to Mike Janko, executive director of NAFEP. For this fee an attorney would transfer the title of your assets to your trust, which is essential to avoid probate. If you find a lawyer willing to set up the trust for a lot less than this—say, $700 or $800—then it means the attorney would simply give you a book of legal documents and leave to you the responsibility of transferring title of your assets to the trust. This is a do-it-yourself approach and should be undertaken only by those who are very familiar with estate planning law. Too often, when people attempt to do this without having proper knowledge of the law, "they fail to fund their trusts and their property goes into probate," Janko points out.

Your will is a very important document, so members of your family need to know where it is kept. It ought to be locked in a safe or fireproof box with other important documents.

A "living will," also known as an "advance directive," is a document intended to give your doctor information and general instructions about what sort of medical care you want, including whether or not you would like "extraordinary" types of treatment. "Extraordinary" treatments could include cardiac resuscitation, mechanical respiration, and artificial nutrition. Some people feel very strongly that they want to die a natural death and want no part of these high-tech treatments. If you are terminally ill or seriously injured and unable to talk, your doctors need to know whether or not you want such treatments. If, for example, you were in a comatose state, would you want to be kept alive on machines indefinitely or unplugged and allowed to die? A living will sets forth your wishes on these matters. The other commonly used advance directive is a document called "durable power of attorney for health care." This names a person to make health care decisions for you if you are not able to do so yourself. You need to assign someone you trust to this role, someone who will honor your wishes about your medical treatment. Both your doctor and your family should have a copy of your advance directive, and an attorney can help you create such a document.

PAYING FOR YOUR CHILD'S COLLEGE EDUCATION

Going to college is important. It is the ticket to upward mobility in the United States. With the rise of the information age, more and more jobs in America are "knowledge based": in order to get a good job, with good benefits, you increasingly need a college degree and often a graduate degree. The marketplace rewards people accordingly. As a March 1998 Census Bureau report, entitled "Educational Attainment in the United States," pointed out, there are big income differences between adults with a bachelor's degree and those who only finished high school. The report noted that those with only high school diplomas tend to have an average annual income of $15,453; those with a bachelor's degree earn an average of $27,689; those with a master's degree, $40,598, and those with a doctoral degree, $42,285. Over a person's entire working career, this amounts to a huge difference. Thus, acquiring an education—both for you and your children—is a major tool for building wealth.

College can be expensive, however, and costs are rising all the time. Since 1992 college prices have risen an average of 6 percent, and for the 1998–99 academic year, annual tuition, fees, and room and board averaged $22,533 at a four-year private institution and $10,458 at a four-year public institution, according to the College Board's Annual Survey of Colleges.

As a result, many low- to moderate-income families are daunted by the prospect of paying for their children's college education. It seems hopelessly unaffordable and way beyond their reach.

But the fact is that college is affordable, even for those with modest means. There is money to help your children go to college, even if they weren't at the top of their class. However, you need to plan ahead about how you will pay for your children's education. Some of you can get a head start on this by beginning to save for your child's college education at the time your child is born: according to Michael Holt, a marketing associate at the investment firm of Invesco, if you fall within certain income limits you can take advantage of the recently created education IRA, which allows you to set aside $500 per child, per year, tax-deferred, to pay for the child's education. You could also set up a Roth IRA, which we discuss in the chapter on retirement planning, to help finance your children's education; it allows each parent to contribute $2,000 per year to the account, and the money can be withdrawn at any time without taxes, penalty, or restrictions, provided that you adhere to specific rules.

As we've discussed, the earlier you start saving, the longer your money will grow thanks to compound interest, and the less money you'll have to invest over time to arrive at your financial target. In the chapter on investing we discuss strategies for you to build an investment portfolio of stocks, bonds, or mutual funds that could be used to help pay for college costs.

If your kids are in elementary school, encourage them to set up their own savings accounts and save for their own college education with money earned from summer jobs and allowances. The Cascade United Methodist Church in Atlanta has such a program for young members of their congregation, run in cooperation with NationsBank. Several other black churches in Atlanta have similar programs as well, and all told, the 1,800 young African Americans participating in the programs have saved more than $170,000.

Some of you may be trying to figure out how to pay for college with children who are already in high school. Don't despair: you, too, will be able to find an affordable solution. As a first step, have your kids talk with the guidance counselors at their school. They have a great deal of information about applying to college and receiving financial aid. In certain cases where a need can be shown, colleges will waive admissions and filing fees. One form can often be submitted for several different grants or loans.

Most student aid—and all aid provided by the federal government— is furnished to students based on their families' ability to pay. So it's worth your while to look into all the different options available. Your children could apply for federal financial aid, such as grants, scholarships, and work-study programs; the federal government also offers several Reserve Officers' Training Corps (ROTC) scholarships to students who are willing to serve in the military after they graduate from college. There are also privately funded scholarship programs as well as university-supported scholarships.

Don't have your children take on excessive amounts of student loans, however. Make sure they will have sufficient earning power to pay back whatever debt they assume. A recent study by the New England Loan Marketing Corporation (known as Nellie Mae), a provider of student loans and financial aid, advised that a payment-to-income ratio above 10 percent to 12 percent of your gross income is "likely to cause hardship."

There are a number of useful sites on the Internet that you or your children can visit to obtain free information about financing a college education:

- www.finaid.org, the Financial Aid Information page, features an online calculator that enables you to figure out how much money college will cost and how much you will need to save to pay for it. There is also a special section called "Financial Aid for Minority Students," which has links to databases, fellowships, and scholarships.

- www.ed.gov/offices/OSFAP/Students, the site for the U.S. Department of Education's Office of Post-Secondary Education, has information about federal student aid programs. You can also call the Department of Education at 1-800-433-3243 and obtain a free copy of *The Student Aid Guide*.

- www.sciencewise.com/molis is the Web page of the Minority On-Line Information Service and has links to institutions, scholarships, and fellowships that serve the minority community.

- www.collegeboard.org is the page for the College Board. The College Board has a worksheet to help you calculate the costs of college. If you don't have access to a computer, you can go to a library and get a book published by the College Board entitled *Meeting College Costs: What You Need to Know Before Your Child and Money Leave Home*.

- www.aascu.org, run by the American Association of State Colleges and Universities (1-202-293-7070), has descriptions of institutions of higher education across the United States, including information on costs and financial aid.

- www.collegenet.com, the Web site for CollegeNet, lists more than 500,000 private scholarships on its database.

- www.fastweb.com, operated by FastWeb, features more than 275,000 scholarships; you can apply for some of them online.

- www.salliemae.com, run by Sallie Mae, provides access to its College Aid Sources for Higher Education database.

- www.acenet.edu, the Web site of the American Council on Education, has information about colleges that offer tuition reductions or special pricing programs, including payment of tuition on the "installment plan," in monthly increments, rather than in one lump sum.

- www.collegeispossible.org is a new site operated by a group called College Is Possible; you can call them at 1-800-433-3243.

DIVORCE

It is a sad but true fact that about half of current marriages in America end in divorce. Divorce can end up damaging a woman's finances more than those of her husband. Although working wives contribute about one-third of their family's total income, women as a group earn less than men, on average: only about 75 cents for every $1 earned by men. Plus, women enter and exit the workforce more frequently, since they are the ones who generally care for children or elderly relatives, and they live an average of about seven years longer than men. One study found that a woman's standard of living declines by 73 percent in the first year after divorce, while a man's standard of living increases by 42 percent.

So you must prepare yourself accordingly. You may want to have a "prenuptial agreement" with your spouse before entering into a marriage. This document will set out the dispensation of each person's assets in the case of a divorce, so you are clear beforehand what might happen to you financially if your marriage dissolves. An attorney who specializes in such documents can prepare one for you.

Once you are confronting a divorce, you need to act calmly where your money is concerned. You need to hire a good divorce lawyer or consult with a financial adviser. In addition, the Consumer Credit Counseling Service (CCCS), a nonprofit group, offers these tips for couples who are in the process of getting a divorce:

- Beware of using money or charge cards as a marital weapon. If accounts are joint, you may end up paying the big money bills.

- Stop using charge cards unless you have the personal income to pay off these expenses in a timely fashion. Do not use credit cards to supplement missing income.

- Save for moving expenses and legal fees. They may be hefty, and you should save and not charge or take new loans—unless you have a secure job and can pay them back as promised.

- Pay utilities on time—especially if they are in your name. If you have to move and resume service, you may be asked to pay security deposits if you have not been a good paying customer in the past. The same goes for rent and mortgage payments. Many landlords request credit bureau reports, and if the payment history is poor, they may refuse to rent to you.

- Do not take out any new joint loans with your spouse. If your spouse doesn't pay, you will have to pay them.

- Write the credit card companies and send a certified letter requesting a new charge card in your name only. According to the Fair Credit Act, they must grant you a credit card equal to the current card's credit limit.

- Protect your divorce judgment. If the divorce papers stipulate your spouse is responsible for the debts, unless you take legal action to remove your name from the original contract, the creditor may still pursue you in court.

- Base all new bills and living arrangements on what you can reasonably afford on your own. Don't depend on child support or alimony when making future income considerations.

- Save what you can, even if it's only $5.

- Read and understand any financial documents before you sign. Make sure your attorney or financial adviser explains all the consequences of a decision, including any penalties for early withdrawals and income tax complications.

- Call the CCCS for free counseling if you have problems paying your debts.

TAXES

In Mark 12:13–18 Jesus spoke to us unequivocally about the importance of paying taxes. Some Pharisees and Herodians approach Jesus and attempt to entrap him in conversation: "And they came and said to him, 'Teacher, we know that you are true, and care for no man; for you do not regard the position of men, but truly teach the way of God. Is it lawful to pay taxes to Caesar, or not? Should we pay them, or should we not?' But knowing their hypocrisy, he said to them, 'Why put me to the test? Bring me a coin, and let me look at it.' And they brought one. And he said to them, 'Whose likeness and inscription is this?' They said to him, 'Caesar's.' Jesus said to them, 'Render to Caesar the things that are Caesar's, and to God the things that are God's.' And they were amazed at him."

You need to pay your taxes, whatever your income bracket. It is your civic duty, and it is the law. However, as long as you use legitimate methods, you should certainly find ways to minimize your tax burden. A financial adviser will be able to help you in this regard. The higher your income, the more taxes you will pay, and thus the more important it is for you to find ways to minimize your tax obligation. You should also factor in tax payments when you draw up your annual budget. Taxes are a regular event, not an accident that happens to you, and you need to plan and budget for them just as you would for the payment of your mortgage or utility bill.

You can also save money by preparing your own taxes rather than paying someone else to do it. For example, you could use tax preparation software, which we discuss in the chapter on using the Internet. Or you could take a course in tax preparation at H&R Block, the nation's number one tax preparation firm. By doing this, not only will you be able to prepare your own taxes very efficiently from now on, but—if you really enjoy it—you could also do tax preparation for others and develop this as a business sideline in addition to your regular job. H&R Block has offices all over the country where you can sign up for tax preparation classes, and the courses range in price from $99 to $295. You can call them at 1-800-829-2000 or visit their Web site at www.hrblock.com/tax.

CARING FOR ELDERLY RELATIVES

There may come a time when you have to care for your aging parents or other elderly relatives in addition to planning for your own golden years. With the aging of the 76 million baby boomers, this is becoming an increasingly important issue. Estimates are that by the year 2000 almost one in five workers will be caring for an older adult.

Currently about 11.5 million Americans need long-term care, which refers to a range of services that includes assistance with the everyday activities of living, such as eating, bathing, dressing, and getting out of bed or a chair. This type of care generally does not involve hospitals but can be provided in the home, in nursing homes for those who are quite frail, or in "assisted living" facilities for those who are more active and require just a moderate level of care.

About 80 percent of people who need long-term care today receive it at home, according to the Long Term Care Campaign (LTCC), a non-profit group. It turns out that the vast majority of elderly people—about 79 percent—prefer to receive care in their own home rather than at a nursing home or other facility. In addition, almost half of all nursing home admissions are for short stays; you have only one chance in ten of staying more than five years in such an institution, according to the insurance industry.

Long-term care is very expensive: the annual cost of nursing home care ranges from about $30,000 to $60,000 per year, and home care averages about one-half to one-third that amount. These days families pay more than one-third of all nursing home costs out of pocket. To pay for care for a loved one, many families "spend down" their assets to the poverty level so that they can qualify for Medicaid, a government program that pays for medical and long-term care for those with limited financial resources. As a result, Medicaid has become the primary payer of long-term care in America. Medicaid pays for 47 percent of nursing home care, but only after families have "spent down" all their assets. By contrast, Medicare, the government health care program for people over sixty-five, covers only 9 percent of nursing home costs and pays just for short-term stays of less than one hundred days.

As we mentioned in the chapter on insurance, it's possible to get insurance policies that cover the cost of long-term care, but they are expensive. Premiums are lower for younger people and higher for older people who seek to buy such a policy. According to the insurance industry, annual premiums in 1995 for a policy covering four years of nursing home and home care were $2,650 if purchased at age sixty-five; but the insurance industry notes that less than one-third of individuals at that age can afford those premiums.

Moreover, given the economics involved, experts say that you need to have a certain minimum level of assets to justify buying long-term care insurance. "Although people buy long-term care insurance for many reasons, the most important reason is to protect your savings," writes Susan Polniaszek in an article in the *Guide to Retirement Living*. "Unless you have considerable assets, you may spend more money on a policy than you have in savings. A seventy-year-old person protecting $20,000 would spend this much in premiums in eight years. An individual should have over $40,000 in savings ($100,000 for a couple) before considering buying a long-term insurance policy."

For more information about how you might finance long-term care, you can call the LTCC at 1-202-434-3744 or visit their Web site at www.ltccampaign.org. To find out about skilled home care, such as having a nurse or other medical professional make house calls for an elderly person, you can call your local Visiting Nurse Association (listed in the phone book) or try the National Association for Home Care at 1-202-547-7424. You may also want to contact the National Health Law Program, a nonprofit advocacy group that is working to insure that low-income people, minorities, and people with disabilities have access to affordable health care (1-202-289-7661; Web site, www.healthlaw.org).

A cheaper alternative to long-term care is "adult day care." This is furnished at centers that cater to old people, providing them with daytime activities, including transportation to and from the home, one or two nutritionally balanced meals, and recreational activities such as bridge or bingo. Some centers sponsor short day trips to museums or other points of interest. Such centers can serve as a social outlet, preventing elderly people from feeling isolated in their homes. In addition, certain programs have a medical component, such as the services of a full-time nurse, social worker, or recreational therapist. And these programs are much less expensive than institutionalizing the elderly. Adult day care averages about $49 per day, or half the price of a nursing home. For more information, contact your local Area Agency on Aging. These local offices can be found in your telephone directory under Aging, Health, and Human Services or Social Services. You can also find out more at your local Social Security office, church, or senior center or by visiting the Web site www.retirement-living.com. Through them you can learn about other initiatives, such as employment programs for senior citizens, volunteers who visit the elderly, and Meals on Wheels, a federally funded program that delivers inexpensive meals five days a week to the home-bound elderly.

BUYING A CAR

Buying a car is one of the major expenses people have in their lives. The most financially prudent thing to do is to pay for a new car outright rather than taking out a car loan and paying finance charges. Furthermore, buying a late-model used car that is in good shape, inspected by a mechanic you trust, will save you much more money than if you were to buy a new car. Keep in mind that once you buy the car, you will need to pay sales tax on the repurchase price, as well as gasoline and repair costs and insurance over a period of years.

Let's say that you have your heart set on a new car. If you decide to get a car loan, be aware of the finance charges involved. Let's assume annual interest rates of 8 percent to 8.5 percent on an $18,000 loan for a new car. The longer the life of the loan, the higher the finance charges you pay: $2,304 for a thirty-six-month or three-year loan; $4,156.80 for a sixty-month or five-year loan; and $5,040 for a seventy-two-month or six-year loan. If you must take out a car loan, to save yourself money choose the shortest possible term of the loan at the lowest possible interest rate.

Before you go into a car dealership, remember that the car salesmen there have one goal in mind: to make you buy a car before you walk out the door, no matter what. They will be very persuasive, but you must not succumb to their pressure. Never buy the first time you go in. Instead shop around and look at what the competitors are offering. When it comes to negotiating your payment options, never reveal what you can afford as a monthly payment. Instead tell them you will negotiate based only on the car's price, not on monthly payments.

You need to be armed with lots of information about car buying before you walk into a dealership. In the business section of the newspaper you can find auto loan rates, and your bank or credit union can give you preapproval for a car loan beforehand. See whether you are able to get any rebates or factory-to-dealer incentives on particular makes or models of cars. Ask your insurance agent how much it would cost to get car insurance on your new vehicle.

You can get lots of good information about buying or selling a car on the Internet. Try www.carbuyingtips.com, run by ConsumerNet Inc., which educates consumers about buying cars. Look on the Internet or check out consumer car guides to find out the invoice price of the car (what the dealer paid to the car manufacturer), because the dealer most likely will not give you that information. To do this online, visit www

.autobytel.com, www.autoweb.com, or www.autovantage.com. Such sites can help match you with a car dealer who is willing to negotiate prices for new or used cars online. According to J. D. Power and Associates, an automotive survey firm, half of all new vehicle buying could be done on the Internet within the next two years. To find a specific make and model in your price range, you can e-mail car dealers with inquiries about new cars. You can find dealers' e-mail addresses by visiting www.dealernet.com for DealerNet or www.nada.com for the National Automobile Dealers Association. You can also visit the Web sites of big dealers directly, such as www.honda.com for Honda or www.bmwusa.com for BMW, to name just two examples. In so doing, you can ascertain the invoice price of all the options that you are looking for, such as a sun roof or leather seats, before you walk into the car showroom. And to determine the trade-in value of your used car, you can visit www.carprices.com or www.edmunds.com.

The Consumer's Almanac counsels car buyers to "make as large a down payment as you can afford and plan to repay the loan as soon as possible." Cash is the least expensive way to buy a car, but two out of three car buyers use credit. Evaluate the manufacturer's warranties and compare what is covered and what is not. Select a car model that is within your price range, one that is not loaded with too many "options" or extras. And buy during the late summer or early fall, just before next year's models arrive, because dealers offer discounts on last year's inventory at these times of the year.

If you want to lease a car, The Consumer's Almanac recommends that you shop around for the best deal and be aware of any costs involved if you end the lease early. The Almanac is published by the American Financial Services Association Education Foundation, which develops materials to help consumers with money management skills. You can call them at 1-202-466-8611 or visit their Web site at www.afsaef.org for more information.

There are going to be some hard times in the seasons of your life. You've got to be ready for them. Having the right financial plan will help you navigate those tough times so you can keep going, keep climbing the "crystal stair" of life, as Langston Hughes, the great writer of the Harlem Renaissance, wrote in his famous poem entitled "Mother to Son":

Well, son, I'll tell you:
Life for me ain't been no crystal stair.
It's had tacks in it,
And splinters,
And boards torn up
And places with no carpet on the floor—
Bare.
But all the time
I'se been a-climbin' on,
And reachin' landin's,
And turning corners
And sometimes goin' in the dark
Where there ain't been no light.
So boy, don't you turn back.
Don't you set down on the steps,
'Cause you finds it's kinder hard.
Don't you fall now—
For I'se still goin', honey,
I'se still climbin',
And life for me ain't been no crystal stair.

CHAPTER 9

Retirement Planning

Our leaders need to incorporate democratic values—the values of IN-clusion versus EX-clusion into a bold vision that challenges people to rise to the occasion, to put their best selves forward, to fully participate in the economic engine that drives our country and that fuels a better quality of life for all of us.

America is graying—and it is doing so at an unprecedented rate. The aging of the baby boomers, those 76 million people born between 1946 to 1964, is a momentous demographic event. One baby boomer turns fifty every seven seconds, according to AARP (formerly the American Association of Retired Persons), a group that represents senior citizens.

Not only is the U.S. population aging; the population of all the world's industrialized countries is graying as well. Economic and technological progress have ushered in declining birth rates and rising longevity. Today, as a result, the elderly account for a mounting percentage of the population in every advanced nation.

Here in America:

- People over sixty-five represent 13 percent of the U.S. population, up from just 2 percent in 1900 and 6 percent in 1950.

- By 2040 about one-quarter of Americans will be elderly, while the neediest age groups—the "old-old" over eighty—will be growing at nearly double-digit rates.

- Many people can expect to live twenty more years after they retire at age sixty-five.

- With medical advances and the revolution in genetic engineering, people may live to be even older—say, 120 or so, reports Human Genome Sciences, the Bethesda, Maryland–based biotechnology firm.

Just as the squirrel stores away acorns for the winter, we all must save and invest for the future. But many people have not saved enough money for retirement, at a time when people are living longer than ever before. Thirty-three percent of African Americans, 42 percent of Hispanics, and 28 percent of workers in the general population said they are not confident that they will have enough money to live comfortably during their retirement, according to a 1999 Retirement Confidence Survey.*

On the plus side, the survey revealed that close to half of African American and Hispanic households, as well as 75 percent of households in the general population, have begun saving for retirement. That's a very encouraging sign. But 51 percent of black households and 62 percent of Hispanic households have not calculated how much money they will need in retirement.

So this is your first step: Before all else, you must figure out how much you'll need once you retire. Experts estimate that you'll require about 70 percent of your preretirement income—and for lower earners, 90 percent or more—to maintain your standard of living when you stop working. You will also need to factor in the effects of inflation. To do that, you can use a worksheet called Ballpark Estimate, published by the American Savings Education Council (ASEC), a nonprofit group. The worksheet is available for free on ASEC's Web site at www.asec.org

---

*The study was co-sponsored by the Employee Benefit Research Institute, the American Savings Education Council, and Matthew Greenwald & Associates.

and also at www.choosetosave.org. You can also phone ASEC (1-202-775-9130) for a free copy of the worksheet. The worksheet assumes that you'll need 70 percent of your current income in retirement; that you'll live to age eighty-seven; and that you'll realize a constant real rate of return of 3 percent after inflation.

Look at what you have today—in terms of savings and other financial assets—and figure out how much you will need to save and invest, over what period of time, to achieve your retirement goal.

You must decide what sort of lifestyle you would like during retirement. Would you like to keep working, and if so, full- or part-time? Or do you want a life of leisure, enabling you to play golf all day? Would you like to stay in your current house or apartment or move somewhere else? How much would that cost you? Whatever your retirement goals, you need to plan now to achieve them. The earlier you start the better, because you will be able to benefit from the time value of money and the magic of compound interest.

Women, in particular, have some special issues they must address in terms of retirement planning, because—on average—they outlive men by seven years; they typically earn less money than men, so their retirement benefits are lower; and they often leave the workforce for a period of time to care for children or aging parents. If you're married, you need to find out which of your sources of income will end when your spouse dies. If you're divorced—and half of all current marriages end in divorce—you may be able to obtain rights to a portion of your spouse's pension benefit. In a private pension plan, this is done through a qualified domestic relations order (QDRO) issued by the court. You or your attorney should discuss this with the administrator of your spouse's retirement plan. The Department of Labor's Pension and Welfare Benefits Administration also has a free brochure entitled "Women and Pensions: What Women Need to Know and Do," which you can get by calling 1-800-998-7542.

You must also identify all your possible sources of income during retirement. Generally speaking, you can view your retirement income as a three-legged stool. One leg is provided by the government, in the form of Social Security; another is provided by your employer, in the form of a pension or profit-sharing plan; and the third—and potentially the most important of all—is your own private savings and investments, including individual retirement accounts (IRAs).

Let's look at all three.

SOCIAL SECURITY

Social Security was designed to provide a safety net during retirement—but nothing more. The maximum benefit allotted to an individual who retires in January 1999 and is age sixty-five is $1,373 per month, or $16,476 a year, according to the Social Security Administration. "That won't allow you to take many cruises," points out Brad Belt, director of international finance and economic policy at the Center for Strategic and International Studies (CSIS), a Washington, D.C., think tank that has proposed reforms of the nation's retirement system. Unfortunately too many people—particularly women—rely on Social Security as their primary source of retirement income.

Added to this, Social Security is facing a massive cash flow problem. Barring some congressional intervention, the Social Security trust fund will begin running a cash deficit in 2015, which means that it will begin paying out more in benefits than it receives in tax receipts. Because other government entities have borrowed money from the fund, it can collect on these IOUs and still keep paying benefits through 2034, according to Belt. But then, beginning in 2034, because of demographic changes resulting in a shrinking workforce and a ballooning number of retired people, "the projections are that people in the workforce would bring in only enough to pay seventy cents on the dollar to beneficiaries," says Belt, who is also executive director of the National Commission on Retirement Planning, sponsored by CSIS.

So don't make Social Security the linchpin of your retirement strategy. View it as simply one leg of the three-legged stool. But keep in mind that despite its problems, Social Security taxes also provide other benefits, such as disability insurance for you, survivor income insurance for your financial dependents, and Medicare, the health insurance program for retirees. Not all people who receive Social Security benefits are re-tirees; about 28 percent are under sixty-five.

To figure out how Social Security will fit into your retirement plans, first find out the amount of benefits you will be entitled to. Your Social Security benefits are based on your earnings during your working ca-reer, but you may also be entitled to benefits as a spouse, ex-spouse, or widow based on your spouse's earnings. You need to have worked a minimum number of quarters to receive benefits—at least forty quar-ters, or ten years—and you need to have earned at least $2,500 in a year. However, your work history doesn't have to be consecutive; it just has to add up to forty quarters. Thus it could include summer jobs, short-term consulting projects, and several years in a nine-to-five job. To get an estimate, you'll need to contact the Social Security Adminis-tration and request a free Personal Earnings and Benefit Statement by calling 1-800-772-1213, or checking their Web site at www.ssa.gov. The agency takes an average of your income from ages twenty-two to sixty-two, not counting the five years that you made the least money, to compute your benefits.

EMPLOYER-SPONSORED PENSIONS

Private pensions have become commonplace over the last several decades and provide an average of 16 percent of the typical senior citi-zen's retirement income. Nonetheless, there's no legal obligation for a company to provide a pension. So you must ascertain whether your em-ployer offers one.

If your company has a pension plan, you need to understand it. Get a description of the plan from your employer. The trend among compa-nies is to provide more and more "defined contribution" savings plans for their employees' retirement, such as the 401(k), in which employees elect to save and invest money for their retirement out of their own pay-checks. This puts a greater onus on the employee to understand invest-ing. By contrast, there is a move away from traditional "defined benefit" plans, because of the costs involved for the large corporations that typ-ically provide them. In this type of plan the employer promises employees a specified monthly pension plan at retirement, usually based on the number of years you worked and your salary.

Find out if you are vested—that is, whether you have worked long enough to be included in your company's pension plan—and what your payout options are. You need to know how much your pension will be and whether it is insured. Your employer can give you an individual benefit statement showing you how much your pension is worth.

Most traditional company and union pension plans are insured by the federal government through the Pension Benefit Guaranty Corporation (PBGC). PBGC pays benefits up to a maximum guarantee if plans fall short. For more information you can contact the PBGC in Washington at 1-202-326-4100. Call up this number, speak with a customer service representative, tell him or her the name of your employer, and the PBGC staffer will then tell you whether your pension is insured by the federal government and, if so, by what amount. You can also get a copy of a free brochure called "Top 10 Ways to Beat the Clock and Prepare for Retirement," published by the Pension and Welfare Benefits Administration, which is part of the U.S. Department of Labor; call 1-800-998-7542.

Some companies have "profit-sharing" plans, which the employer may or may not decide to fund, depending on how profitable the company has been in a given year. The amount can range from 2 percent up to 15 percent of your salary. Find out if your employer offers such a program.

You need to obtain pension information from all your previous jobs and find out what happens to your pension if you retire early or change jobs. You should keep your employment and pension-related documents with other important papers.

A highly effective way to provide for your retirement is by placing money in tax-deferred accounts. Investment earnings are not taxed while they remain in the account, which helps your savings grow even faster. This means money that would have been paid in taxes is reinvested, earning additional returns for you. You pay income tax on both contributions and earnings at the time of withdrawal; but if you withdraw money before you are eligible to, you'll have to pay a big penalty.

Over the years, the extra earnings can substantially increase the assets
in your account. For example, if you invested $10,000 at 8 percent an-
nually and you were in the 31 percent tax bracket, at the end of twenty-
five years the investment would be worth $50,000 if placed in a
tax-deferred account. However, it would be worth only $38,000 if the
interest were taxed each year. (Source: Ibbotson Associates.)

The leading tax-deferred retirement plans to choose from are
401(k)s, individual retirement accounts (IRAs), simplified employee
pension (SEP) IRAs, savings incentive match plan for employees (SIM-
PLE) IRAs, and Keoghs. Religious, charitable, educational, and other
nonprofit groups offer 403(b)s, while government institutions, local
schools, and state university systems use 457 plans, both of which resemble 401(k)s.

Since its creation in 1982, the 401(k) has become the fastest-growing
retirement plan in America. A well-designed 401(k) can help companies retain talented employees and can also secure a nest egg for you,
the employee, in your old age.

"These plans make good business sense," says David Wray, president
of the Profit Sharing/401(k) Council of America, a Chicago-based trade
group that has focused on defined-contribution plans for fifty years.
"Plus, electronic systems and technology are bringing down the administrative costs of these plans to smaller companies."

The numbers of employees enrolled in 401(k)s has been climbing
steadily. In 1996 there were 24.6 million participants in 220,000 such
plans, with $1 trillion in assets under management, according to Wray.
But, he predicted, by the end of the year 2000 that will double to $2
trillion in assets, with more than 400,000 plans and over 38 million
people enrolled.

Although nearly all large companies with over 5,000 employees have
such plans, Wray said the fastest growth in the industry is coming from
small to midsize firms—those with 50 to 500 employees. This trend
was demonstrated in 1996, when the average-size company participating in a 401(k) plan had 285 participants.

Thanks to 401(k) plans, employees can save rather painlessly for retirement. The maximum you can currently contribute to a 401(k) is

$10,000 a year or 15 percent of your income, whichever is less. Contributions are deducted automatically from an employee's paycheck, which makes it easier for many people to save. Many companies match their employees' pretax contributions, which amounts to free money for you. And the plans are portable: employees can take them with them if they change employers.

Moreover, there are major tax benefits to be gained from a 401(k). Contributions are set aside on a pretax basis, meaning that they are deducted from the employee's pay before taxes are calculated and withheld. Thus 401(k) plans lower your taxable income, thereby reducing the amount of current federal and state income taxes you pay. In addition, you pay no current income tax on contributions or ongoing investment earnings, until you withdraw the money at age 59½.

These plans offer an array of other advantages. Employees can watch their savings soar over a period of years, thanks to the benefits of compounding. Just a small investment, over time, can grow impressively. For example, $100 invested monthly over thirty years—or $36,000—at an 8 percent annual rate of return becomes $150,030. And employees are increasingly offered a wide array of investment vehicles to choose from in their 401(k)s—ranging from conservative bonds and mutual funds to more aggressive equity investments, small- and medium-cap funds, and more.

It can be a dazzling array of choices. But keep in mind that if you're young and have at least thirty years before you retire, you can afford to take more risks with your portfolio. You can therefore afford to have a heavier investment in aggressive growth stocks. As you get closer to retirement, you can recalibrate your portfolio accordingly and move toward a more moderate-risk portfolio in midlife and a conservative one just before you retire. We discuss those principles further in the chapter on investing.

If your company offers a 401(k), be sure to take advantage of it. About 30 percent of 401(k) plans allow you to vest immediately; others require that you work at a firm for one year before you can qualify for benefits. You need to find out from your employer how quickly you can be included in their plan. Your employer can show you what you would save by age sixty-five, at a 7.5 percent rate of return, contributing just 1 percent or 2 percent of your paycheck a week, including company matching amounts. This serves as a powerful enticement for you to participate in such a program.

It is possible to become a millionaire by investing in your company's 401(k) plan. An investment of $10,000 a year in a 401(k), growing at a compound interest rate of 8 percent per year for thirty years, will turn into $1.1 million. Just a small difference in interest rates, compounded over thirty years, can have a major impact on the amount of money you end up with. For example, $10,000 a year for thirty years at 6 percent compounded interest becomes $800,000, while at a compounded interest rate of 10 percent, it turns into twice as much: $1.6 million. (Source: Equifax, Inc.)

"Invest as much as you can in your company's 401(k)," urges Michael Holt, an African American who works as a marketing associate for Invesco, an Atlanta-based financial services firm. He gives seminars about retirement planning all around the country. "If your company has a matching program, take full advantage of it," he advises. "If, for example, your company puts up 5 percent of your total contribution, put that up and match it. Do it! This is money given to you with no strings attached."

At many companies, thanks to computers, employees can monitor their accounts automatically. At other firms employees can access information about their accounts twenty-four hours a day using a touch-tone phone. Some firms offer complete 401(k) account information on the Internet—and, indeed, online access is becoming an industry standard.

In addition, some companies have audiocassettes that explain their retirement plan in different languages, as well as ongoing financial education seminars and automated enrollment by phone. At your company there may be a benefits planner, personnel expert, or union representative who can tell you about all the aspects of your employer-sponsored retirement plan. Go talk to that person. Don't be afraid to ask for help.

As we've seen, 401(k) plans offer many benefits. But a vexatious dilemma confronts the industry: How do you get all the employees in a company to participate?

At present the 401(k) industry has only about a 77 percent participation rate among all the eligible employees out there, notes Wray. If all the eligible employees did participate, it would be to everyone's benefit, he points out, by helping a larger number of people finance their retirement and bringing down the administrative costs for the company running the program.

By not participating, about 25 percent of people eligible to receive tax-free growth and matching contributions from their employer are choosing not to save. And saving money, as we have told you, is a key step to securing your financial future. As the Jamaican proverb puts it, "Save money, and money will save you."

These people are simply leaving money on the table—and this is a tragedy. Reasons vary as to why eligible employees won't contribute to a 401(k). About three-quarters of them say they simply can't afford to save anything. Many are single parents—typically women—raising kids on their own and earning small salaries.

A lot of them claim they just don't understand money. Some say they can't even balance their checkbook. Still others don't trust institutions to invest their money for them. Or they want to put their money in other investment vehicles.

Don't let yourself fall victim to one of these excuses. Join in your company's 401(k) plan.

Another thing: Beware of taking your 401(k) money and squandering it before retirement. This is an all-too-common practice among employees who switch jobs, take their 401(k) with them, but then spend the money instead of transferring it to the new employer's program. A whopping $42 billion slips through the cracks every year in this manner.

We know it's tempting: you could go out and remodel your kitchen or buy a new sport utility vehicle with that $30,000 from your 401(k). And that might be keenly gratifying in the short term.

But consider the long-term consequences. What is the value of your 401(k) program if you don't keep money in it? This is like eating your seed corn—the seed you've planted for your retirement. If you do this, when you retire in twenty or thirty years you won't have any harvest. Your field will be barren. "For whatever a man sows, that he will also reap," as the Bible teaches us.

Moreover, if you spend your 401(k) prematurely, you'll have to pay a substantial penalty, as well as taxes. There's a 10 percent federal tax penalty for early withdrawal, and possibly a state penalty. You could end up losing a significant amount to penalties and taxes. A much better strategy is to either transfer it to your new employer's 401(k)—if they offer one—or roll it over into an individual retirement account, which we'll discuss next. "You need to stay on your path and your plan," says Holt. "You have to be sure that you look at the full picture and not just day to day."

Henry Ford is a man who looked at the full picture. Ford, who is fifty-eight, worked for thirty years in a factory run by the Euclid division of General Motors—now known as Euclid-Hitachi. The factory manufactured heavy construction equipment. Ford never went to college but worked his way up in the firm to become a white-collar salaried employee—one of the 4 percent of African Americans in the company at that time who attained such a post. Thanks to his steady investments in Euclid's 401(k), beginning in the mid-1980s, he's looking forward to a comfortable retirement. And he's also made it his mission to go out and educate other African Americans about the virtues of investing.

Ford did not bring any prior investing experience to the table. Quite the contrary. "As a teenager, at age eighteen, I thought the stock market was where they ran cows through," he recalls. "None of my friends invested in the stock market. I never heard my family or friends talk about stocks." Nor did he receive any instruction about personal finance in high school. He grew up in a middle-class neighborhood in Cleveland, and his father died when he was ten years old. To keep the family afloat, Ford's mother worked at National Malleable, a factory that made castings, and died when she was just forty.

Ford awoke to the stock market through his company—thanks to GM's taxable stock ownership program, which he participated in beginning in the early 1970s. It was a precursor to the 401(k). Under the program, Ford could buy GM stock with after-tax dollars, and at the end of the fifth year the company would kick in fifty cents for each dollar that Ford contributed, thus increasing the size of his stock holdings. He also reinvested all the dividends. By 1974 when he was making about $200 a week, he had fifteen shares, worth around $1,000. At that point he was married and had a young son.

His interest was piqued in stocks—so much so that he joined the National Association of Investors Corporation (NAIC), a nonprofit organization that since 1951 has been helping promote grass-roots investor education through the launching of investment clubs. Ford began avidly reading their magazine, *Better Investing*. He started reading the financial pages of the newspaper. "It got easier to understand," he explains. "After you have some exposure to it, it becomes a part of you."

A shock came, however, when Ford went to NAIC's annual conference in 1977. "There were about five hundred people at that conference," he recalls. "Perhaps a half dozen were African Americans. They were definitely underrepresented. That was tragic to me. There were no Hispanics, either. The racial disparity was so obvious that it really absorbed me."

Ford wrote to Tom O'Hara, the chairman of NAIC, expressing his concerns. "Their response was positive and well thought out," notes Ford. The NAIC gave him the title "special representative to the NAIC," beginning in 1983. With that, Ford went out and contacted *Black Enterprise, Ebony,* and a number of other black publications, as well as black churches and schools, bringing them the message about investing.

"There's a lot of distrust by African Americans toward investing," Ford observes. "They want to put their hands on what they own"— which is why they like investing in houses and real estate. They also like to show off their fancy houses or cars. Whereas, Ford pointed out, an asset that is more abstract, like "a stock certificate or statement—we tend not to understand or trust."

In 1985, when he was making $30,000 a year, Ford began participating in Euclid's 401(k) plan and stayed in for the long haul. "I was practicing what I preached," he explains. "The company would kick in up to fifty cents on the dollar." Today, thanks to regular saving and investing in the company's 401(k), Ford has built up a nest egg of $100,000 and is looking forward to a comfortable retirement.

"My major savings is from the 401(k), built up over ten years with Euclid," he observes. "I put in 6 percent of my annual salary, and they matched it with 3 percent." Ford also invested it in mutual funds and regularly monitored the returns on his money.

In 1987 he won the NAIC Investment Education Award at the organization's national conference. *Black Enterprise* magazine had contacted O'Hara and told him that Ford's efforts were really making a difference with their readership. They hailed Ford as a pioneer. Most recently he has taken a position in Cleveland as part of the Rainbow/PUSH Coalition's Wall Street Project.

"Some people argue that black people don't have the means to invest," says Ford. "My feeling is we don't have enough money *not* to."

INDIVIDUAL RETIREMENT ACCOUNTS (IRAs)

Let's say your company doesn't offer a 401(k). Then what should you do?

You could suggest that your employer start a retirement plan. Certain small employers can set up SEP-IRAs. Self-employed individuals can do the same. For information on how to create one, you need to order the Internal Revenue Service Publication 590 by calling 1-800-829-3676.

You could also open an individual retirement account (IRA) for yourself. Anyone with earned income can do so. An IRA allows you to set aside money on a tax-deferred basis. Individuals can contribute up to $2,000 a year, and married couples with only one working partner may contribute a maximum combined contribution of $4,000. If you don't have a retirement plan, or are in a plan and earn less than a certain amount, you can also take a tax deduction for your IRA contributions. And if you earn less than $25,000 a year, even if you do have a 401(k) plan at work, you can still contribute to an IRA and get the full deduction. You can then invest the money in your IRA in an array of investment vehicles, including stocks, bonds, annuities, mutual funds, Treasury notes, and bank CDs.

IRAs were created by Congress in 1974, and in the past year there have been some very beneficial innovations in these plans. Nonworking spouses can now make a full contribution—up to $2,000 a year—to a traditional IRA. There are also fully deductible contributions for spouses not covered by a retirement plan.

Not only has the traditional IRA been enhanced, but a new tax-free IRA has been created: the Roth IRA. You can put in a maximum of $2,000 a year and must pay taxes on it when you make the contribution to your account. But earnings can be taken out tax- and penalty-free, as long as you've held the account for at least five years and met one of these criteria: reached age 59½; made a first-time home purchase; become permanently disabled; or (in the case of a request by your beneficiary) died. The Roth IRA is more flexible than the traditional IRA and requires no mandatory withdrawals, beginning at age 70½.

Thanks to these innovations, IRAs have become much more than retirement tools. They now allow individuals to save for a variety of major goals over their entire lifetime.

Both the traditional and the Roth IRAs permit penalty-free withdrawals for major life events. Thus you can use the money to pay for higher education for yourself, your spouse, your children, or your grandchildren; to buy a first home or pay for extraordinary medical expenses; or to pay for health insurance premiums in case of long-term unemployment.

The Roth IRA can also be used for estate planning. Because it doesn't require distributions at any age, investors can leave their estate intact for their heirs. Your heirs can inherit assets from a Roth IRA free of income tax, provided the five-year requirement is met. In a traditional IRA heirs have to pay income taxes on inherited assets.

Senator William Roth (R-Del.), chairman of the Senate Finance Committee, was the architect of the new IRA that bears his name. Congress included these accounts as part of the huge tax overhaul enacted in 1997.

The Roth IRA is right for some investors, but not for others. For one thing, you must be in the appropriate income bracket. To make the conversion from a regular IRA to a Roth IRA, you must have an adjusted gross income of $100,000 or less, whether you're single or married. Then, once you've made the conversion, there are provisions governing how much you can contribute to it each year. An individual can contribute the maximum annual amount to a Roth IRA—namely, $2,000 per year—if that person earns less than $95,000 per year. Those who earn more than $95,000 and less than $110,000 may make a partial contribution. Married couples with joint income of up to $150,000 can contribute the maximum amount; those earning up to $160,000 can make a partial contribution.

Let's say you already have a traditional IRA but want to convert it to a Roth IRA. You've got $50,000 in your current IRA, and you're in the combined federal and state 33 percent tax bracket. By converting it, you'll owe $16,500 to the IRS on the conversion alone by April 15, 2000. You need to have the money on hand to pay this tax bill if you're going to do the conversion. The best option, for those who want to reduce the tax bite on the conversion, is to convert your traditional IRA to a Roth IRA over a period of years. You could convert one-quarter of your IRA each year over a period of four years, for example, and that would reduce the tax bite correspondingly.

Still other factors to consider, when contemplating a conversion, include what your future tax bracket and income will be, how long you plan to be in the workforce, and what type of estate planning you wish to do. It's not an easy decision. Each person has a different set of circumstances that needs to be analyzed.

When all is said and done, some people still derive benefits from a traditional IRA. Other individuals, particularly married couples, will benefit most from a combination of the traditional IRA and the Roth IRA.

Still others, who run small businesses, may want to explore a SEP-IRA or SIMPLE IRA. The SIMPLE (Savings Incentive Match Plan for Employees) IRA is similar to a mini-401(k). Employers with one hundred or fewer employees, as well as self-employed people with no employees, can set up one of these tax-deferred retirement plans. Each employee may divert $6,000 a year of his or her pay into such a plan.

In addition, employers are required to match, dollar for dollar, employees' contributions to a SIMPLE IRA, up to a maximum of 3 percent of the employee's salary. If you're self-employed and not incorporated, you could also set up a Keogh plan, which allows you to make a tax-deductible contribution up to a certain percentage of your income. The funds grow tax-free until they're withdrawn.

For those who want a vehicle to help pay for their child's college degree, the education IRA may be a good option. The education IRA allows you to set aside $500 per child per year, tax-deferred, to pay for your child's education, if you fall within certain income limits.

Another variant is the rollover IRA, which people may utilize when they retire from a job or leave an employer. If you are covered by your employer's retirement plan at work, and are about to receive a distribution from that plan, you may be eligible to establish a rollover IRA. A rollover IRA enables you to postpone any current tax liability on the distribution and allows your funds to grow on a tax-deferred basis until you begin to withdraw them.

Because of the wide variety of IRAs and other retirement vehicles that currently exists, you may want to hire a financial adviser to be your guide. In the chapter on investing we discuss how to go about finding a financial planner. A financial adviser can work out different scenarios for you, using your financial and income data, to produce a calculation showing you the value of a Roth IRA and a traditional IRA on an after-tax basis, for example, at the end of a certain number of years.

If you have access to the Internet, you can also go online to various Web sites run by investment firms, such as www.franklin-templeton.com, or www.vanguard.com, and use their electronic worksheets to figure out which IRA makes the most economic sense for you. These worksheets ask you a series of questions, such as your annual income, years before retirement, and expected future tax bracket. Then the worksheet automatically calculates for you the amount of money you would have in your account, from a traditional IRA as well as the other types of IRAs, after a set period of years.

The choice of an IRA should be dictated by your particular circumstances, including income, tax bracket, number of years before retirement, and risk tolerance. The ideal combination for you might be a couple of different types of IRAs, along with a separate IRA for your spouse. Such a combination can provide maximum flexibility in your retirement planning.

The IRA, when used correctly, can become the crown jewel in your retirement portfolio.

ANNUITIES

Annuities are contracts sold by insurance companies, brokerage firms, banks, and other financial service organizations. They provide the benefits of tax-deferred saving and are thus similar to traditional pensions. You can contribute to an annuity and avoid current taxation, thereby helping your savings grow faster than they otherwise would. The money that you put into an annuity is called the "premium." You must pay taxes on it. But once the money is in the annuity, all of its earnings—whether from interest, dividend income, or capital gains—grow tax-free. Most variable annuities also offer some type of death benefits, which insure that your beneficiaries will receive no less than the total value of investments that you made, regardless of what happens to the stock market and the value of your subaccounts. Fees on a variable annuity usually amount to about 1.25 percent of assets for administrative fees, according to Annuities Online (www.annuity.com). Companies also usually charge an annual flat-dollar fee for a variable annuity, varying from $20 to $40 per year, and there is the annual expense ratio of the subaccounts—that is, the fees charged by the mutual funds and other money managers who invest the funds. You need to look at all these costs closely, then determine whether buying an annuity makes sense for you. Jane Bryant Quinn, the financial columnist, writes, "You have to hold a variable annuity for 12 to 20 years or more before your gains from tax deferral outweigh the higher taxes and expenses you have to pay."

SAVINGS AND INVESTMENTS

Your own assets are an increasingly important part of your retirement plan, so it's vital that you start saving early and invest wisely. Thanks to compound interest and the time value of money, which we have discussed, you could invest just $1,720 a year, every year, starting at age twenty-five, and assuming an 11 percent average annual return—the average return on stocks over the seventy-one-year period from 1926 to 1997—you'd have $1 million by age sixty-five. That's right: $1 million.

Starting as early as you can is key. The beauty of starting young is that most of your eventual $1 million will be from appreciation, rather than from money that came out of your own pocket. If you start later, at age forty, for example, you'd have to invest $8,770 every year at the same rate of return to end up with $1 million. You would have invested a total of $219,250 of your own money to arrive at $1 million by age sixty-five, but if you had started at age twenty-five, you would have had to invest just $68,800.

We discuss other ways that you can maximize your returns on your portfolio in the chapter on investing.

Determine whether your mortgage will be paid off by the time you retire. If you own your home outright, and find yourself "house rich" and "cash poor," you could do a reverse mortgage and thereby generate a stream of income from your house. Essentially, a reverse mortgage allows those aged sixty-two or older to turn their home into a source of money. A lender advances you an amount of money based on the value of your home, either through regular payments or a lump sum payment. The lender is paid back the full amount of the loan plus interest when the elderly owner moves away permanently or dies. Be careful to find a reputable lender to do a reverse mortgage for you, as there have been cases of unscrupulous firms defrauding people of their homes. To find respectable companies that make these sorts of loans, call the Department of Housing and Urban Development at 1-888-466-3487. You may also want to contact the National Center for Home Equity Conversion at 1-800-247-6553. In addition, you can order a free copy of *Money from Home: A Consumer's Guide to Home Equity Conversion Mortgages,* published by the Federal National Mortgage Association (Fannie Mae), by calling 1-800-732-6643.

Another important issue to consider is health insurance. Since Medicare probably will not cover all of your health care costs, you will need to determine the best program for your retirement. In the chapter on insurance we cover this in more detail. In addition, find out if you can cash in, borrow against, or convert life insurance policies into money.

You must continue to study, review, and revise your plans throughout your working career, as your circumstances change. We've shown you the importance of budgeting over your entire lifetime, and that includes budgeting for retirement. The following chart shows three different income scenarios for a typical retiree's budget: the first one assumes an income of $7,226 a year; the second, $10,226; and the third, $15,078. Using these income levels as a guide, you can see how much experts advise that you spend on different areas of your budget every month, such as food, housing, and transportation. This will give you a general idea of how you might allocate your money in retirement.

Retiree's Budget

Component	Low	Intermediate	Higher
Total Budget	7,226	10,226	15,078
Monthly Income	602	852	1,256
Food	182 (30%)	242 (28%)	304 (24%)
Housing	198 (32%)	283 (33%)	442 (35%)
Transportation	46 (7%)	89 (10%)	163 (12%)
Clothing	20 (3%)	34 (3%)	52 (4%)
Personal Care	17 (2%)	24 (2%)	35 (2%)
Medical Care	90 (15%)	91 (10%)	92 (7%)
Gifts, Contributions, & Life Insurance	26 (4%)	51 (6%)	93 (5%)
Other	23 (3%)	38 (4%)	75 (5%)

Source: The National Foundation for Consumer Credit.

Michael Holt at Invesco has given seminars all around the United States to African Americans about the importance of saving for retirement. He's addressed the Coalition of Black Investors and a variety of black churches, among other groups. "A lot of people in our community still feel they can't participate in these types of activities, such as IRAs and 401(k)s," he comments. "We have a history to overcome, a generation of children and families behind the economic curve."

When the U.S. economy takes a downturn, he points out, African

Americans are affected more severely than the general society, because as a group they earn less than whites.

Moreover, many in the younger generation of black Americans have access to education and amounts of income their parents never had. So they need instruction on how to manage their funds. Too many black Americans stick their money in low-yielding savings accounts or CDs—the things they know best—when they could be reaping much higher yields by investing more aggressively.

Holt teaches them that with consistency and discipline they can build a sound retirement portfolio. "Sacrifice now for a bigger payoff later," he tells them. "You can make a minimal sacrifice today for a big payoff later."

For single people, he advises: "Just because you have access to income doesn't mean it all has to be spent. We go out and buy houses, cars, clothes, and take trips, without properly saving and planning. Most people in America are living paycheck to paycheck."

For married people with children, Holt emphasizes that "retirement planning is something you do together. There needs to be a joint understanding of the financial plan"—and that includes retirement planning.

"This is one thing that couples often don't talk about," he continues. But they need to discuss college planning for the children, as well as financial planning for the entire family. "That really needs to be a strong conversation, and it needs to be looked at constantly," Holt points out. He advises couples to start planning and investing even before their child is born. Then invest aggressively, with an eighteen- to twenty-year time horizon, before the child goes off to college. He's a great proponent of the Education IRA.

Once you've embarked on a sound program of saving and investing for retirement, you need to stick with it. Although starting earlier is always preferable, it's never too late, even in your fifties, to begin saving for retirement. Make changes in your lifestyle so you won't fall off the path.

"Take one vacation a year instead of two," advises Holt. "Cut back on shopping. You need to adjust your perspective, since you're playing catch-up."

He concludes: "Understand that it's never too late. Learn as much as you can. And make this a way of life."

CHAPTER 10

Avoiding Scams: Don't Let Anyone Use You for a Cat's Paw

Too many working poor people choose a bear lottery over the bull market. How come? Because the lottery is advertised all over—on the bus, on billboards, on TV. These people choose floating gambling boats over stable banks. This idea is fed by fear, ignorance, and greed. People who play these high-risk games are afraid of the bull market. They're ignorant of it. They think the bull market is something for the elite. The scam artist plays on your greed. That person will tell you: "Here's how to get something for nothing. Here's how to beat the system."

One day the Monkey had done got some chestnuts and put in the open hearth—the fire, you know—to roast 'em. And 'bout time they got roasted, he went to pull 'em out, and he stuck his foot in that fire and it burned his foot. He didn't want to lose his chestnuts, so the Cat was laying down there purring and carrin' on. He say, 'Cat, lend me your paw a minute; I'll showed ya a trick.' So the cat won't thinking; he reached over there and let 'im take his paw. And he took his paw and reached over there and raked them chestnuts outa the fire and burned the cat's paw, see.

"So the saying is: 'Better watch! Don't let anybody use you for a cat's paw!' "

—*Shuckin' and Jiving: Folklore from Contemporary Black Americans*

———————

Don't let anybody use *you* for a cat's paw.

The United States has the strongest, most vibrant economy in the world. Along with that, this country has a record number of con artists who will try to cheat you of your money in any number of creative ways.

Americans lose about $1 billion a year to investment fraud, according to the Federal Trade Commission (FTC). Con artists are very creative. They will come at you from all different directions: through an infomercial on TV, an ad in a newspaper, a door-to-door salesman, a spot on the radio, a phone call, a flyer in the mail, or a Web site on the Internet.

Although the U.S. economic system is fundamentally honest, there simply aren't enough regulators to prosecute all the shysters out there. The sad reality is that most people who get ripped off never see their money again or, at best, collect a fraction of what they lost.

So your best defense is to be alert, on your guard, and well informed. You must avoid getting ripped off in the first place.

Because most Americans are ill informed about investments, this makes them easy prey for con artists. A national survey of investor knowledge and habits, produced by the nonprofit Investor Protection Trust (IPT) in 1996, found that fewer than one in five U.S. investors was financially literate. Two out of three people did not have a financial plan. And nine out of ten of those with brokers or financial planners had never even checked out the credentials of their financial professionals.

This is nothing short of a "national epidemic of financial illiteracy," according to the IPT study. Investors need to know that "if you don't understand what's going on with your investments and you rely blindly on the advice of strangers, you are openly courting investment fraud and abuse," states Mark Griffin, former IPT trustee and director of the securities division of the Utah Department of Commerce.

Forewarned is forearmed, so in this chapter we will discuss some of the more common frauds out there, how you can avoid getting ripped off, and what to do if you have been victimized.

AFFINITY MARKETING SCAMS

In this type of fraud the con artist becomes acquainted with you at a club, fraternal organization, or church that you may belong to. The person befriends you in a social setting and wins your trust, as well as that of your friends in the same group.

"A successful swindler will be extremely polite, dress in expensive clothes, and may work out of impressive offices with prestigious addresses," observes Stephen L. Diamond, who was securities administrator for the state of Maine when he made his comments in a 1996 article in the Associated Press. The individual then persuades you and your friends to invest in a scheme offering exceptionally high rates of return, with no risk.

Whenever anybody says "very high rate of return, and no risk," beware. There is no such thing. The higher the risk, the higher the reward. This is a basic, inviolable principle of finance. No investment scheme has ever existed, nor ever will, that can defy this.

The Better Life Club is a recent example of an affinity marketing scheme that met with a calamitous ending. Robert N. Taylor, an African American, launched the scam in Washington, D.C., in 1993 and targeted other African Americans as his victims, "posing as a financial savior of the downtrodden," according to the Securities and Exchange Commission (SEC). He cast a wide net and eventually roped in about six thousand investors from around the country, who put up a total of about $48 million.

Taylor lured people by telling them that funds deposited with him in an "advertising pool" would be doubled every ninety days, through investments in 900 numbers and other lucrative ventures. He told them there was no risk at all attached to these investments, which promised a stunning compounded one-year return of up to 1,500 percent. Each investor was encouraged to put in an amount ranging from $200 to $4,000, or even more. Investors were given commissions to bring in new recruits.

Like many con men, Taylor was quite charismatic. He published a newspaper called *The Better Life News,* which sang the praises of his operation. He traveled around the country and held "wealth-building" seminars in cities like Los Angeles, Chicago, Philadelphia, Atlanta, and New York. Over two hundred people showed up at one such event in Lafayette, Louisiana. He sold guidebooks and tapes. The club brochures claimed to help members "end the paycheck-to-paycheck existence." In his persuasive pitch he offered African Americans what appeared to be an incredible opportunity to gain the economic security denied them elsewhere.

But it was all a scam. It turned out that this was an illegal "Ponzi" scheme, a classic type of swindle that has gone on in America since the early days of the twentieth century. There is no legitimate business activity generating revenues in these sorts of operations. Instead investors' money is simply used to pay off earlier investors. At some point the schemes get too big, the promoter can't raise enough money from new investors to pay off the old ones, and the whole thing collapses. Lots of people lose money in the process. The Better Life Club owed investors over $50 million, but it had only $2.7 million in the bank. Taylor had already spent between $540,000 and $1.2 million of investors' money on a house, a swimming pool, cars, and trust funds for his children. And the rest of the money was distributed among some twenty-seven different bank accounts. The SEC successfully brought a case against Taylor, who ended up going to prison for three and a half years in 1997.

A pyramid scheme, which you may have heard of, is akin to a Ponzi scheme, in that both rely on an inexhaustible stream of funds from new investors to stay afloat, and neither one has any legitimate business activity to back it up. The pyramid scheme works like a chain letter. The promoters are at the top of the pyramid-shaped flow of money and can theoretically make money and recover their investment as they sell "distributorships" to other investors. Initially it appears that it could go on forever and everyone could make money. But because of the mathematics behind it, the number of investors needed to keep the pyramid scheme working quickly exceeds the population of the United States. And the whole thing collapses.

Ponzi schemes and pyramid schemes are different from legitimate, "multilevel" marketing arrangements like Mary Kay Cosmetics. The key is whether the promoter is telling the truth about the product or service offered. You could have a legal operation, sell a legitimate product, and make money—and it may also involve constantly recruiting new investors or associates.

That's why it's very important for you to investigate whatever opportunities are offered to you. You need to be able to ferret out the bad from the good. If you're unsure whether an investment that has been offered to you is legitimate, you can call the SEC's special toll-free investor hot line at 1-800-732-0330. The hot line is available twenty-four hours a day and is updated constantly as new developments occur. That way you can find out if any lawsuits or disciplinary actions have been brought against companies or individuals that have proposed investments to you. You can also report shady practices to the SEC.

In addition, you can call your state securities regulator and make a similar inquiry. To find out the name of that person, call the information department of your state government or contact the North American Securities Administrators Association (NASAA), an umbrella group for state securities regulators. They work at the state level to police abuses. You can call them at their Washington, D.C., headquarters: 1-202-737-0900. NASAA also has an investor hot line that has helped thousands of investors and publishes an informative book called *Investor Alert*.

They warn investors to resist high-pressure salespeople who urge you, "Tomorrow will be too late!" or, "Act now because there will soon be a long waiting list of others who want to take advantage of this golden opportunity." Be suspicious of "inside information," hot tips, and rumors that supposedly will give you a leg up on other investors. And before making a commitment, get a professional opinion from your attorney, stockbroker, accountant, or other reliable consultant.

Slow down, ask questions, and get written information. Take notes so you'll have a record later, if need be, in case the situation leads to a legal dispute.

According to the SEC, here are the ten questions you should always ask before making an investment:

1. Is the investment registered with the SEC and the state securities agency in the state where I live, or is it subject to an exemption?

2. Is the person recommending this investment registered with my state securities agency? Is there a record of any complaints about this person?

3. How does this investment match my investment objectives?

4. Will you send me the latest reports that have been filed on this company?

5. What are the costs to buy, hold, and sell this investment? How easily can I sell?

6. Who is managing the investment? What experience do they have?

7. What is the risk that I could lose the money I invest?

8. What return can I expect on my money? When?

9. How long has the company been in business? Are they making money, and if so, how? What is their product or service? What other companies are in this business?

10. How can I get more information about this investment, such as audited financial statements?

(Source: SEC Office of Investor Education and Assistance.)

PREDATORY LENDING

Predatory lending—which seeks to cheat victims out of their home or other assets—is on the rise, thanks to a number of factors such as a relaxed regulatory climate and the immense profitability of such scams. Anyone can fall prey. However, senior citizens are often targets, because they own their own homes and thus have a large amount of wealth concentrated in their properties. Also, anyone who has a bad credit history—and this includes many low-income people—are potential targets. Because they get turned down for loans from conventional lenders, they are often thrust into the hands of the shady, "subprime" lending market, as it is called.

"It's a significant problem," asserts Senator Charles Grassley, chairman of the Senate Special Committee on Aging, who held hearings in April 1998 on Capitol Hill about how predatory lending hurts the elderly. "There's big money to be made by the lenders." The Iowa Republican added that "a few bad apples" have tainted the otherwise honest lending industry. Other cases of alleged abuse are being investigated around the country by the Justice Department, FTC, legal aid lawyers, and state attorneys general.

The abuses may take several forms. One popular variant is known as "equity stripping," whereby unscrupulous lenders refinance a homeowner's mortgage at very high levels of interest, with the ultimate goal of seizing the equity in the individual's home. Another is "flipping," which consists of refinancing the homeowner's mortgage multiple times at higher and higher rates. A third technique is "packing," whereby the loan is larded with expensive and unnecessary extras, such as insurance policies, thus making the loan more costly.

Except in cases of forgery or falsification of documents, much of what is considered "predatory lending" is legal. And consumers certainly have a responsibility to read what they sign. But unscrupulous lenders target the unsophisticated and the elderly, talking them into decisions that are unwise for them.

You need to be aware that this goes on and watch out for it.

Senator Grassley predicted that predatory lending will rise, fueled by the explosion in the home-equity business. Home-equity loans have skyrocketed, from $1 billion in 1982 to $600 billion in 1996. There have been over one hundred thousand examples of equity stripping in twenty states. With the aging of the baby boomers, that figure is projected to increase.

Gael Carter, a homeowner who lives near Tyson's Corner, Virginia, fell prey to such a scam. She's a fifty-five-year-old widow on Social Security disability whose last job was in 1978, as a night cleaning lady for movie theaters. She suffered from high blood pressure and liver problems. Too ill to testify in person, she recounted her tale from a hospital bed, via video, as testimony at Sen. Grassley's hearing.

Carter unwittingly became a victim of lending fraud when she bought a remote-controlled toy car for her son in 1994. She paid for the $1,000 toy at a hobby shop and was given an installment loan financed by a Texas-based finance company.

Over the next year, she said, the finance company "kept giving me advice on my finances and getting me to take out loans with them." Each time they told her they would consolidate all her bills and put all her finances in order, and "that just wasn't true," she said ruefully. The company said they would help her pay for her daughter's wedding and lower her total monthly payments through a series of seemingly simple loans.

When she was first approached by the lenders, Carter was paying off a $50,000 mortgage on her home of thirty-five years at 6.7 percent, according to her attorney. The house was appraised at $194,000.

Carter testified that after signing a series of loans with the Texas-based company, "by the end of January 1995, I owed them payments totaling $328,322. I was scared to death I was going to lose my home."

One of the finance company salespeople told Carter that she had to have a $100,000 life insurance policy in the loan, although she had never asked for such a policy. Nor did the salesperson tell Carter that she would be paying finance charges for the cost of the insurance over the entire fifteen years of the loan, even though the insurance was good only for ten years. The upshot: Carter ultimately was saddled with three home-equity loans by late fall 1994.

"What the company told me over the phone about what they were doing turned out to be a lot different from what they did, as I later learned," she said.

Some finance company employees are under enormous pressure to meet quotas regarding loan volume, repeat business, and insurance sales. Thus they will go to great lengths to get business, sometimes even committing forgery or sending you a "live check" in the mail that you can cash immediately. Once you do, that instantly puts you on the hook to them. These checks often carry interest rates as high as 25 percent. And they target people such as those who are having a hard time paying their bills. One ex-employee at the finance company Carter dealt with said the saying around the firm was "A loan a day, or no pay."

The company denied the charges, contending that they make millions of loans around the world, 98 percent of which are paid off on time by consumers. Furthermore they have begun circulating new consumer guidelines. Nonetheless, Carter is suing the firm as part of a class-action lawsuit in Dallas.

Stephen Brobeck, executive director of the Consumer Federation of America, a nonprofit advocacy group, said that no matter what form such solicitations take—whether they be "live" checks or other tactics—they are potentially dangerous because they open the door to excessive credit.

"The nation is awash with consumer credit," Brobeck told *The Washington Post*. "There is not a household that can afford more debt that doesn't have ready access to it" through conventional lending avenues, he added.

For their part, lenders defend their practices. They point out that the majority of home-equity borrowers are satisfied with their loans. According to a 1994 survey done by the University of Michigan's Survey Research Center in Ann Arbor, 95 percent of all home-owners with home-equity lines of credit and 89 percent of those with traditional home-equity loans said they were satisfied with the loans they received.

What can you do to protect yourself? Contact the FTC Office of Consumer & Business Education at 1-202-326-3650 or visit their Web site (www.ftc.gov) and get their free pamphlet entitled "Home Equity Loans: Buyer Beware." AARP (formerly the American Association of Retired Persons) also has informative brochures on predatory lending as it affects older people. You can call them at their Washington, D.C., headquarters: 1-202-434-3470.

Experts also advise the following:

- If you do need a home loan, shop around and get one from a legitimate lender. By using the Internet, scanning rates advertised in your newspaper, or simply calling local loan brokers, you can find a better deal than what you've been offered through a "live" check in the mail.

- Be wary of anyone who calls you on the phone or comes to your door offering you an unsolicited home loan.

- Never sign anything you don't understand. Never sign under pressure. And never sign a document with any blank spaces.

- The Truth in Lending Act allows you, for any reason or no reason at all, three days to back out of any credit transaction in which you think your home has been used as security.

- If you think you've been victimized, call your state attorney general's office or the nearest legal aid office.

PAYDAY LENDING BUSINESSES

In chapter 1 we warned you about the perils of check-cashing store-fronts, which will lend you money against your paycheck. To avoid their high fees, keep your money in a bank, credit union, or S&L.

Payday lending companies have sprouted up all over the country, growing to nearly 8,000 in 1999, from 300 about seven years ago, according to *The New York Times*. At least twelve national chains have sprung up in this industry. They have names like "Check into Cash," "Check 'n Go," and "Fast Cash." Their revenues have grown from $810 million in 1998 to $1.44 billion in 1999. They target the poor, who need small sums of money to get over a financial hump, like paying for car repairs. Most commercial banks do not make loans for less than $1,000, and often low-income people have poor credit, so they can't get a loan from a commercial bank anyway.

You can fall into a dangerous spiral with these lenders. In a typical example, for a fee of $30 they will advance you a two-week paycheck of $100. You have to write them a check for $130, which the lender agrees to hold until your next payday. But the $30 fee amounts to an annual interest rate of 780 percent, according to consumer advocates. And if you fail to make the payment in two weeks, you might be forced to turn to another payday lender, and another, and another, bouncing around, racking up more and more debt, borrowing from one to pay the fees of the next.

Frequenting payday lenders could be your ticket to bankruptcy. In chapter 2 we told you about how personal bankruptcy has hit an all-time high in the United States.

A credit card would be a much better solution. As *The New York Times* reported, a $30 fee for a two-week $100 loan, renewed for two more weeks, costs $60 a month. On the other hand, a credit card available to people with poor credit might have a 3 percent fee for a cash advance, plus an annual interest rate of 19.8 percent, or about $2 a month on $100, for a total fee of $5 a month. This, by the way, is a better deal than what you would receive if you were to pawn something you owned at a pawnshop or buy something at a "rent to own" place. They, too, have the system stacked in their favor.

Jean Ann Fox, director of consumer protection at the Consumer Federation of America, told *The New York Times* her view of payday lenders: "There's nothing wrong with small loans at reasonable interest rates, reasonable terms, and reasonable collection practices. But these practices are designed to keep you in perpetual debt."

FRAUD ON THE INTERNET

The Internet, as we discussed in chapter 7, brings great promise for individual investors and entrepreneurs. But it's also fraught with peril, because it provides a new way for crooks to get to you—one that crosses worldwide borders. Con artists can crop up one day on a Web site, seduce you into sending your money, and then vanish into the ether of cyberspace. The elusiveness of the medium makes such scams particularly hard to unmask. Plus, it's a jurisdictional nightmare for regulators, since the scam artists can operate worldwide, and different sets of laws apply in different parts of the world.

Three years ago the first instance of a fraudulent investment scheme on the Internet was discovered, and by mid-1999 the FTC had brought eighty-three cases against fraudulent Internet claims.

The FTC is the U.S. government's principal agency for setting policy pertaining to American commerce and the Internet. It's an independent government watchdog agency with enforcement powers and has two primary responsibilities: an antitrust division, which insures that U.S. businesses don't engage in anticompetitive or monopolistic behavior, and a consumer protection side, which seeks to prevent unfair or deceptive trade practices.

Many of the online frauds that the FTC uncovered are "get rich quick" schemes. One offered an investment in fake action/adventure movies. Another was a Web site that purported to sell Viagra. And a third went by the official-sounding name of the "U.S. Consumer Protection Agency." The site had a logo similar to that of the FTC. For $1,000 people could "buy" a consumer protection franchise—which proved to be bogus.

Still other Internet investment frauds involve people who tout an exciting, "hot" new company in a chat room on a legitimate investors' Web site, such as Motley Fool. The con artists aim to bid up the price of a bogus company, prior to an initial public offering, for example, and get unwitting investors to buy shares in what proves to be a sham operation. A "chat room" is a common area in cyberspace where people meet to have online discussions. It is not an official part of a Web site such as Motley Fool. Nor is there any guarantee that any of the claims made by the people in a chat room are true.

Fraud on the Internet is hard for regulators to prosecute, because it spans so many legal jurisdictions. Which country's laws will govern Internet transactions, and who will be responsible? It's a thorny issue that the FTC and other government agencies are currently hashing over.

To date, 80 percent of worldwide Internet traffic originates in the United States—but over the coming years the amount generated in other countries is expected to grow dramatically. Thus the Europeans and Japanese have begun querying the FTC about appropriate ways to regulate commerce on the Internet, as well as suitable consumer protection laws for the new medium. Other countries are moving to emulate the American regulatory model of consumer protection, because they have seen that it allows for a more flexible and dynamic economy than their own system.

"People are looking to the United States for economic leadership, because our models are working very well. E-commerce and high tech are the leading edge of our economy," explains Mozelle Thompson, a commissioner at the FTC in Washington. "Other countries are beginning to jump on the bandwagon and are looking to us for guidance."

Thompson, an African American, is currently involved in negotiating high-level consumer protection guidelines for international behavior on the Internet.

To protect yourself from fraud over the Internet, the SEC Office of Investor Education and Assistance advises the following:

- Don't believe everything you read online. And don't assume that people online are who they say they are.

- Download and print a hard copy of any online solicitation that you are considering. Make sure you have a copy of the Internet address, in case you need to use it later.

- Check with your state securities regulator or the SEC and ask if they have received any complaints about the company, its managers, or the promoter.

- Ask the online promoter where the firm is located. Call that state's secretary of state and ask if the company is incorporated with them and has a current annual report on file.

- Don't assume that your Internet service provider has approved or even screened the investment. Anyone can set up a Web site or advertise online, often without any check on its legitimacy.

- Before you invest, always obtain written financial information, such as a prospectus, annual report, offering circular, and financial statements. The prospectus is a required document that should disclose all the facts and risks involved in the offering. Compare the written information with what you've been told online. Beware if you're told that no written information is available. That's a red flag.

THE LOTTERY

Ask many low-income people how they plan to make half a million dollars in the course of their lifetimes and most will tell you: "I'm going to win the lottery."

So they go into their local convenience store, betting on the numbers every day, in search of a phantom. They make this the centerpiece of their financial planning. They think they are going to win enough to make their next car payment or pay off their mortgage or go on a fancy vacation. They think this is going to solve all their problems.

This is complete and utter folly.

As we've discussed, saving and investing even small amounts, steadily over your entire lifetime, is the best way to create wealth. Trying to hit it big by winning the lottery is sheer nonsense. The chance of winning is infinitesimal.

Let's say you did win, however. Even then the lottery has tricked you. Although this type of gambling is government sponsored, it is deceptive, because the payoffs are advertised in a misleading manner. A typical $1 million jackpot is taxed and paid out over a twenty-year period. Because of the time value of money, which we told you about in chapter 1, if this money were taxed at a 40 percent rate and adjusted for inflation, winners would receive only about $318,000 in real dollars. Thus the government fails to disclose the real interest rates and costs associated with the lottery.

Lotteries disproportionately hurt the poor. According to a *New York Times* analysis of lottery spending in New Jersey, published May 22, 1999, people who live in the state's lowest-income ZIP code areas spend more than five times as much of their money on lottery tickets as do people who live in the highest-income ZIP code areas. And the lottery is New Jersey's fourth largest source of revenue. For every $10,000 of annual income earned in lower-income areas, $108 was spent on taxes and $111 on the lottery. This is why the lottery is often called "a tax on the poor." The *Times* reported:

"The analysis is consistent with those in other states that have shown that as a percentage of household income, poorer people in cities and rural areas alike spend much more on the lottery than do people in high-income brackets. Living from paycheck to paycheck, they are easily captured by the notion that the lottery can fulfill their basic financial goals."

For example, on the South Side of Chicago, which suffers a high poverty rate, Reverend James Meeks, pastor of Salem Baptist Church, found that one district in his neighborhood alone spent $75 million a year on lottery tickets.

Lotteries, as well as other forms of legalized gambling, are spreading like wildfire in the United States. Gambling is the fastest-growing industry in the country. Americans spent $600 billion on it in 1998—more than they spent on clothes and cars and groceries. And they lost $50 billion gambling that year, according to the National Gambling Impact Study Commission, a panel appointed by President Bill Clinton and Congress that spent two years studying the issue. It can be addictive for some folks. The number of pathological gamblers in the country has risen to about 2.5 million people; another 3 million are problem gamblers, and 15 million adults are at risk for problem gambling. "There is no end in sight" to the growth of gambling in America, according to a recent report issued by the commission.

The Bible warned us about worshiping "the golden calf" and falling prey to idolatry. "Shun the worship of idols," St. Paul taught us in Corinthians 10:14. "You cannot drink both the Cup of the Lord and the cup of demons. You cannot partake at the Table of the Lord and at the table of demons."

Corinth was the capital of the Roman province of Achaia, and at the time Paul visited it, in A.D. 54, the community was famous for its trade, its festivals of worldwide renown, its wealth, and its luxury. But it was grossly immoral. St. Paul wrote a letter to the members of the Christian Church at Corinth, advising them thus:

"No temptation has come upon you that is not common to mankind. God will not fail you, and He will not allow you to be tempted beyond your strength; but when He sends the temptation, He will also provide the way of escape, so that you may have the strength to endure."

CHAPTER 11

Entrepreneurship: A Time-Honored Road to Wealth in America

There is a story I often tell that I heard when I was growing up in South Carolina. There were two drunks—one black, one white—sitting at the railroad station, drinking wine. The more they drank, the better they felt. And when they got real high, one drunk said, "I think I'll buy this railroad." Then the other drunk turns to him and said, "I don't think I want to sell it. Have a drink on me."

The point is that until the person who owns the railroad and the train is at the table, they're just talking trash. We must empower the disenfranchised, so that they have something to offer in this deal. Those with the power of money, infrastructure, and know-how and those with the untapped power of money, market, talent, and location must see a mutually beneficial relationship.

The unique promise of America is the opportunity to make a fortune in your own lifetime by starting a business and taking it right to the top. This is not just folklore; it really happens.

More than 80 percent of American millionaires are people who accumulated their wealth in one generation. As the best-selling book *The Mil-*

lionaire Next Door pointed out, they were people who pulled themselves up by their own bootstraps. Typically they created a business and made a fortune in the process. Or they were highly paid corporate executives.

Consider Madame C. J. Walker, a successful cosmetics manufacturer who became the first black woman millionaire. Born in 1869 to ex-slave parents in Delta, Louisiana, Sarah McWilliams—as she was named—was orphaned at the age of seven, married C. J. Walker at fourteen, and was left a widow with a small child at the age of twenty. She worked as a laundress in St. Louis and, by literally saving pennies, eventually built an empire in retail cosmetics. She designed hair care products exclusively for African American women, which were widely sold in the United States, Central America, and the Caribbean. Under the name of Madame C. J. Walker, she became famous for her new hairstyling pomade, added a complete line of toiletries and cosmetics, employed thousands of people in her plants, and established many Walker schools of beauty across the country. In 1917 she built a mansion in New York City on Broadway called Villa Lewaro, where she entertained the rich and famous. She was the Mary Kay of her day.

During the era of legal segregation, entrepreneurial businesses thrived in the black community. In 1923—just seventy-six years ago—African Americans owned twenty-two million acres of land, seventy-eight banks, one hundred insurance companies, and twenty thousand other business enterprises. Today African Americans own businesses in greater numbers than ever before: a total of 620,912 black-owned businesses existed in the United States, as of 1992, according to the Census Bureau. And that figure continues to grow at a record pace. In 1997 it was estimated to have reached 880,000, based on figures from the Small Business Administration (SBA). Changes in the laws and victories by the civil rights movement have empowered us. There are opportunities today that our ancestors never had. If we go at it with the right spirit, we can achieve entrepreneurial successes beyond our forefathers' wildest dreams. And if you feel that you've been held back by the traditional business establishment, you can break out on your own and start a company. You may make a fortune in the process.

There are still serious issues, such as access to capital, that have stifled growth and denied economic opportunity to black, brown, and red people in America. Their skills have been underutilized, and their communities have suffered from a lack of investment. Our challenge is to even the playing field, expand the marketplace, embrace the assurances of the American dream, and allow all of us to realize life, liberty, and the pursuit of happiness. We need to eliminate the bitter legacy of segregation that still holds back black business professionals when they seek to borrow money to grow their companies and are forced to pay higher interest rates than their white counterparts.

Minority entrepreneurs are a slumbering giant that needs to be awakened in communities around the country. People with a vision can capitalize on their own local markets, figuring out the right products and services to sell there. They can launch companies in their own neighborhoods, create jobs for their own people, and generate wealth for themselves as well as others.

In May 1999 President Bill Clinton and Vice President Al Gore announced a new program that would make giant strides in empowering America's underserved communities. It's called the New Markets Initiative and is designed to encourage private investment in inner-city and rural areas. Among other features, the plan would set up America's Private Investment Companies (APICs), which would leverage up to $1.5 billion in investments in new businesses targeting inner-city and rural locales. APICs are modeled on the Overseas Private Investment Corporation, which the United States has used successfully to help promote growth in emerging markets overseas. For years our country has encouraged private businesses to invest hundreds of millions of dollars in developing nations such as Thailand, Indonesia, and the Philippines. It's high time we did the same here at home, right in our own backyards, where the potential market is bigger and there is no political risk.

Consider this: If black people, as a group, were to invest just 5 percent of the $500 billion that they make every year in income, that's $25 billion that could be plowed back into our communities. And what a rich harvest we could reap from that! Think of it: You can build your own factories, finance your own institutions, educate your own youth, liberate and dignify your own race. Hispanics could do the same, capitalizing upon their $350 billion in annual buying power.

Starting your own business is not an easy path. According to the Small Business Administration, half of new businesses fail within four years of inception. Being an entrepreneur requires a high level of motivation, discipline, and risk taking. The risk involved is not for everyone. But for those who take the plunge, the rewards can be substantial, both financially and psychically.

Mel Farr is an African American who became an entrepreneur after a career as a professional athlete. He now runs the largest black-owned business in the country, the Mel Farr Automotive Group.

Margarita Perez is a Puerto Rican woman who grew up poor. But she was a diligent student and a hard worker and now manages tens of millions of dollars in corporate pension funds as head of Fortaleza Asset Management.

Nick Hockings, an Ojibwa Indian, launched a promising tourism business on his reservation in the north woods of Wisconsin by re-creating authentic tribal campgrounds.

And Alex Bambara, an African immigrant, came to America about a decade ago with just $150. Today he's a successful chef, launching an upscale bakery with projected revenues of $150,000 a year.

Each of these people has a unique story, but there are classic lessons that can be culled from all of them. All had drive and determination. All developed a marketable skill or talent over a period of time. And all took a calculated risk, launching their own companies, all the while sharpening their skills so they could do better and better.

It's hard to make it as an entrepreneur—and it's even harder when you're black, brown, female, or a Native American. You have to work that much harder. You have to be even more determined than your white male counterparts. But ultimately success can be yours, as the stories of these people so amply illustrate.

We'll tell you how they made it, and at the end of this chapter we'll discuss some resources available to help you decide whether to go the entrepreneurial route.

MEL FARR: FROM ATHLETE TO AUTOMOTIVE EMPIRE

When Mel Farr Sr. was growing up in Beaumont, Texas—in the southeastern part of the state, on the Gulf coast—it rained a lot. His father, who worked on a semitruck, couldn't pour concrete when it rained. So his salary fluctuated, depending on the weather. In addition, his father ran a used-car lot, where he repaired automobiles and sold them.

Mel Farr learned firsthand from his father how to be an entrepreneur. He saw how someone's salary could go up and down. He knew his father's hourly wage rate and, every day, computed how much money he made. From his mother, who was a real stickler about paying the bills and keeping a budget, he learned the importance of maintaining good credit.

As a young man, Farr was a talented football player. In 1963, when he graduated from high school, he decided to go to college in the North, because at that time southern universities were not recruiting black athletes. "They were not recruiting any African Americans south of the Mason-Dixon line," he recalls. "So I applied to schools outside the 'Cotton Curtain.' "

He ended up attending the University of California at Los Angeles, then graduating from the University of Detroit in 1971 with a degree in political science. In 1967, playing for the UCLA Bruins, he made the All-American team. He was the number one draft choice of the Detroit Lions and was the NFL's Rookie of the Year for the 1967 season. He enjoyed a meteoric rise and became a well-known, highly paid professional athlete.

But then the injuries started. During his second and third years playing in the NFL, he hurt his knees. In his fourth year he had operations on both knees and dislocated his shoulder. By then he had a wife and two children to support. There came a moment of truth, which all star athletes have to face. He knew he could not continue playing professional football indefinitely. The question popped into his mind: What will I do next?

"I decided to find myself a job," recalls Farr. So he went to the Ford Motor Company and had an interview with a high-ranking executive there in the late 1960s. The Ford executive gave him two options: Either do some public relations work for the company and make a lot of money in the short term or work in the dealer development division for just $200 a week. Working in dealer development was less glamorous, but it would enable him to learn the retail and wholesale end of the business.

Farr asked to think it over. He ultimately decided to take the $200-a-week job and build his career skills. So for the next seven years, beginning in 1971, he worked at Ford, developing his talents in the automotive industry, while continuing to play football for the Detroit Lions.

Then, in 1974, at the age of twenty-nine, he decided to retire from football, a career that was paying him $100,000 a year at the time. "I wanted to do something else, and be more than a football player," recounts Farr. "I wanted to be an entrepreneur."

He had saved much of his earnings from professional football, so he took the money and bought a bankrupt automotive dealership in Oak Park, Michigan—a white suburb—in 1975. Despite the fact that the dealership had been bankrupt twice, Farr saw that it was in a great location. He had confidence in his own knowledge of the automotive business. He knew he could turn it around.

"I had prepared myself," recalls Farr. "I had developed the skills. I was very, very sure of my talents."

And turn it around he did. Just three years later President Jimmy Carter invited him to the White House to attend a dinner for the leaders of the top one hundred African American–owned businesses in the country.

Farr, at age thirty-three, was the youngest person there. His corporation was the sixteenth-largest black-owned business in the United States. Today, twenty-two years later, the company ranks as the largest

African American–owned business in the country. The Detroit-based Mel Farr Automotive Group has annual sales in excess of $600 million.

"In order to accomplish this, you've got to work on some skills," he says. "You need the talent. Most of us don't want to pay the price. That's why we're not successful. You have to make these sacrifices."

With that talent, he continued, you can discover a market. You can create a product. "Talent is the most important thing man has," he concludes. "And the greatest gift we can give back to God is the utilization of that talent."

All of his dealerships are currently in suburbia, with just one dealership in the urban market. But Farr plans to take his business in the future to the underserved market in the inner city. In 1999, he pointed out, African Americans will spend a total of roughly $500 billion. Of that, $50 billion is spent on used cars. "It's a huge market," asserts Farr. "But no major force in the community has taken advantage of that marketplace."

In the city of Detroit—the automotive capital of the world, where Farr's company is headquartered—45 percent of the people have no transportation and 70 percent work outside the city. There's a crunch now going on, forcing people off welfare into work. To go successfully from welfare to work, you need job training, day care, transportation, and a job. In an area where residents are labeled "bad credit risks," abandoned by major automotive insurers, Mel Farr has taken the risk of leasing cars. And he has done so very successfully. People need the transportation; they must have it. So far about five hundred customers have leased cars on a one-week basis, and none have defaulted.

Farr has made a big push into leasing used cars to poor people with no credit or bad credit who have been turned down by other automotive dealers. If they miss a payment, the car simply won't start, thanks to a computerized "on-time" payment device inserted in the dashboard, which can be controlled from Farr's headquarters.

In Mel Farr's opinion, the four things an entrepreneur needs to be successful are a market, a product, talent, and capital. We have the market and the talent in America's underserved communities, and we have lots of products we could potentially bring to market. But to realize that potential, we need access to capital. Our current corporate leaders are victims of myopia and cultural blindness, and they travel in small, intense circles. We need to expand the circle.

The time is ripe for minority-owned entrepreneurs to step forward, build their own companies, and serve their own markets, which they know best. "We don't have an African American company yet that's a billion-dollar company, and that's a shame," Farr commented in a recent speech before the Coalition of Black Investors conference in Detroit.

Minority communities have historically been devastated by a lack of capital, which can be seen just by driving through them.

"The grass is green in suburbia," observes Farr. "Tall buildings are going up. Jobs are there. Mass transit systems have been developed to serve them. But in the African American community, there is blight. Businesses are closed down. We have no investment going into our neighborhoods." He likened it to a tree that grows crooked if it's fenced in by barbed wire and not given sunlight and water.

"We as African American entrepreneurs should go back into the area we came from and invest in it," he says. "Kids will only emulate what they see—a drug dealer driving a BMW, a pimp in a Cadillac. That's all they see.

"We've got to understand what the Statue of Liberty means, what freedom is all about," he continues. "We didn't see it. When we came over, we were in the bottom of the boat.

"We've got to dispel that illusion that we can't be good businessmen. That's an illusion. We can't let that illusion stop us from being motivated," he adds. "We can do more. . . . What force is more dynamic than love? A dynamic power, moving out into the world and doing something original."

MARGARITA PEREZ: RISING TO THE TOP IN ASSET MANAGEMENT

Atop a glittering skyscraper in downtown Chicago is the office of Fortaleza Asset Management, which manages tens of millions of dollars of corporate pension money.

It's a far cry from Caguas, Puerto Rico, the impoverished little town on a tropical island where Margarita Perez, the founder and CEO of the firm, grew up. Her parents separated when she was a baby, so she was raised by her grandfather, grandmother, and aunt in a tiny four-room house.

"We were from a low-income family," recalls Perez. "But it was kind of a mixed neighborhood. Some folks were doing better than others. And it was my observation that those who did have their own home and had jobs and were doing a little better than us—much better than us— had something in common. In my little eyes, I could see that common element was education. All of them had at least a high school diploma, which was a big thing."

This observation kindled in Perez the determination to get a good education—that, along with the admonitions of her strong-willed grandmother, who was instrumental in raising the girl. Perez's grandmother intoned: "You're a woman, and things will be tough for you as you grow up. So always make sure you can stand on your own two feet wherever you go."

As a young girl Perez excelled in school. Because her parents both re-married, she has seven half siblings, none of whom has gone to college. Thus she had no role models in her family as she was growing up and, in fact, was regarded as somewhat odd by most of her family and her contemporaries.

"I was looked at as, I guess, a little different—a little too ambitious," explains the forty-five-year-old executive, clad in a smart-looking business suit. "As I was growing up, girls normally just got married and their husbands took care of them. And I saw things differently. Mostly because of what I had seen my grandmother go through. I wanted to be able to stand on my own two feet, as she used to tell me. And I just didn't see a difference between what men and women could do."

At the age of fourteen Perez moved to the mainland United States, which she viewed as the land of opportunity. Her father was residing in Chicago, working in a Florsheim shoe factory, making shoes. So she came to live with him in June 1968. "I loved Chicago," she comments. "It was a beautiful, clean city, and friendly. This has been home ever since." When she arrived, she spoke only Spanish, but within a year and a half she was fluent in English.

Perez went to DePaul University, where she received an undergraduate degree in accounting. She couldn't afford the tuition, which was $7,000 a year at the time—amounting to her father's entire annual salary. So right after high school she went to junior college for the first couple years, then found out that the Borg Warner Corporation, a diversified manufacturing conglomerate, would pay tuition expenses for employees as a benefit of employment. The company made air conditioners, auto parts, armored trucks, and chemicals, among other things.

Perez got a job working in the firm's treasury department while she attended college. "I learned a lot. That was a great experience," she recounts. "Good people. Minorities all had opportunities to move up at Borg Warner. I never saw a problem. They gave me every opportunity to grow up."

And grow up she did: Perez ended up spending fifteen years at the company. Her employer assigned her a variety of tasks. She started out reconciling cash transactions, then moved into cash management, which consisted of investing the firm's daily excess cash into commercial paper. Perez also did some foreign exchange hedging, covering their receivables coming in from different countries, and did forward contracts in different currencies.

Borg Warner paid her tuition as she went to college full-time. The firm also paid for her to get a master's degree in business administration in international business and finance, as well as a certified public accountant degree.

She recalled, with pleasure, the time one of her white male bosses, who was the treasurer of the company, called her into his office "and gave me this whopping increase in salary," based on her outstanding performance at the firm. "I was just the happiest woman on earth," remembers Perez. "I went home and I was so happy."

Toward the end of her stint there, by the early 1980s, Perez was assigned to help manage some $4 billion of Borg Warner's pension funds,

$300 million of which was invested in the stock market. "When I was senior enough, they let me do that," she recalls. "I kept moving up the scale."

She and a partner spun off in 1990 and started their own asset management company, building on the skills she had acquired at Borg Warner. The new company, Fortaleza, has mutual funds and also manages institutional pension money. Borg Warner became one of her big clients, giving the firm $30 million to manage. She got another $30 million from other clients, bringing the total under management to $60 million.

Fortaleza means fortress, as well as fortitude, in Spanish. Perez likes to think of the firm as a fortress against the vicissitudes of the marketplace.

Today the firm has eight employees, including two African Americans and three Mexican Americans, plus Perez. She financed the company by putting her own money into it, as well as that of three ex–Borg Warner executives, who are still shareholders. One was the ex–chief financial officer (CFO), another was a senior vice president, and the third was the CFO. "They've all seen my work and knew that I was focused," explains Perez. "So they all trusted me and gave me the money." All of them were white men.

Perez would like to see more African Americans, Hispanics, and women involved in the money management business. To this day, when she goes to national conferences in her industry, the events are dominated by white males.

Her advice to low-income people who are trying to enter the field is simply this: "Get an education. That should be your number one focus," she says.

"I didn't have a penny to my name, yet I found a way," continues Perez, whose accomplishments have landed her a seat on the Governor's Commission for the Status of Women in Illinois. "I found out there are employers like Borg Warner Corporation—a full-time employer—that will pick up your tuition. That's how I did it. I was also willing to work late at night and stay up until two in the morning doing worksheets for accounting. And I got up the next day and gave it a full 100 percent. So where there's a will, there's a way. If you really want to get a better education, there's nothing that should get in your way."

––––––––––––

Mel Farr and Margarita Perez are examples of entrepreneurial successes who chose to play in the big leagues of corporate America. But there are other folks who are succeeding on a smaller scale. Rather than running multimillion-dollar companies, they aspire to make it on a local level, right in their own communities.

NICK HOCKINGS: NATIVE AMERICAN ENTREPRENEUR

Nick Hockings is such a person. A full-blooded Ojibwa Indian, he grew up on a northern Wisconsin reservation in Lac du Flambeau, or "Torch Lake." The French fur traders, who were early settlers in the region, gave it that name when they saw the torches on the lake as the Ojibwa speared fish at night.

The town is nestled in Wisconsin's north woods, a scenic region that has more lakes per square mile than any other place in the United States. Every year tourists from the surrounding states flock there to fish, swim, and go boating. In recent years the casino built on the Indian reservation has also proven a great draw.

Hockings, a tall, slender man with a gray ponytail, devised a way to capitalize on the region's booming tourism while helping to preserve the traditions of his tribe. Along twenty acres of Moving Cloud Lake, he has re-created authentic Indian campgrounds. There are birch-bark wigwams; handmade bows, arrows, and baskets; cedar sleds; tepees and willow fish traps. Everything is handmade. Visitors can stroll along a rustic trail and see how Indians once lived in the region, before the white man came. "It's a way of life that honored the earth and natural resources," explains Hockings.

He hosts a variety of students, families, and others who pay $7 apiece to view the site. There's also a large, grassy field where people can pitch a tent, stay overnight, and dine on Ojibwa food served by tribal women.

The site is called Wa-Swa-Goning, which was the Ojibwa name for the whole region, meaning "the place where they spear fish by torchlight." Hockings believes that it's the only such Indian-owned-and-operated village in the United States. It's open during the summer months and closed the rest of the year. Thus far he receives about 5,000 visitors a season but hopes to grow that number by increased advertising, along with a Web site.

During the off-season, Hockings earns money by giving lectures about traditional Ojibwa life to schools and universities and donning tribal regalia to perform in "pow-wows" or ceremonial dances. Some of his clients include the College of DuPage, Illinois State University, and Rock Valley College, which send students to the camp to learn about Indian culture firsthand. He's also launched the Wa-Swa-Goning Dance Theater, which does performances around the state.

Hockings was driven by a mission. "I wanted to start something up that would be positive for the tribe," he says. "I wanted to do something to educate people and present our culture." When he was growing up in the 1940s, none of the schools taught courses on Native American culture. He grew tired of the misrepresentations of Indian people that he had seen in the popular culture. In reality, he said, the Ojibwas were semi-migratory people who traveled around much of northern Wisconsin. They had strong religious beliefs. They were always open to other cultures.

"Racism and prejudice will dissipate if you're open to other cultures," Hockings contends. "I have had black kids from Jamaica up here, and they sang very beautiful songs. I have had white college kids from the suburbs, and they spent two or three days here, camping. I taught them to chop down birch trees, peel off the bark, and make a wigwam. I hold this place open to everybody."

The village is located near the casino. Hockings figured that if five thousand people a week went to the nearby casino, which is run by the tribal council, and 10 percent went out of their way a third of a mile to see a real Indian village, then he would have steady profits. Thus far he's breaking even, but he hopes to enhance revenues in the future.

"The hardest thing about it is not building the wigwams or re-creating an Indian village," says Hockings. "The hardest thing about it is, if you put up a sign that says you're open at ten A.M. to five P.M., you damn well better be there from ten to five. And there's no excuses for not opening up. There's none. If you have a business and you're advertising something, you'd better be able to fulfill."

Hockings, who is fifty-seven, has worked with Wisconsin government programs to help get his business off the ground. Jerry Rayala, a small business consultant at the Great Lakes Inter-Tribal Council, assisted him on financial matters, such as establishing a bookkeeping system and maintaining it. Rayala, who is white, works with eleven other tribes in the council.

Hockings bought the eighty-acre site for $60,000 a few years ago, after putting about $20,000 down, and said the operation paid for itself in five years. Building the campground required very little capital investment, since he relied on help from volunteers and used materials from nature. He has no debt and lives in a fully paid-for tribal home with his wife, who hails from a branch of the Sioux tribe, and three grandchildren, whom he is raising.

He also moved away from the reservation for a few years and picked up some business skills in the process. He worked in a Wisconsin print shop, where he eventually became part owner, learning how to run the presses and do artwork and layout. He also resided in San Francisco during the late 1960s.

"I always felt business was more than just one thing," Hockings explains. "It had to be all-inclusive. For instance, you put in a grocery store, you get people to come to the grocery store, pretty soon the gas station starts up. Then pretty soon a garage starts up, and pretty soon this, and pretty soon that."

A recovered alcoholic, Hockings became sober by joining Alcoholics Anonymous. He said most of the people he grew up with on the reservation suffer from drinking problems, including his nine brothers and sisters. It's an expression of despair, not unlike drinking and drug use by the disenfranchised of every community.

Sitting on the porch of his log cabin at the campground, two deer hides are drying in the sun on the side of the little building. Hockings hopes his venture will encourage both the young and the old on the reservation. He knew he was on the right track when he brought a group of about twenty tribal elders with him on a tour of the place. They were enraptured.

"Finally," they told him, "someone has done this."

ALEX BAMBARA: WEST AFRICAN IMMIGRANT

Alex Bambara was a prince in his West African homeland, Burkina Faso. His father was the king of the village of Bambara. "But I was a very poor prince," Alex says with a laugh. He grew up on a farm near Bobo-Dioulasso, the second biggest city in his country, and had nine brothers and sisters. They raised cows, chickens, goats, and sheep.

Nine years ago, seeking his fortune, he bought a plane ticket to New York City and arrived in America with $150.

When it came to pursuing a career, Bambara's father taught him a piece of African wisdom that always stuck with him: "Never leave the prey that you can get. Get that before you follow the bigger prey. Kill the deer first—then go after the elephant."

It's a strategy Bambara has followed with great success in America. He started small, then worked his way up. First he got a job as a dishwasher in a Tex-Mex restaurant called Stetson's in Washington, D.C. French was his native language, and he was fluent in various African tongues such as Mali, Mossi, and Gouroussi, but he spoke very little English. So he got the job by walking around with a small piece of paper that read: "I'm looking for a job. Any available?"

The chef at the restaurant was an African from Ghana. They hired him, and for six months he was in charge of cleaning the basement, doing the dishes, and mopping the entire restaurant until three A.M. every morning. "I was so happy," recalls Bambara. "I loved it. Everybody was so nice to me." He made $4 an hour and shared a one-room apartment with another guy from Burkina Faso. They paid $200 a month in rent, and Bambara managed to save $80 every month. He opened a savings account at a local bank.

From there Bambara decided to go after bigger prey. He landed a job at I Ricci, a fancy, award-winning Italian restaurant in Washington, D.C. President George Bush, his wife, and other dignitaries counted themselves among the patrons. Bambara was making $8 an hour in 1990. They rotated him around in different slots in the kitchen, so he learned how to fry, do vegetables, make ice cream, bake bread, prepare fresh pasta, and concoct gourmet desserts.

He took to this role with gusto. While growing up in Burkina Faso, Bambara had always loved to cook. His aunt taught him to make bean bread from black-eyed peas, and "froufrou," a puffy African bread fried in oil. In addition, thanks to the French influence in Burkina Faso, he had grown up surrounded by *boulangeries,* or French-style bakeries, aromatic with freshly baked baguettes of bread.

He loved to bake so much that he sometimes forgot what time it was. The hours flew by.

Every two weeks Bambara made $500, and every month, like clockwork, he saved $500. He put it all in the bank. This was a new experience for him. "In Africa, we never learned to save or invest," he explains. "We keep the money at home."

Bambara married an American woman who had worked with the Peace Corps in Africa, and by 1992 had obtained legal status as an American citizen. They now have two children, a boy and a girl, and have bought a house in Alexandria, Virginia, near Washington, D.C. She is a professional at the Environmental Protection Agency.

After his stint at I Ricci, Bambara, who is now thirty-six, helped open the Firehook Bakery in Alexandria, where he worked three years, refining both his culinary and business skills. Every day he would be at the bakery from six A.M., and some mornings he would be there as early as three A.M. to start baking. There he learned how to make over thirty varieties of bread, including European artisanal breads, as well as specialty pastries, tiramisu, and cookies. He saw what a lucrative business it was. The owner was grossing $3 million a year.

"I learned so much there that I was able to start consulting," explains Bambara. "They sent me to Colorado, Chicago, and Minneapolis to open bakeries. I became sort of important." People would pay $20,000 to $30,000 to have him come and do a two-week consultation on the intricacies of gourmet bread making.

He discussed how to shape the dough, divide it, and control the temperature, among other niceties. All this, despite the fact that he had never attended cooking school.

"If you learn something special, you become very valuable," he explains. "Even if you're not a college graduate. People treat you like a professor."

After this he set his eyes on still larger quarry: a business of his own. Currently he's sharing kitchen space with a cafe called Aunt Meme's Bakery & Cafe in Alexandria. An Armenian couple owns the place.

Bambara comes early, at three A.M. every day, and bakes bread for them as well as for his own clientele. Then he delivers bread, pastry, scones, and cookies to his thirteen customers each day in his white Honda Accord. His customers include restaurants and coffeehouses. All told, he's making about $5,000 a month from this arrangement.

But his big plan is still in progress. Bambara has been working with the local Small Business Development Center (SBDC), to create a business plan, complete with revenue projections over the next several years, so that he can qualify for a bank loan. He wants $81,000 so that he can hire three employees. Demand is so brisk for his baked goods that he projects annual profits of $150,000 two years from now, once he gets the additional staff. Bambara has projected revenues of $7,000 a month on wholesale and retail bread, plus $4,000 on cooking for a gross of $11,000, before expenses. Expenses will be about 28 percent of that, including the wages of his bakers—about $13 an hour. But the profit margins are hefty in this business: 55 percent.

At the SBDC Bambara was matched with a mentor, Jack Parker, a retired vice president of a local bank, who walked him through all the steps involved in writing a business plan and obtaining a bank loan. And it was all free, under a program run by the Small Business Administration.

From $150 to $150,000 in a little more than a decade. The big quarry is finally coming into range.

"In this country, if you want it, you can make it," he summarizes. "Pick up a skill and put your heart into it. You really have to sacrifice time and pleasure for what you want to accomplish in the future. You have to tighten your belt and do it. But if you're tough, you can succeed.

"This," he concludes, "is a dream that is really happening."

Maybe you have a dream—an idea to build a business, however large or small. Maybe it is selling baseball cards over the Internet. Or bottling spring water from the mountains, out in the country where you live. Or exporting used American cars to Africa.

Following are some of the resources available to you, as a burgeoning entrepreneur, to help you take that dream and turn it into a profitable business:

THE U.S. SMALL BUSINESS ADMINISTRATION

Your first stop is your local Small Business Development Center (SBDC), run by the Small Business Administration (SBA). The SBA has 1,000 Small Business Development Centers all over the country, in every state, and on Indian reservations as well. This is a one-stop assistance center that provides a wide variety of information and guidance to small business.

These centers offer free or low-cost mentoring and counseling sessions with seasoned business professionals and are run in partnership with local universities, chambers of commerce, and economic development corporations. They can give you an idea as to how viable your business might be. They can teach you about every aspect of business, whether it be marketing, management, accounting, finance, exporting, or obtaining capital.

Retired professionals, in an SBA program called the Service Corps of Retired Executives (SCORE), can give you expert advice at these places. You can meet with a veteran in your industry, who can give you the lowdown about how to make your company succeed. SCORE volunteers can meet with you at a local SBA office or at a SCORE office, of which there are almost eight hundred across the United States.

The SBA may also be able to provide your business with a loan guarantee. To find the SBDC nearest you, check out the SBA Web site at www.sba.gov, or call their SBA Answer Desk at 1-800-8-ASK-SBA.

In addition, the agency runs 346 Small Business Investment Companies (SBICs), which provide equity capital, long-term loans, and management assistance to small businesses that qualify. To be eligible, the SBA requires that your company have a net worth of $18 million or less and profits of not more than $6 million for the past two years.

The SBDC has various types of business plan software that you can use free. Using the software helped Alex Bambara develop a viable business plan, which then enabled him to approach a bank about getting a loan.

Some of the centers are geared specifically toward the needs of minorities and women. For example, Ofelia Arellano, a forty-two-year-old Mexican American, went to the SBA's Minority Business Resource Center in San Diego. She worked as a dean at a local community college but dreamed of opening a small business selling shaved-ice desserts in El Centro, California, near San Diego. It was to be called Ice Dreams. She knew the desserts—which are topped with flavorful syrups like mango, tamarind, and coconut—are very popular with Latinos, who are the primary residents of the area.

Like most entrepreneurs, she had problems obtaining capital. At the SBA center veteran business counselors met with her and advised her to try writing her business plan with the aid of some software. She tried out various makes of software free at their facility before settling on Business Plan Pro, made by Palo Alto Software. She ended up buying the Windows-based software for $99.

Bingo. Arellano landed an SBA-guaranteed loan of $50,000 in just three days from the Bank of Coronado, a local community bank. She used the money to construct a building for her shaved-ice business on an empty lot she owned in El Centro. Since she started in July 1997—with various members of her family chipping in to work at the store—Ice Dreams has exceeded her revenue estimates. She hopes to eventually expand and open other stores around the state.

Arellano credits the business plan software with being instrumental in winning the financing. Business Plan Pro has a generic business plan you can customize to fit your particular company; using prompts that pop up on the computer screen, it guides entrepreneurs step by step through all the elements needed to construct a plan. "Business Plan Pro was my tutor," asserts Arellano, who had no business background prior to undertaking this venture. Moreover, the plans can be modified as the business progresses, to ensure that entrepreneurs are meeting their targets one year, two years, or five years down the road. When used correctly, the business plan can grow and evolve along with the company and provide a road map for the entrepreneur.

Business plan software comes in a variety of formats, offering something for everyone. And for those lacking an MBA or knowledge of finance, accounting, or some other specific business discipline, such software can provide a helpful tool to ensure that you cover all the bases before approaching a lender for financing—which is the most common usage for a business plan.

According to PC Data in Reston, Virginia, an independent consulting firm that tracks software sales, the best-selling business plan software packages in America are Jian's BizPlan Builder (1-800-346-5426; Web site www.jianusa.com), which costs $89.95, and Palo Alto Software's Business Plan Pro (1-800-229-7526; Web site www.palo-alto.com), which sells for $99.95. Between the two of them they've captured about 85 percent of the retail business plan software market.

Business plan software varies a great deal, so try out several before buying and find one that's right for you. You can do this free at various SBICs around the country, and you can often do so at the business sections of local libraries or universities.

THE U.S. DEPARTMENT OF COMMERCE

Let's say your dream is to start a company and sell your products all over the world. You want to be involved in international business. And why not? Already one in seven U.S. jobs is trade related—a figure that is expected to grow with the continued globalization of the world economy.

Then you need to go to the U.S. Department of Commerce, which is set up specifically to promote U.S. exports. They can give you free advice about any country in the world where you want to do business.

The International Trade Administration, which is part of the Commerce Department, has programs for small and medium-size entrepreneurs. Their Trade Information Center (TIC) is a clearinghouse of information that works with people who are ready to export. Before you contact them, you will want to get your business plan, your product, and your company all hammered out at your local SBDC (see previous section). The Commerce Department also has about fifty-three export assistance centers around the country that can work with you. You can speak with a trade specialist at one of these places who will counsel you about the best market for your product or service anywhere in world.

The TIC has market research information and services to help you find agencies or distributors of your product in foreign countries. In addition, for each foreign country they have a country commercial guide, which lists ten to fifteen product categories that are the best prospects for U.S. companies that want to do business there.

The National Trade Databank, issued by the Commerce Department, is the world's largest source of trade information. It offers one-stop shopping for monthly trade data from over forty federal sources, putting you in touch with the very latest market research reports, business conditions in almost every country in the world, trade leads, and contacts. It is available at federal depository libraries; can be accessed through the Internet at STAT-USA's World Wide Web site (www.stat-usa.gov); or can be purchased on CD-ROM for $575 for an annual subscription of twelve monthly issues. If you're serious about doing business overseas, this may be a good investment for you, and you can deduct the fee as a business expense on your income taxes.

The Commerce Department can be reached in Washington, D.C., at 1-800-USA-TRADE. To get export information, ask for the International Trade Administration or visit their Web site at www.ita.doc.gov.

THE U.S. DEPARTMENT OF LABOR

Maybe you're trying to figure out what industry would be the best one for you to go into. You'll want data on fast-growing occupations in the United States, as well as their salaries. To find this out, get in touch with the Bureau of Labor Statistics, which is part of the U.S. Department of Labor. Every other year they publish *The Occupational Outlook Handbook,* containing salary and employment data on 750 occupations, updated quarterly. You'll be able to see which occupations are growing and which are shrinking. This book will also tell you what training you'll need to go into a particular occupation. You can call 1-202-512-1800 to get a copy of this book, which costs $42 in paperback, $46 in hardback, and $28 in CD-ROM for online use. You can also search this data on the Web site of the Bureau of Labor Statistics, at http://stats.bls.gov/oco-home.

THE NETPRENEUR PROGRAM

Let's say you want to start a digital business and become a player in the fast-growing field of electronic commerce. You would like to launch a Web site and sell products in cyberspace.

A first step would be to contact the Morino Institute Netpreneur Program, a nonprofit organization set up to spur the creation of online businesses. Although the group focuses primarily on businesses in the greater Washington, D.C., area, if you live outside that region, you can also participate by visiting their Web site (www.netpreneur.org), subscribing to Netpreneur News, joining their discussion groups, and participating in their online events. It's a tremendous educational opportunity.

The group was founded by Mario Morino, a self-made multimillionaire who was founder of the Legent Corporation. Morino grew up poor, the son of a coal miner in western Pennsylvania, and decided—once he made his fortune—that he would give back to the community by trying to bridge the gap between the technological "haves" and "have-nots" in society.

The group's networking events in the greater Washington, D.C., area draw enthusiastic crowds of three hundred to nine hundred attendees. Investors and strategic partners are matched up with promising netpreneurs. Deals are made. Business gets done. People share information and help one another.

You can call the Morino Institute in Herndon, Virginia, at 1-703-757-7421.

These are just a few of the many resources available to you as an aspiring entrepreneur. There are many others, and you can get referrals about them from some of the organizations we have just mentioned.

The key: Act on your dreams. If you want to start a business, there are a number of places that can help you.

And don't delay. As African American novelist Terry McMillan—author of *Waiting to Exhale,* which became a best-seller and a major motion picture—put it: "Can't nothing make your life work if you ain't the architect."

CHAPTER 12

The Importance
of Educating the Young

*What shall we tell our children? Tell them we always moved to a higher
vision with nonnegotiable ideals and faith in God. As long as we were
morally centered and did not faint in the heat of battle we prevailed.
Tell them there are rivers and hills in front of us, but there are mountains and oceans behind us. Tell them we must still heal the breach, the
gap between Wall Street and Harlem and Appalachia. Tell them we
must choose the challenge of development over the rhetoric of despair.
Tell them we must resolve the contradiction between Wall Street, the
capital of capital, and Harlem, de-capitalized on the same island between the same two rivers in the same city.*

As part of the fourth movement of our Freedom Symphony,
we must bring the message of financial empowerment to
every child in this country—black, brown, red, or white.
Everyone must be included. As Dr. Martin Luther King said, equal opportunity in America requires not only entry into the marketplace and
access to jobs, but also the education of our young people.

We at the Rainbow/PUSH Coalition are carrying out Dr. King's vision.
As part of that effort, we have partnered with the Securities Industry As-
sociation, the leading trade group in the securities industry, to bring the
Stock Market Game to our children. The Stock Market Game is an edu-

247

cational initiative offered by many schools across the country, sponsored and distributed by the Securities Industry Foundation for Economic Education. Hundreds of thousands of students play the game during each school year.

The Stock Market Game gives students an opportunity to manage an imaginary $100,000 portfolio over a ten-week semester. Teachers report that the program has tremendous motivational value and is a unique way to introduce young people to a market-based economy. The program is available to all grade levels but works best in grades four through twelve. About seventy-five children, ranging in ages from six to eighteen, of Rainbow/PUSH employees are learning from the Stock Market Game. When they complete the course they'll be given $200, which they must use to invest in stocks.

Among other things, students learn how business firms are organized; how to choose and buy stocks; how to use the daily newspaper as a source of financial information; how daily events affect our economy; how investment contributes to economic growth; and how supply and demand operate in real markets.

Student teams compete in geographic, regional competitions, as well as statewide contests. Winners can receive cash awards; recognition at a regional awards dinner; and even a trip to New York City, including tours of the stock exchanges. Those interested should contact the Rainbow/PUSH Coalition (the phone number of the Chicago headquarters is 1-773-373-3366); call their local school and inquire if the program is offered; or visit the Web site of the Securities Industry Foundation for Economic Education at www.smg2000.org.

We want to teach our children from an early age how to save and grow, not spend and sink. This needs to start when children are young. They, in turn, can pass on these skills from generation to generation, building wealth over time.

Maceo Sloan, an African American multimillionaire whose ancestors were among the founding families of the North Carolina Mutual Life Insurance Company (NCM) in 1898, is a prime example of how this can be accomplished. Because of his family's sound financial management, NCM today ranks as the nation's largest black-owned life insurance company. The Sloan family handed down their financial expertise over four generations, providing Maceo Sloan with a foundation from which he could create such innovative ventures as the Sloan Financial Group, Inc., a diversified financial services company that he runs, whose subsidiaries manage assets in excess of $4 billion. Sloan is also chairman of New Africa Advisers, the first American investment firm in post-apartheid South Africa and the first black-owned institutional investment adviser on the African continent. And he is chairman and chief executive officer of NCM Capital Management Group, Inc., which provides equity, fixed-income, and balanced portfolio management services to clients from all sectors of the institutional investment management industry. Finally, he is chairman of the Rainbow/PUSH Wall Street Project.

"I've been around business and investments my whole life," says Sloan. And he started learning about it at home, from his parents.

We can all start learning about finance and investments—whatever our age, whatever our background, whatever our race or gender. And we can pass on that knowledge to our children and our children's children. We can continue the "how to" tradition of the civil rights movement. Over time we can accumulate wealth and build bridges between Wall Street and Harlem, Wall Street and Appalachia, Wall Street and the barrios of south central Los Angeles, Wall Street and all the underserved communities in America.

Teaching our young people sound financial management skills begins at home. Consider the case of Richard Anderson Jr.

He's a seven-year-old boy, and like most kids his age, he spends a lot of time romping around enthusiastically. But he is not just any seven-year-old boy. He is an investor.

Today he's clad in a gray pinstripe suit, along with tiny black loafers with tassels on them: a young executive in miniature. And why not? Anderson already has the distinction, at his tender age, of having rung the bell to open the New York Stock Exchange, as well as having given a speech about investing at the Coalition of Black Investors conference in Milwaukee.

His father, Richard Anderson Sr., of Brooklyn, New York, works as a certified financial planner and decided, along with his mother, that he would imbue his young son with a knowledge of investments at an early age. Thus whenever young Richard misbehaved, his father took away his cartoon privileges on television and instead made him watch CNBC for a couple of days.

"He started to pick up the language," explained the senior Anderson. "Every discipline has a language."

Pretty soon young Anderson could recite the names of all thirty companies on the Dow Jones Industrial Average (DJIA). The DJIA is an indicator of thirty blue-chip stocks to measure the general increase of stock prices. Young Richard got so he wanted to spend his allowance on investments instead of toys. He logged on to the Internet at his family's home computer, typed in the name of a company, and began researching it. He became an enthusiastic proponent of investing in companies that he understood. For example, Nike: young Anderson saw lots and lots of people wearing Nike sneakers. He began looking into the company and decided it was a good investment. Richard Jr. also likes Hasbro, a toy manufacturer whose products he enjoys playing with, and the Chuck E. Cheese restaurant chain, another company that he patronizes.

"My investment strategy is to look at each industry and see which company is the best one," explains the seven-year-old. "A really great company needs three things: 1) great leadership and management; 2) great products and services, at a reasonable price; and 3) great customer service that just keeps getting better and better."

Young Anderson also understands the rudiments of how the economy works. "There is such a thing as the inflation monster," he comments. "If you don't invest your money, the inflation monster will eat it." His current investment portfolio consists of mutual funds as well as an S&P 500 index fund.

Learning about finance and investments has become a family ritual in the Anderson household. Father and son regularly watch *Wall Street Week,* a popular show about investments hosted by Louis Rukeyser, and listen to investment tapes, such as *The Wall Street Journal* video series. The senior Anderson also tapes various financial shows, such as the *Nightly Business Report*, which he and his son then watch together.

His father stresses the urgency of teaching young people financial literacy so they will be able to provide for themselves in retirement. Because of advances in medicine, people are living longer and longer and may spend as much as one-third of their lifetime as retirees. But they're not saving sufficient resources to finance their lengthy retirements. One-third of people who currently retired at age sixty-five have less than $10,000 in savings.

"If we don't promote economic literacy and entrepreneurialism, who will take care of them?" asks the elder Anderson.

An understanding of personal finance is one of the most important skills that you will ever pass down to your children. It is as important as learning to drive a car—for without such skills, they will be unable to navigate the twists and turns of life's financial highways. And as we learned in the chapter on investing, starting young is crucial to building a nest egg, because by saving and investing just small amounts of cash, you can build a great fortune by the age of your retirement, thanks to the time value of money.

Armed with this knowledge, many parents from minority backgrounds, like the Andersons, have begun to impart financial literacy to their children at an early age. When possible, they invite members of their extended family, such as grandparents and other relatives, to participate. In this fashion they are handing down valuable money management skills, which will enable their children and their children's children to build wealth over many generations.

Duane and Carol Davis, cofounders of the Coalition of Black Investors, are examples of parents who have begun educating their children at a young age about the crucial importance of investing. Their six-year-old daughter, Taylor, already has a $35,000 investment portfolio, while their son, Duane II, age four, has $25,000; the portfolios were set up when each of the children was born and have been added to steadily ever since. Thus far the parents have been investing in stocks and mutual funds for their children's accounts. But gradually the kids are being trained to assume this role. For example, this Christmas Taylor picked her first stock.

"For us, it's become a family affair," explains Davis, a certified financial planner who lives in Winston-Salem, North Carolina, where he works as vice president/investment counselor at First Union Brokerage Services, Inc. "My mother-in-law is setting aside $1 a day for the kids in a savings account. If you put $1 a day aside for a child from the day he or she is born, assuming a 10 percent rate of return, that individual will have $2 million by age sixty-five."

Davis sent a note to his mother-in-law that read: "Thanks for making your grandchildren millionaires!"

The Davises also put $1,000 in a variable annuity—a onetime, $1,000 investment—as a gift, for each of their children. "Assuming it grows at 12 percent a year, this onetime gift will be worth $500,000 by the time they're sixty-five," points out Davis. "Most parents are not able to give their kids a gift of $500,000 outright. But a variable annuity is one way that you can do it, over a period of time." He urges parents, grandparents, and others to give children in their family gifts of stocks, mutual funds, Education IRAs, annuities, or other investments, for Christmas and birthdays. Such gifts help build the child's long-term wealth and educate the child about the value of investing.

Both his kids get paid every month to do their chores. Then they take their money out of the piggy bank and make a deposit in a real bank. "There are a lot of things you can do for your kids to get them involved," says Davis. "You lead by example. If the parents aren't doing it, the kids won't do it, either."

Still another example of a parent who has trained her children from early on about savings and investment is Margarita Perez, head of Chicago-based Fortaleza Asset Management, whom we met in chapter 11. She's been married for twenty-five years and has two children, Christina, age seventeen, and Anthony, age eleven. Already she's gotten them into the habit of saving and investing. A few years ago she went to First Chicago Bank and asked them if she could open an account for her kids. They said she could, with as little as $10 for an initial deposit. Each child gave the clerk a check for $10. Every time they made some money from doing household chores or the like, they added to their accounts, so they grew over time.

"My daughter has got a nice little account now," comments Perez. "It's not a lot of money, but for a seventeen-year-old she's got close to $2,000 that she has put in there with her own money.

"I teach them things like filling up a piggy bank," she continues. "When it's full, half of it goes to Anthony, half goes to her, and we go to the bank with it and they make a deposit with it, you know? It's simple things, but it teaches the kids the value of money. And come Christmastime, she'll take out $100 and buy gifts, and then she thinks about replenishing it. So it's a good discipline."

Her daughter may even be able to pay for college when the time comes, or at least finance part of the expenditure.

Her kids have seen the power of compound interest, from putting even $5 or $10 away on a regular basis in their savings accounts.

Perez also advises starting off early to train your children about the stock market. Whenever possible, she takes her kids with her to work-related conferences, so they can learn the lingo of finance. She even introduces them to the managers of some of the companies she works with. And by way of a reality check, she and her husband occasionally drive the kids through the blighted neighborhoods of Chicago and show them how the poor people live.

"We live in Park Ridge here, and they go to good schools and they've been sheltered," she explains. "But we take them through those neighborhoods. And even when we are on vacation sometimes, we take the detour so that they can see how not everybody lives in a nice little suburban home. They need to see that."

Lack of knowledge about investing is a problem in the Latino community, in her view. Perez recounted stories of wealthy Puerto Rican businessmen she had met who had a few million dollars in real estate assets. But they were not invested in the stock market. "It amazes me that they've been so successful, yet they still mistrust the market because they don't know it," she says. "They've never been exposed to it. And exposure is everything in life."

We've discussed some ways that families can educate their children about financial topics at home. But there are also a variety of nonprofit groups, camps, government initiatives, church programs, and public-private partnerships all over the United States that aim to promote economic literacy among young people. Many are targeted at low-income children. We'll highlight just a few of them for you.

The state of Wisconsin has some extremely innovative programs to foster financial literacy in children. The Youth Enterprise Academy is one of them. This is a ten-day summer program for ninth and tenth graders in the public school system, conducted at the University of Wisconsin's Milwaukee campus, which teaches young people the basics of economics and capitalism. They learn how a market economy works, including such key concepts as profit, supply and demand, and opportunity cost. In addition, they study personal finance, savings, investing, credit, and the importance of investing for life from the National Association of Investors Corporation (NAIC). The students use the NAIC stock selection approach as their methodology. Leadership skills are also stressed, and students who successfully complete the program receive $500 in U.S. savings bonds.

Those who graduate from the Youth Enterprise Academy can then join the Youth Enterprise Investment Club. Thus far there is just one such club, with twenty-five to thirty kids as members. So popular was this first club, however, that plans are afoot to start more.

Cassandra Horton, a young black woman who is a high school junior in Milwaukee, is president of the club. "We meet every three weeks and discuss which stocks we hold," she explains. Currently the club has some shares of America Online, among other companies. "We've been meeting since September, and it's a wonderful experience," she adds. "It's a wonderful way to teach kids about the importance of savings and investing."

The club often invites guest speakers, some of whom work in the broker-age industry, who can shed light on different aspects of investing.

"We could do this program on a larger scale," says Dr. Mark Schug, director of the Center for Economic Education at the University of Wisconsin's Milwaukee campus. "We want to export the program around the state and perhaps nationally."

———————

Every July the Bull and Bear Investment Camp takes place in Kansas City, Missouri. The atmosphere evokes the frenzy of Wall Street—complete with the noise, energy, and intensity of high-flying traders. The camp is a week-long clinic for fourth to twelfth graders on the economy, business, and investing conducted by Douglas Coe, an African American who is president and chief executive officer of Moody Reid Inc., an investment firm in Kansas City. Now in its sixth summer, Coe's camp includes a mock stock market, role-playing sessions that simulate labor-management talks, team and individual competitions for "Douglas Dollars," and an auction in which students bid against each other with their winnings. "Douglas Dollars" are paid to students for attendance, punctuality, and participation.

The whole thing is free. Coe started the camp in 1994 to expose inner-city youth to the investment world. He holds a BA from More-house College in Atlanta, Georgia, and has worked in the investment in-dustry since the age of twenty-one. He's formerly associate vice president of investments at Kemper Securities, Inc., a major Wall Street firm, and in 1996 he was named one of the one hundred most influential African Americans in Kansas City by the *Kansas City Globe*.

"Each year, the camp grows bigger and bigger," comments Coe. "Every year, I'm pleasantly surprised how much the kids really like learning about money management and how the financial markets function."

He got the idea for the camp because he noticed that every summer there were many different "outdoors-type" camps for kids in Kansas City: football camps, baseball camps, camps where you could go swim-ming, hiking, or horseback riding. "They train the kids' bodies," Coe points out. "But where are the camps that teach their minds?" Only a

handful of kids will have enough talent to be professional athletes, he
continues, but everyone needs to understand financial planning. Such
was the impetus for the Bull and Bear Investment Camp.

Coe's teaching methods empower the students and transform them
into decision makers. The kids are divided into two teams, called the
Bulls and the Bears. Each team invests a hypothetical $100,000 dollars
in imaginary stocks that mirror real-life companies on Wall Street. In
addition, each team has portfolio managers, analysts, traders, and an
economist who share three main objectives: to earn money, maximize
investment returns, and protect assets from potential risks.

The companies are fictional but reflect real-life firms. Each day Coe
reads hypothetical news events to the teams about these firms. Based on
this information, the students make investment decisions. For example,
there is Spike (as in Nike) Shoes Inc., which is having trouble with
threats that basketball legend Michael Jordan, who stars in Spike commercials, might retire. There is CyberSoft Inc. (as in Microsoft), a huge
software company struggling with an antitrust investigation that might
hold up release of its Doors 98 software. There is Big Daddy's Records,
a make-believe record label that just signed a recording contract with
the recently deceased rap star Tupac Shakur. What will his death do to
the stock price of Big Daddy's Records? The Bulls and Bears mull over
these news stories carefully before making their investment decisions:
buy, sell, or hold.

Other team members, playing economists, get an update from Coe
on the likelihood that the Federal Reserve would raise interest rates at
its upcoming meeting, as well as tips on what the Fed action, or inac-
tion, would mean to the market.

Huddled closely around conference tables last summer, the group of
young investment managers, traders, market analysts, and economists
on the teams took to their tasks with gusto. After only two days in the
mock market, the Bears' portfolio was up to $178,195. The Bulls had
$168,500. Even though their stock portfolios were make-believe, you
couldn't tell it from the participants' zeal.

The camp also teaches the importance of setting goals, both financially and professionally. Career topics include professional opportuni-

ties in the financial services industry; development of a sound relationship with a banking institution; and the importance of helping others learn about finance (as part of "Each One Teach One!" seminar).

"I've waited all year for the camp!" crows Aubree Collins, a black high school senior in Kansas City. "I really had a good time and learned a lot last year. So I wanted to come back and learn even more about investing again." Last year, before attending the camp, Collins had spent three weeks traveling overseas. So she brought some foreign currency to the Bull and Bear Camp for the other children to see. It provided a great opportunity for the students to discuss the Euro, the single currency introduced in Europe in January 1999. In fact, this summer's camp will offer a new segment centered on global and international investing.

The camp also addresses the following themes:

- Understanding the importance of saving and investing.

- Cash alternatives: certificates of deposit, savings accounts, and checking accounts.

- Global and international investing.

- How to establish an investment account.

- Investing in common stocks and bonds.

- The power of tax-deferred compounding.

- How to analyze the financial markets and national economy.

- How to develop an effective investment plan.

- How to use dividend investment plans.

- How to evaluate corporate takeovers and mergers.

"You have to give back," Coe concludes. "We reach levels in our professional careers and think that writing a check to some good cause is adding value. But we could add so much more value to these kids' lives by sharing with them what we know." Coe hopes to replicate the camp in cities all over the country.

Many young people of high school and college age or older can learn about professional careers in business and finance by contacting the National Black MBA Association. The Chicago-based organization hosts an annual career fair, in which some 350 companies and more than 10,000 people participate. You can call the organization at 1-312-236-2622 for more details.

There are also summer internships available at various banking, consulting, and financial services firms for minority candidates. Contact Sponsors of Educational Opportunities (CSEO) at 1-212-979-2040.

You could also whet your children's appetite for business and investing by getting them a subscription to certain media publications tailored just for them. *Black Enterprise* magazine—which has chronicled the achievements of African American businesspeople for thirty years—now has two bimonthly newsletters, geared especially for children and teenagers:

KidpreneursNews, ages eight to twelve. This is a brand-new publication that covers basic business ideas, money and investing, stocks, bonds, and stories of child entrepreneurs. The May 1999 issue, for instance, describes how two African American girls, both age twelve, successfully launched a printing company in Irvington, New Jersey, called C & C Printing, using greeting card software and a $500 investment from one of their mothers. The newsletter, along with membership in the Kidpreneurs Club, costs $20, and you can subscribe by calling 1-877-KID-PREN. The club membership features coupons, gifts from different sponsors, and T-shirts. You may want to order the publication in bulk if you are a teacher, for use in the classroom. Bulk orders feature a discount: $6.50 per copy for 10–99 orders; $5.50 for 100–499; and $5 for over 500. There are also teacher's supplements for *KidpreneursNews,* which cost $6.50 each. You can e-mail them at kidpreneurs@blackenterprise.com and read about the newsletter at *Black Enterprise's* Web site (www.blackenterprise.com).

Black Enterprise for Teens, ages thirteen to eighteen. This publication covers many of the same topics as *KidpreneursNews* but adds information about preparation for college, job opportunities, careers, and celebrities. Five-time Grammy winner Lauryn Hill graced the cover of the May 1999 issue, and an article described her community activism, including a nonprofit organization called the Refugee Project, which she founded to enhance the lives of youth in the New York City and New Jersey areas. Another article listed useful Web sites for finding financial aid grants and college scholarships. Club membership, including a subscription to the newsletter, is $20. Bulk orders feature discounts.

"We're the only company that targets African American kids and encourages them to start businesses," says Melvin Crenshaw, Kidpreneurs' program manager. *Black Enterprise* also presents annual awards for the best entrepreneurial businesses run by young African Americans. Starting in the year 2000, *Black Enterprise* will host a one- to two-week camp to teach children about entrepreneurialism, featuring special guests from the business world.

For Latinos, *Hispanic Business* magazine—now in its twentieth year—also has a publication to encourage young people in business pursuits. It's called *SuperOnda,* which means "Big Wave" in Spanish. It's geared toward high school and college students and debuted in January 1999. It aims to give Latino students the direction and information they need to make positive choices, both in their educations and their careers. The premiere issue offered articles on how to get a job in the computer industry, the entertainment business, and the Coast Guard, among other features. A one-year subscription (eight issues) costs $9.95. The Web site is www.SuperOnda.com.

Hispanic Business also presents Entrepreneur of the Year awards and is running an essay contest on the subject "How will I win as an entrepreneur in the 21st century?" Entrants must write a three hundred- to five hundred-word essay, and winners will receive a free trip to Washington, D.C.

The Jumpstart Coalition, based in Washington, D.C., is another major resource of programs going on all over the country in the realm of financial literacy. The two-year-old nonprofit group maintains a vast database of information, which is a clearinghouse of all the educational curricula and materials in personal finance in the United States. You can search their database by topic on their Web site at www.jumpstartcoalition.org; just click on "Educational Materials." If you are not hooked up to the Internet, you can phone them at 1-888-45-EDUCATE or 1-202-466-8604 and ask them to do a database search for you.

Jumpstart was founded three years ago by several nonprofit groups involved in the financial services industry and economics education. Today it has eighty-three national organizations as members, including the National Endowment for Financial Education, based in Colorado; the American Bankers Association in Washington, D.C.; and the Economic Literacy Initiative in New York City.

"We don't want people to re-create the wheel," explains Dara Duguay, executive director. "There's so much curricula for personal finance already out there—about 250 different ones in all." If people simply see what's already available, they may be able to adapt some of it for their own needs, whether it be for a school program, a church initiative, or some community group.

Jumpstart is on a mission to make personal finance a required course in American public schools. This will require changes at the state level, since curriculum decisions are made on a state-by-state basis. The organization views this as a pressing need in American education.

"Currently, 90 percent of students sail through school learning nothing about personal finance," comments Duguay. Jumpstart aims to change all that. And they feel pretty confident about the likelihood of their success. "More than eighty groups together, working as one, opens doors," she points out. The White House has become interested in their program, and the U.S. Department of Education has agreed to work with Jumpstart to make personal finance part of the curriculum in American schools.

Jumpstart also has special curricula designed for low-income people.

There are also some outstanding programs to teach children entrepreneurship. The National Foundation for Teaching Entrepreneurship (NFTE—pronounced "Nifty"), founded in 1988 by Steve Mariotti in New York City, looms large among them. This organization is a youth development program that operates in schools, as part of after-school community settings, and through summer partnerships with colleges and community groups all over the country. NFTE's goal is to help low-income youth develop a set of marketable and transferable skills, as well as experience the first step in owning a business, through the establishment of a sole proprietorship. Children learn to read a balance sheet, write business plans, and calculate return on investment. Their "mini-MBA" course also teaches them about supply and demand, cost benefit analysis, record keeping, the present and future value of money, advertising and marketing, and other elements of starting a business.

NFTE currently works with five thousand kids a year but hopes to vastly expand the numbers of participants all over the country. Its current clientele is composed of 55.9 percent African Americans, 17.1 percent Hispanic, 5.7 percent Asian, 13.5 percent white, and 7.8 percent other groups. About equal numbers of males and females participate.

"The program works," asserts Mariotti, a former teacher in a tough neighborhood of New York City, who holds an MBA from the University of Michigan. "Can you teach entrepreneurship? The answer is a resounding 'yes.' There's a craft, a frame of mind, to do this. And you can teach it to people." Mariotti noted that in a recent national contest recognizing the top twenty-five entrepreneurs in America under age twenty, the majority were African American and nineteen were NFTE kids.

The efficacy of the program is further corroborated by a new study of NFTE alumni begun in 1993 by Brandeis University. The study found that

- NFTE raises the number of young people who have ever run a business by sixty-three youth per one hundred.

- in a post-program survey, 33 percent of respondents said they were still running their own businesses.

- of this 33 percent, most were making enough money from their businesses to pay themselves a monthly salary.

- 70 percent of older NFTE graduates went on to postsecondary education—a higher percentage than the national statistic for high school graduates.

Nonetheless, warns Mariotti, "you don't want to encourage people to go into business before they're ready." NFTE gives young people—most of whom are eighteen or younger—the requisite skills before they launch their own enterprise. For information, call their headquarters at 1-800-FOR-NFTE or visit their Web site at www.nftebiz.org.

If you live in a rural area, and you or your children want to learn about entrepreneurship, you can contact Rural Entrepreneurship Through Action Learning (REAL Enterprises), based in Durham, North Carolina. REAL is a nonprofit group that offers entrepreneurship courses in over three hundred predominantly rural high schools, community colleges, and elementary and middle schools in thirty states. They stress learning through doing. As part of the coursework, participants size up their entrepreneurial abilities, analyze their community, and identify a business that would fill a niche in their local economy. Then they research and write a business plan for their enterprise and have the opportunity to actually run the venture. State or regional REAL organizations and a local community support team assist REAL instructors and students along the way. The idea is that you don't have to move away from your small town to be successful.

Since 1991 REAL has

- provided entrepreneurial training for over 7,500 high school students and adults in predominantly rural communities in 30 states.

- trained nearly 700 instructors in the use of REAL's curriculum, from the elementary school level through post-secondary education.

- taught young people how to create businesses in fields such as computer sales and service, craft studios, sustainable agriculture, furniture making, welding, Internet marketing, and lawn service. In North Carolina alone, REAL participants started 212 new businesses and expanded 132 existing ones, generating total new sales revenue of over $5 million and creating 280 full- and part-time jobs.

- worked with many women, minorities, and low-income people.

Consider Maxwell, Nebraska, for example—a little town of 285 people on the Great Plains. Four teenage girls renovated a dusty old house in 1997 and made it into a brightly lit, secondhand store called The Original Source, which sells vintage items. Jonie Gosnell, a seventeen-year-old who was one of the founders of the shop, said, "We want people to say, 'Hey, you're from Maxwell, where they have that cool store.' " The girls were able to launch their business thanks to a Maxwell High School class on entrepreneurship, along with a REAL program.

About 90 percent of rural high school students leave their farm and ranch communities after graduation, and roughly half of Nebraska's university graduates leave the state, according to the Nebraska Rural Development Commission. So programs like REAL may provide ways to stem the tide of this "brain drain" and keep these small towns alive.

You can phone REAL at 1-919-688-7325 or visit their Web site at www.realenterprises.org.

Business and finance have traditionally been thought of as a male domain. But Girls Inc., a New York–based nonprofit group, has a mission of teaching girls how to become financially independent adults. It is the nation's leading advocacy group for girls. For over fifty years the organization—formerly called the Girls Clubs of America—has provided educational programs to millions of American girls, particularly those in high-risk, underserved areas. In fact, nearly two-thirds of the girls they serve come from households with incomes below $20,000 a year; 61 percent belong to racial and ethnic minority groups; and over half are from single-parent households, most of which are headed by women.

Girls Inc. has a useful pamphlet entitled "Money Matters: An Economic Literacy Action Kit for Girls." It's free. In it there are discussions of budgeting, saving money, investing, useful Web sites, and entrepreneurism. There are inspiring nuggets of information, such as the fact that in 1996 approximately 8 million women-owned businesses employed more than 18 million people and generated $2.3 trillion in sales in the United States. Moreover, the number of women business owners increased by 78 percent between 1992 and 1996.

The group also offers tips on how to raise financially savvy girls. "Prince Charming is a myth," reads one of the tips. "Most women will work for pay for a large portion of their adult lives and will need to support themselves, their families, and often their aging parents. Encourage your daughter to think about meaningful and interesting career opportunities, as well as her financial goals and responsibilities."

For information, call Girls Inc. at 1-212-509-2000 or visit their Web site at www.girlsinc.org.

Some black churches have taken the lead in educating young people about personal finance. For example, at Cascade United Methodist Church in Atlanta, kids can open interest-bearing savings accounts at the church and make regular deposits with as little as $25. The church has 3,500 members of the congregation and more than 800 kids. Since Cascade launched the program in April 1997, the children—from babies all the way up to eighteen-year-olds—have deposited tens of thousands of dollars, according to Milton Brown, an African American who is founder and executive director of Good Choices, Inc, a nonprofit agency in Atlanta that is working to create a level playing field economically for inner-city youth.

"We ran the Cascade program as a pilot project for one full year, to determine the viability of the program," says Brown. "And we were blown away by the results. Over 600 young people opened accounts. That gave us all the ammo we needed to expand the program."

Good Choices partnered with NationsBank to create the program and is replicating it at black churches in Atlanta and other cities across America. So far, as of May 1999 the 1,800 kids participating in the program at black churches around Atlanta have deposited more than $170,000.

At Cascade United Methodist, the children are using their accounts to save for their college education, among other goals, says Brown. "There are no check-writing privileges with these accounts," he explains. "Instead, this is a long-term savings account. We encourage parents to understand that it's not a Christmas club type of account, where you save money for Christmas gifts and then withdraw it. It's not like that. This is for a long-term goal, such as paying for college."

The pastor at the church, Reverend Walter Kimbrough, enthusiastically embraced the idea. Along with encouraging the savings accounts, the church also hosts monthly seminars for young people about the importance of saving and how to manage your money. Plus, the program has been virtually cost-free for the church to run.

Still another outstanding program that can educate your children about business is Junior Achievement (JA).

Based in Colorado Springs, Colorado, Junior Achievement is a national program that for eighty years has focused on educating young people about business and economics. The organization was founded by Horace Moses in 1919, who saw what 4-H was doing for rural students and decided that city kids needed the same type of opportunity.

"Our original program was an after-school one," explains Nancy Brown, vice president of research and development at the organization. "Kids learned how to start a business, produce something, and sell it."

Junior Achievement today has a full portfolio of programs, reaching 3 million students from kindergarten through twelfth grade, at 168 offices across the country as well as overseas. The organization trains volunteers from the business or professional worlds about how to use JA's materials, then these individuals work in partnership with teachers. At the high school level, Junior Achievement has internship programs to teach kids business skills. The program allows kids to run their own companies under the guidance of seasoned business mentors. To find a Junior Achievement office near you, you can either visit their Web site (www.ja.org) or call them at 1-719-540-8000.

For Bruce Goode, an African American who grew up in Cleveland, Ohio, Junior Achievement proved to be a turning point in his life. He grew up in working-class neighborhoods on the east side of town and in the Kinsman area, near the public housing projects. Goode's father was a house painter, and his mother worked nights as a maid, cleaning bathrooms in government buildings. After his parents separated in 1960, his mother and her six children moved in with the kids' grandparents and some cousins. It was a hardscrabble existence.

"My mother made do with what she had," recalls Goode. "My parents earned next to nothing." His father squandered much of his paycheck on drinking. The family didn't have a bank account, and what little money they did have, they kept in a drawer at home.

Goode attended one of the city's worst high schools, ranked at the bottom in academic achievement. Around his neighborhood, as he grew up in the 1960s, Goode saw black guys his age on the street, selling drugs and shooting people. Some young men were in wheelchairs from being shot; others were murdered in gunfights.

Goode is reminiscing about all this, attired in an elegant business suit, sitting in a posh corporate office atop a skyscraper in one of Cleveland's fanciest business districts. The view from the window is fabulous. The entire city of Cleveland unfolds below. Goode works as managing director of the Key Corp., a major money management firm, where he runs a fixed-income portfolio totaling $1.3 billion. He's been with the company for twenty years.

How did he make the trajectory from his blighted neighborhood to the pinnacle of Cleveland's business community?

"What sparked my interest in business was the Junior Achievement program," explains the executive. It was sponsored by the Cleveland Business League, a group of black businessmen from the city in the late 1960s—the same time as race riots were wreaking destruction across much of Cleveland and entire neighborhoods were being burned to the ground.

Junior Achievement created hope against this backdrop of destruction. Under the program, kids created a business, wrote a business plan, then went out and sold stock in the new company to their friends and family. Young people then ran the company with the money they raised from their stock sale. All of this was done under the tutelage of real-life business professionals who were assigned to mentor the kids.

Paul Hamilton, a black businessman in Cleveland, was Goode's adviser. Goode devised the idea of creating a company that made coat hangers. He sold stock at the beginning of his sophomore year for $1 a share to friends and family members. By the end of the year, thanks to good management, the company was profitable and Goode was able to pay each shareholder $1.25.

"That's what really piqued my interest in business," comments Goode. There was also a stockbroker who came to Goode's high school and told the students that stockbrokers were in the top 5 percent of wage earners in America—yet another tantalizing statistic.

Goode went on to major in finance at the University of Toledo. A well-to-do white attorney in Cleveland named Ralph Gibbon helped finance his college education and remains Goode's "godfather" to this day. "I talk to him regularly," says Goode. Goode found him through a neighborhood center, where a group of local kids who were trying to go to college were seeking sponsors.

There was racial discrimination along the way—some blatant, some subtle. It continues to this day, according to Goode. But he persevered; he maintained a B-plus average in finance in college. It was a struggle, because when he was growing up there were no books at home. He found himself competing with white, suburban, middle-class kids who had gone to prep schools and were overqualified. To keep up, Goode teamed up with another young black man from Toledo. "We helped each other make it through," he recalls.

After graduation Goode worked in the brokerage business, and in 1975 he married. His wife is a deeply religious woman, and with her guidance, Goode said, the Lord saved him in 1974.

This religious conversion sparked a strong desire in him to make a contribution to the community. Although he earns a good salary and could live in a fancy suburb and go to a posh church if he chose, Goode has instead elected to live in Cleveland's inner city. He is minister of a small congregation of about forty people, in addition to his job at Key Corp. The parishioners represent a cross-section of folks—nurses, construction workers, and retired people among them. He also works with forty other churches in his district and conducts financial seminars for various churches in Cleveland.

"We live in the house that my wife grew up in, so we could give back to the community," he explains. His church is called Christian Hope, and he can see it from his front porch.

For Goode, his career in financial services and his ministry complement one another.

In his view, the right relationship with Jesus Christ "brings all other relationships into order"—including financial ones. At his church he tries to inculcate sound financial practices among the congregation. He encourages them to create a financial plan, to save for retirement, and to tithe 10 percent of their income as well. "If God gives you the wherewithal to tithe, He's also given you the wherewithal to leave a component for savings," explains Goode. "God is not silent on your financial participation. He speaks to these issues."

Goode tells young black kids whom he works with on the Cleveland Scholarship Program: "Find something legitimate to do. Learn something about it. And set your sights high." He also ministers to white colleagues whom he has met at Key Corp.

"Racial healing really needs to deal with individuals," Goode says as he rises to leave. "What really would help is more people understanding that it's not a person's race that makes them what they are. It's the character of people. You have to get them to be good Christians. That's where it all begins."

One of the best ways we can uplift our young people is by telling them inspiring stories about those who triumphed over great odds.

John Johnson is such a person—the founder of Johnson Publishing Company, the largest black-owned publishing company in the world. He grew up poor, during the twenties and thirties, in the segregated town of Arkansas City, Arkansas, where blacks were only allowed to work as domestics or laborers on the Mississippi River levee. They were the children and grandchildren of slavery, locked in a sharecropping system that kept them perennially broke. His father was killed in a sawmill accident when Johnson was eight, and he was raised by a stepfather. His mother, Gertrude Jenkins, worked as a domestic and a cook. She struggled and sacrificed for her son's education. She infused her son with a vision of what could be, rather than what was.

"My mother never went beyond the third grade. Yet she was the best educated person I ever met," writes Johnson, in his stirring autobiography, *Succeeding Against the Odds*. "She was daring, she was caring, she believed you could do anything you wanted to do, if you tried. She gave me that faith and that hope, and that has guided my life."

For five years, his mother worked as a cook in a levee camp so they could get money to go to Chicago, where Johnson could attend high school, because there was no black high school in Arkansas City.

"She'd always believed that there was a solution to every problem, and that the solution was in God's hands, not human hands," continues Johnson. "But she believed also, and with equal fervor, that God helped those who helped themselves."

She did not believe in the doubters. She believed you could win, if you had the courage to run the race. She kept on working and dreaming and saving.

Thanks to her financial prudence, Johnson was able to get a bank loan of $500 in 1942 to start his first magazine, *Negro Digest.* In those days, there were few banks that made loans to black people. But Johnson got the loan, using his mother's new furniture as collateral.

And with that money, he went on to build an empire. He founded *Ebony* and *Jet,* magazines that chronicled the successes of African Americans in all walks of life; he created other ventures, including Fashion Fair Cosmetics, Supreme Beauty Products, and the American Black Achievement Awards television program; and he became chairman and chief executive officer of Supreme Life Insurance Company, where he began his career as an office worker.

It can be done.

"Victory," as John Johnson's mother always told him, "is certain if we have the courage to believe and the strength to run our own race."

INDEX

actuarial tables, 71
adjustable-rate mortgages (ARMs), 61
adult day care, 182
advance directives, 173
affinity marketing scams, 209–12
aggressive growth funds, 133
Alliance for Community Media, 154
American Association of Individual Investors, 99
American depositary receipts (ADRs), 107
American League of Financial Institutions, 17
American Savings Education Council (ASEC), 188–89
American Society of Home Inspectors, 55
American Stock Exchange (Amex), 106, 107, 165
amortization, 59
Anderson, Richard Jr., 249–51
annual percentage rate (APR), 42, 43, 61
annual reports, 108–10
annuities, 203
Arellano, Ofelia, 241–42
Ariel Capital Management, 98–99, 126
asset allocation, 131–32
athletes, professional, 157–58
ATMs (automated teller machines), 18
auto, purchase of, 182–84

auto insurance, 80–82
auto loans, 183

back-end loads, 134
balanced funds, 133
Bambara, Alex, 226, 237–40
banking, software, 146–47
bankruptcies, personal, 44, 50–51
banks:
    community development, 17–18
    depositing money in, 16–20, 24, 137
    interest paid by, see interest
    Internet services, 18
    investment, 104
    opening an account, 19
    selecting, 18
bear markets, 101
Better Life Club, 209–10
Bible, see Scripture
BizPlan Builder, 242
Black Enterprise, 258–59
Blazers Youth Center, 154
bonds, 23, 104, 113–19
    call feature of, 117
    discount, 116
    government, 117–18
    interest rates and, 115–17
    junk, 115
    maturity of, 115
    municipal, 118
    mutual funds, 113–14
    prices of, 116–17
    ratings of, 114–16
    tax advantages of, 114
    Treasury, 113, 117
    yields of, 115–18

Brazier, Rev. Arthur, 36
brokerage firms, 107–8, 135–36, 147
Brown Capital Management, 126, 128
budgeting, 26–30, 45
    for retirement, 205
    software for, 146
Bull and Bear Investment Camp, 255–58
bull markets, 101
burial societies, 72
Burns, Matilda, 3–4
Business Plan Pro, 241–42

Caldwell, Rev. Kirbyjon, 36
call feature, 117
capital, democratization of, 6–7, 12
capital appreciation, 101
capital gains taxes, 56
capitalism, 7, 33, 100, 103
capitalization, market cap, 106–7
capital markets, 103, 104
CardTrak, 43–44
car insurance, 80–82
car loans, 183
car purchase, 182–84
Carter, Gael, 213–15
Carter, Jimmy, 70
cash dividends, 101
cash equivalents, 136–37
cash surrender value, 75
cash value life insurance, 76
CCCS (Consumer Credit Counseling Service):
    on avoiding credit problems, 52
    on budgeting, 26, 28, 30

CCCS (Consumer Credit
    Counseling Service)
    (cont'd):
  on divorce, 178–79
  on repayment of debts,
    42–44, 46
  services of, 44–45
CDs (certificates of deposit),
    137
Center for Teaching
    Entrepreneurship,
    Milwaukee, 30–31
certified financial planners
    (CFP), 137–38
Chapman Company, 126
Chapter 7 bankruptcy, 50
Chapter 13 bankruptcy, 50
check-cashing fees, 16, 18,
    216
checking accounts, 16, 17,
    19, 24
children:
  college for, 38
  costs of having, 30
  teaching about finance,
    40; see also education
  trustees for, 172
churches:
  burial societies of, 72
  as community computer
    centers, 155
  finance taught in, 36–38,
    41, 54
  insurance information
    from, 96
  savings programs in, 175
  young people taught in,
    264–65
civil rights movement, 6–8,
    12
Coalition of Black Investors
    (COBI), 99, 126, 251
COBRA (Consolidated
    Omnibus Budget
    Reconciliation Act of
    1986), 82
codicils, 171
Coe, Douglas, 255–58

Coker, Bisi, 151–52, 155
collateral, defined, 46
collection agencies, 45, 51
college, see education
Commerce Department,
    U.S., 242–44
common stock, 102, 103
community access centers,
    151, 153–55
Community Connections,
    58
Community Technology
    Centers' Network
    (CTCN), 154
comparative market analysis
    (CMA), 63
compound interest, 20–21,
    204
computers, see Internet
Computers in the 'Hood,
    151–52, 154–55
con artists, see scams
condominiums (condos),
    59–60
Consumer Credit
    Counseling Service, see
    CCCS
Consumer Federation of
    America, 78
Consumer Information
    Center, 65
contingent deferred sales
    charges, 134
convertible preferred shares,
    103
cooperatives (co-ops), 60
Corinthians I 10:14, 221
Corinthians I 13:11–12, 40
Corinthians II 9:6–9, 96
corporate bonds, 113
corporations:
  annual reports, 108–10
  board of directors,
    110–11
  bond issues, 113–19
  cash dividends, 101
  foreign, 107
  limited liability, 100

  new shares issued by, 104
  publicly traded, 111
  stock ownership,
    100–101
  ticker symbols, 111–12
coupon bonds, 115–16
credit, 33–52
  applying for, 49, 51
  APR and, 42, 43
  avoiding problems, 52
  consumer, 45
  cost of, 42, 43
  defined, 44
  forms of, 44
  unacceptable, 36
  unemployment and, 36
  uses of, 48
credit cards:
  borrowing money on, 43
  hidden fees of, 43
  multiple, 45
  paying off, 37–38, 41–44,
    46, 52
  secured, 43–44
credit history, 49, 213
credit rating, 44, 45
credit report:
  contents of, 49–50, 51
  copies of, 47–48
credit-reporting agencies,
    47–48, 49
credit score, 51–52, 55
credit unions, 17; see also
    banks

Darricarerre, Yolanda
    Robinson, 156–57
Davis, Carol, and Duane
    Davis, 125–26, 251
day trading, 102, 161–62
death:
  estate planning, 170–73
  intestate, 170
  and trusts, 171–73
  and wills, 171–72, 173
death benefit, 74, 75, 77
debit insurance policies,
    72

debt, 33–52
  avoiding problems, 52
  and bankruptcy, 44,
    50–51
  collateral for, 46
  collection agencies and,
    45, 51
  control of, 38–40
  cosigning loans, 45–46
  credit rating and, 44, 45
  installment, 45, 52
  interest on, 42–43
  prioritizing of, 46–47
  refinancing of, 47
  repayment of, 37–38,
    41–44, 46, 52
  secured, 46
  unsecured, 46
debt counselors, 46
"Debt Free in 2003"
  (Meeks), 37, 40, 41
debt instruments, *see* bonds
direct deposit, 18
disability insurance, 85–87
discount bonds, 116
discount brokers, 135, 136
discretionary spending, 28
distance learning, online,
  150, 164–65
diversification, 132–33
dividend reinvestment plan
  (DRIP), 136
dividends, 101, 103, 111
dividend yield, 110
divorce, 177–79
dollar cost averaging, 133
Donovan, Kyle, 122–24
Douglass, Frederick, 12
Dow Jones Industrial
  Average, 120–22
durable power of attorney
  for health care, 173

"earnest money," 64
earnings per share, 108–9
earthquake insurance, 80
Ecclesiastes 3:1–2, 169
Ecclesiastes 10:19, 127

education, 247–70
  church-based, 36–38,
    264–65
  in entrepreneurship,
    261–64
  Gates scholarships,
    153–54
  in investments, 255–58
  Junior Achievement,
    265–69
  online, 150, 164–65
  paying for, 174–77
  periodicals, 258–60
  in personal finance,
    251–55, 260–62
  Stock Market Game,
    128–29, 247–48
  student aid, 175–76
education IRA, 174–75, 202
elder care, 180–82
Eldercare Locator, 87
electronic commerce,
  155–58
electronic communication
  networks (ECNs), 166
entrepreneurship, 223–45
  Bambara, 226, 237–40
  capital markets and, 103
  children and, 258–69
  Commerce Dept., 242–44
  defined, 100
  Farr, 226, 227–30
  Hockings, 226, 234–37
  Labor Dept., 244
  minority, 7, 224–26
  Netpreneur, 244–45
  New Markets Initiative,
    225
  Perez, 226, 230–34
  SBA and, 226, 240–42
  software for, 241–42
  teaching of, 261–64
Equifax, 47, 49–50, 51
equities, 102
equity, 23, 56–57, 61, 104
equity analysts, 108–9
equity stripping, 213
estate planning, 170–73, 200

estate taxes, 74, 170–71
executor/executrix, 171–72
expenses:
  fixed, 28, 52
  for home buyers, 61–62
  income to exceed, 30
  keeping track of, 28
  variable, 28

"Fannie Mae" (Federal
  National Mortgage
  Association), 57, 59,
  60, 62, 204
Farr, Mel, 226, 227–30
Federal Reserve System,
  118, 119–20
finance company scams,
  214–15
financial goals, 24–26,
  28–29, 52
financial plan, 24–32
  becoming debt-free, 52
  budgeting in, 26–28
  discretionary spending in,
    28
  emergency fund in, 29
  goals and, 24–26
  spending patterns, 28
financial planners, 99,
  137–39
financial prudence:
  church teaching, 36–38
  lack of, 44
  lessons of, 3–5
  in Scriptures, *see*
    Scriptures
  software for, 146
fixed-rate mortgage, 60–61
Flake, Rev. Floyd, 36
flipping (scam), 213
flood insurance, 80
Ford, Henry (retiree),
  197–99
401(k) plans, 193–99
  advantages of, 194
  changing jobs, 196–97
  Internet information
    about, 148–49, 195

403(b) plans, 193
457 plans, 193
"Freddie Mac" (Federal
    Home Loan Mortgage
    Corporation), 57, 59,
    60, 62
front-end sales charges, 134
FTC, 215, 217–19
Fuller, Millard and Linda,
    69–70

gambling, legal, 220–21
Gates, Bill, 153–54
general obligation bonds,
    118
Godwin, Lemond, 5
Goe, Kathy, 67–70
Goode, Bruce, 266–69
government bonds,
    117–18
Grassley, Charles, 213–14
gross income, defined, 59
growth funds, 133
growth investing, 135

Habitat for Humanity,
    69–70
health insurance, 82–85
    co-payment for, 83
    retirement and, 204–5
health maintenance
    organizations (HMOs),
    83–84
Hispanic Business, 259–60
Hockings, Nick, 226,
    234–37
home:
    appraised value of, 56
    buying, 63–64
    cost of, 59
    owning, *see*
        homeownership
    selling, 64
    structural features, 64
home-equity loans, 56–57,
    59
HomeFree-USA, 53–55, 66
home inspection, 55, 64

homeownership, 53–70
    borrowing money for, 58;
        see also mortgages
    down payment and, 62
    equity of, 56–57, 61
    expenses of, 61–62
    hints for, 54–56
    insurance, 78–80
    minorities and, 57–58
    net worth and, 56
    predatory lending and,
        212–16
    tax benefits of, 56
home service insurance
    policies, 72
Horton, Cassandra, 254–55
HUD (Housing and Urban
    Development), 59, 60,
    64, 66, 204
Hughes, Langston, 185

income, gross, 59
income funds, 133
Independent Insurance
    Agents of America
    (IIAA), 90
index funds, 135
industrial insurance, 72–73
inflation:
    bonds and, 118
    and retirement savings,
        24, 188
    and time value of money,
        23–24
inheritance, probate and, 74
initial public offering (IPO),
    103
inspection, home, 55, 64
installment debt, 45, 52
institutional shareholders,
    103
insurance, 71–96
    agents, 89, 90, 95
    black-owned firms,
        90–93
    buying, 89–96
    car, 80–82
    direct-market, 94

disability, 85–87
disaster, 80
health, 82–85
homeowners, 78–80
industrial, 72–73
information sources,
    89–94, 96, 149
liability, 81
life, 73–78
long-term care, 75,
    87–89, 181
mortgage (decreasing
    term), 76
policy, defined, 71
private mortgage, 62–63
Insurance Information
    Institute, 89
interest, 19–23
    APR of, 42, 43, 61
    bonds and, 115–17
    calculating, 21n
    changing rates of, 61
    compound, 20–21, 204
    on credit card debt,
        42–43
    on deposits, 16
    fluctuating, 19–20
    mortgages and, 23, 55,
        59, 60–61, 65
    Rule of 72 and, 20, 22
International Association of
    Financial Planning,
    137–38
Internet, 145–68
    access to, 152–55
    car buying or selling on,
        183–84
    college finance
        information on,
        176–77
    fraud on, 217–20
    home buying on, 63
    insurance information on,
        84–85, 89–90
    international scams on,
        218–19
    investing online, 159–63
    IRA information on, 202

online banking services, 18
personal finance software, 146–50
intestate deaths, 170
investment banks, 104
investment clubs, 139–43
Investment Company Institute, 134
investments, 125–43
asset allocation in, 131–32
basics of, 129–37
in bonds, 23
brokerage firms for, 107–8, 135–36
buy and hold strategy of, 102, 129
cash equivalents, 136–37
children and, 249–51, 255–58
direct, 136
diversification of, 132–33
dollar cost averaging in, 133
financial planners for, 137–39
growth strategy for, 135
income from, 130–31
on Internet, 159–63
Internet frauds, 217–18
money-market accounts, 20, 22, 137
mutual funds, 37–38, 133–35
objectives of, 129
online advice on, 148
proportion of, 131
questions about, 212
real estate, 23
retail, 103
for retirement, 203–6
return on, 101
risks of, 131, 132
scams in, 208–21
in stocks, 22, 23
tax-deferred, 192–93
time horizon for, 129–31
value strategy for, 135

IRAs, 193, 199–203
choosing, 202–3
education, 174–75, 202
Internet information about, 202
for nonworking spouses, 200
Roth, 175, 200–201
SEP, 199, 201–2
SIMPLE, 201–2

Jackson family, 4, 5
jobs:
computer skills needed for, 151, 154, 156
401(k) and, 193–99
Internet information about, 150
knowledge based, 174
John I 2:15–17, 52
Johnson Publishing Company, 269–70
Jones, Chiffon*, 33–34, 36, 38–40
Jumpstart Coalition, 260–61
Junior Achievement (JA), 265–69
junk bonds, 115

Keogh plans, 193
KidpreneursNews, 258–59
King, Rev. Martin Luther Jr., 7–8, 12, 37, 247

Labor Department, U.S., 244
Lewis, John, 12
liability insurance, 81
life estate trusts, 172–73
life events, 169–85
buying a car, 182–84
college education, 174–77
divorce, 177–79
elder care, 180–82
estate planning, 170–73
Roth IRAs for, 200
taxes, 179–80

life insurance, 73–78
borrowing money against, 75, 76, 77
cash surrender value of, 75
cash value, 75, 76–77
death benefits of, 74, 75, 77
fixed installment payments, 74–75
interest only arrangement, 75
lump sum arrangement, 74
policy term, 75
term, 75–76, 77
universal, 77
whole, 76–77
limit orders, 106, 162
liquidity, 20, 22, 108
living trusts, 172–73
living wills, 173
load vs. no-load funds, 134
loans:
amortization of, 59
car, 183
cosigning, 45–46
home-equity, 56–57, 59
on life insurance policies, 75, 76, 77
payday, 216–17
payment-to-income ratio of, 176
predatory, 212–16
prequalification for, 60
student, 176
see also mortgages
Long Term Care Campaign (LTCC), 180, 182
long-term care insurance, 75, 87–89, 181
lottery, 207, 220–21

McCarty, Oseola, 169
McGriff, Deborah, 139–43
margin, 163
Mark 3:27, 37
Mark 12:13–18, 179

market capitalization, 106–7
market timing, 131
Martin, Jade*, 65–67
Matthew 25:14, 15–16, 19, 23
maturity:
  defined, 40
  yield to, 116, 117
Medicaid, 87, 181
Medicare, 87
Meeks, Jamella, 40–41
Meeks, Rev. James, 34–36, 37–38, 40–41
monetary policy, 119
money:
  bank deposits, 16–20
  borrowing, see loans
  budgeting of, 26–30, 45
  depreciation of, 23–24
  "earnest," 64
  growing of, 13–32
  interest earned on, 16
  as liquid, 20, 22
  love of, 127
  purchasing power of, 23–24
  risk and reward of, 20, 22
  time value of, 23–24, 129–30, 204
money-market accounts, 20, 22, 137
Morino Institute, 245
mortgage-backed securities, 57
mortgages, 53–70
  adjustable-rate, 61
  approval of, 58
  credit score and, 55
  early payment of, 38, 40, 65
  equity stripping and, 213
  fixed-rate, 60–61
  insurance and, 62–63, 76, 78–80
  interest and, 23, 55, 59, 60–61, 65
  Internet information on, 149

  for low- to moderate-income persons, 58–61
  monthly payments of, 59
  packing and, 213
  points and, 55
  preparation for, 54–55
  prequalification for, 60
  profit motive and, 56
  questions about, 56
  refinancing of, 63, 64–65, 213
  reverse, 204
  subprime lenders, 58–59
"Mother to Son" (Hughes), 185
multilevel marketing plans, 211
municipal bonds, 118
mutual funds, 22, 133–35
  balanced, 133
  bond, 113–14
  income vs. growth, 133
  index, 135
  Internet information on, 149
  investment in, 37–38
  load vs. no-load, 134

Nasdaq Stock Market, 105, 107, 165
National Association of Insurance Commissioners (NAIC), 77, 88, 89
National Association of Investors Corporation (NAIC), 136, 139–40, 198–99
National Association of Personal Financial Advisors (NAPFA), 99, 137
National Association of Securities Dealers (NASD), 106
National Association of the Self-Employed, 83

National Bankers Association, 58
National Black MBA Association, 258
National Center for Home Equity Conversion, 204
National Committee for Quality Assurance (NCQA), 84, 89
National Council of State Housing Agencies, 58
National Flood Insurance Program, 80
National Foundation for Teaching Entrepreneurship (NFTE), 261–62
National Insurance Consumer Helpline, 89
National Partners in Homeownership, 58
NCLC (National Consumer Law Center), 46, 47
Netpreneur program, 244–45
net worth, 24–25, 56
New Markets Initiative, 225
New York Stock Exchange (NYSE), 105, 107, 129, 165

packing (scam), 213
parables, see Scriptures
parents, aging, 180–82
par value, 115, 116
payday lending businesses, 216–17
Pension Benefit Guaranty Corporation (PBGC), 192
pensions, 191–99
  becoming vested in, 192
  changing jobs and, 192
  profit-sharing, 192
  see also 401(k) plans
P/E (price/earnings) ratio, 110, 113
percent yield, 112

Perez, Margarita, 226,
230–34, 252–54
PITI, defined, 59
policy term, 75
Ponzi schemes, 210
portfolio, *see* investments
preauthorized payments,
18
predatory lending, 212–16
preferred provider
organizations (PPOs),
84
preferred stock, 102–3
premium, defined, 71, 203
prenuptial agreements,
177–78
Presley, Elvis, 11, 32
price/earnings (P/E) ratio,
110, 113
principal, defined, 59
private mortgage insurance
(PMI), 62–63
probate, avoiding, 74,
172–73
profits, defined, 100
profit-sharing plans, 192
prospectus, 104, 134
Psalm 37:21, 37
pyramid schemes, 210–11

Rainbow/PUSH Coalition,
248
real estate, investing in, 23
real estate agents, 63
REAL (Rural
Entrepreneurship
Through Action
Learning), 262–64
retail investors, 103
retirement, 187–206
annuities, 203
Ballpark Estimate
worksheet, 188–89
budgeting for, 205
early, 192
health insurance and,
204–5
income during, 189–90

inflation and, 24, 188
Internet information
about, 148–49
investments and savings
for, 203–6
IRAs, 199–203
pensions, 191–99
Social Security, 190–91
tax-deferred plans for,
192–93
revenue bonds, 118
reverse loads, 134
reverse mortgages, 204
risk vs. reward, 20, 22,
101–2, 115, 118, 131
Rodgers, Redonna, 30–31
Rogers, John, 98–99, 126
ROTC scholarships, 175
Roth IRAs, 175, 200–201
Rule of 72, 20, 22

S&P 500 Index, 122
savings:
automatic deductions for,
28–29
bank accounts, 16, 17,
24, 175
budgeting for, 29
financial goals and,
25–26, 28–29
inflation and, 24, 188
lack of, 45
protection of, 181
for retirement, *see*
retirement
tax-deferred, 77, 203
savings and loan
associations (S&Ls),
17; *see also* banks
SBA (Small Business
Administration), 226,
240–42
scams, 207–21
affinity marketing,
209–12
on the Internet, 217–20
lottery, 220–21
payday lending, 216–17

Ponzi schemes, 210
predatory lending,
212–16
pyramid schemes,
210–11
questions about, 212
state securities regulator
and, 211
SCORE (Service Corps of
Retired Executives),
240
Scriptures:
Corinthians I 10:14, 221
Corinthians I 13:11–12,
40
Corinthians II 9:6–9, 96
Ecclesiastes 3:1–2, 169
Ecclesiastes 10:19, 127
John I 2:15–17, 52
Mark 3:27, 37
Mark 12:13–18, 179
Matthew 25:14, 15–16,
19, 23
Psalm 37:21, 37
Timothy I 6:8, 127
securities:
fixed-income, 23
mortgage-backed, 57
Securities and Exchange
Commission (SEC),
104, 107, 111, 150,
211, 219–20
self-employment, health
insurance and, 82–83
SEP-IRAs, 199, 201–2
shareholders, 101–4, 111
shopping, as addiction,
33–34, 36, 45
short-term debt, 115
SIMPLE (savings incentive
match plan for
employees), 193,
201–2
Sloan, Maceo, 248–49
Small Business
Administration (SBA),
226, 240–42
Smith, Barkin' Bill, 13–14

Social Security, 86–87, 190–91
speculators, 102, 161
Standard & Poor's 500 Index, 122
stock:
  average annual returns of, 130
  and bonds, 23, 114
  common, 102, 103
  company offerings, 104
  individual ownership of, 103, 104
  initial public offerings of, 103
  listed, 107; see also stock market
  mutual funds, 22, 37–38, 133–35
  over-the-counter, 108
  preferred, 102–3
  split, 109–10
stockbrokers, 107–8
stock exchanges, 104–5, 107, 108
  education in, 129
  ticker symbols, 111–12
stockholders, 101–4, 111
stock market, 97–124
  bull and bear, 101
  capitalization of, 106–7
  corrections of, 129
  day trading, 102, 161–62
  double-action trading, 105
  of the future, 165–68
  gambling vs., 127, 161
  indexes of, 120
  information sources, 97–98, 111–13

limit orders, 106, 162
market orders, 106
publicly traded companies on, 100–101
return on investment in, 37–38, 101
risks, 101–2, 107, 127
supply and demand, 105
Wall Street and, 106
Stock Market Game, 128–29, 247–48
stock quotations, 111
student aid, 175–76
subprime lending market, 58–59
Sullivan, Rev. Leon, 7
SuperOnda, 259
Supplemental Security Income (SSI), 86
supply and demand, 19
  in stock market, 105
Surviving Debt (NCLC), 46, 47

Tardy, Benita, 25–26
tax-deferred savings, 77, 192–93, 203
taxes, 179–80
  capital gains, 56
  estate, 74, 170–71
  software for, 147
Taylor, Robert N., 209–10
Teach Me Some Cents, 30–31
term insurance, 75–76, 77
13 Scribes, 151–52, 155
Thomas, Isiah, 157–58
time value of money, 23–24, 129–30, 204

Timothy I 6:8, 127
tornado insurance, 80
Treasury bills, 23, 117, 137
Treasury bonds, 113, 117
trusts, 171–73

underwriters, 104
unemployment, 36
universal life insurance policies, 77
Urban League, 153

value investing, 135
Veteran Affairs, U.S., 60
Veterans' Administration, 63
virtual college, 164–65
volatility, 132, 163

Walker, Mme. C. J., 224
Walker, Rev. Wyatt, 36–37
Wall Street, 106
Wall Street Journal, The, 111–13
whole life insurance, 76–77
Williams, Rev. Hosea, 12
wills, 171–72, 173

yield:
  bond, 115–18
  dividend yield, 110
  percent, 112
  risk vs., 115
Youth Enterprise Academy, Wisconsin, 254–55

Zarb, Frank, 165–68
zero-coupon bonds, 115–16